# SUR

## THE

# YEAR 2000

# COMPUTER

# CRASH

## It's too late to fix all the software!

# David Wm Brown

**A Flying Kiwi Plain English Guide for the Ordinary Person**

**Flying Kiwi Press / Trafford Publishing**
**Victoria BC  Canada**

## Surviving the Year 2000 Computer Crash

The author and the publisher have used their best efforts in the research and preparation of this book. All reasonable attempts have been made to establish the accuracy of the facts reported, and opinions given are those sincerely held on the basis of available information. Advice is given in the sincere desire to help protect the reader from possible difficulties associated with the year 2000 computer problems, and is given strictly as advice, to be weighed, evaluated and further researched by the reader before any decisions are made. The reader will be fully and solely responsible for any such decisions made on the basis of information or opinions contained in this book. The author and the publisher make no warranty of any kind, expressed or implied, with regard to the information contained in this book. The author and the publisher shall not be liable in any event for incidental or consequential damages in connection with, or arising out of, the furnishing or use of this information.

Canadian Cataloguing in Publication Data

Brown, David Wm (David William), 1944-
   Surviving the year 2000 computer crash


   Includes bibliographical references.
   ISBN 1-55212-224-7

   1. Year 2000 date conversion (Computer systems)--Social aspects.  I. Title.
QA76.76.S64B76 1998      363.34'97          C98-911146-6

## TRAFFORD

**This book was published "on-demand" in cooperation with Trafford Publishing.**
On-demand publishing is a unique process and service of making a book available for retail sale to the public taking advantage of on-demand manufacturing and Internet web marketing.

Suite 2, 3050 Nanaimo St., Victoria, B.C. V8T 4Z1, CANADA

| | | | |
|---|---|---|---|
| Phone | 250-383-6864 | Toll-free | 1-888-232-4444 (Canada & US) |
| Fax | 250-383-6804 | E-mail | sales@trafford.com |
| Web site | www.trafford.com | TRAFFORD PUBLISHING IS A DIVISION OF TRAFFORD HOLDINGS LTD. |

10      9      8      7      6      5      4      3      2      1

## Credits:

Produced by TechStyle Industries
Printed in Canada by Trafford Publishing, a division of Trafford Holdings Ltd.

To my mother-in-law, Nieves Prado Francisco,
a woman of courage, strength, dignity and grace,
whom I am proud to call *Inang*.


To her firstborn,
the late Luis Prado Francisco,
my *Kuya*.


And to those who died in Baguio, the *Wahine*, and the Edmonton tornado,
when I was there.

I trust your story may help others to survive.

### Ordering Information

*Surviving the Year 2000 Computer Crash* may be ordered in single or multiple copies from:

**Trafford Publishing**
#2 - 3050 Nanaimo St., Victoria BC  V8T 3P7  CANADA
Phone: 250-383-6864    Fax: 250-383-6804    Toll-Free: 1-888-232-4444
Internet: www.trafford.com/robots/98-0043.html

Multiple copies may also be ordered from:
**Flying Kiwi Press**, ATTN: Y2k Orders,
3998 Wolf St., Victoria BC  V8N 3P7  CANADA
Phone:250 - 477 - 3617
Internet: flyingkiwipress@home.com

*Volume and trade discounts apply.*

## By the Same Author

### "Acres of Fire"

A novel, a coming-of-age with a difference, release middle of 1999.  As a complement to *"Surviving the Year 2000 Computer Crash"* it spans from the Summer of 1999 to the Spring of 2000, and is set against the worst-case scenario of a world gone mad.

"There is terror and violence everywhere, as civilization falls apart when the computers all stop.  A young girl is forced to grow up rapidly as she experiences fear, pain and loss, and finds unexpected love amid the chaos."

Flying Kiwi Press        flyingkiwipress@home.com
Trafford Publishing      www.trafford.com

### "An Introduction to Object-Oriented Analysis, Objects in Plain English"

*Published February, 1997.*

The author's entire teaching career has been a constant search for textbooks his students could actually read and learn from. *"An Introduction to Object-Oriented Analysis, Objects in Plain English"* was his first book, written to fill that need.  Though primarily

aimed at second-year MIS, Computing Science, Business, and Computer Systems students, it is also intended for practising computer professionals who need to upgrade to the new techniques, and business and professional persons who wish to learn about information systems design.

This is the only Object-Oriented book so far:

- Written in plain, everyday English,
- With a strong business bias, and
- Written as a textbook engineered for students to learn from.

Brown, David (1997), "An Introduction to Object-Oriented Analysis, Objects in Plain English" New York, NY: John Wiley and Sons.  ISBN  0471110280      www.wiley.com
http://catalog.wiley.com/ss.1256953645index.cgi?script=remsrch&query=An+Introduction+to+Object-Oriented+Analysis

# Table of Contents
## in Brief

# Table of Contents

# Chapter 1: What Problem?

## Imagine this:

It's December 31, 1999. Your friend Diane has an office three floors up, looking out over Times Square New York. It's 11:58 p.m., and from Diane's office, you and a few other guests are watching half a million people crammed into the streets below, waiting for the Millennium. As midnight draws near, the crowd begins to chant, just like they do every New Year. You can hear them through the window, as well as on a portable radio behind you. "10, 9, 8 . . . " The noise comes clearly through the window glass. They're working up to a frenzy. "4, 3, 2 . . . " – Just one second to go! – "One, Zero!!!" A roar begins to rise from the crowd.

## *And the lights go out.*

The cheering chokes off suddenly. Times Square is in total blackness, and so is every building in Manhattan. After a moment of awful silence, a different kind of noise swells and rises from the people. A horrified murmur quickly becomes a muted babble of fear, punctuated by screams. People begin to stumble around, trying desperately to head toward the streets leading out from the Square. But most can't move anywhere in such a crush of bodies. Here and there you see the flare of a match or lighter. Few and far between, you see the steady lights of those who were smart enough to bring along a flashlight.

*Could this actually happen? I hope not. But when you think of just how much we depend on computers these days, you have to wonder what might happen if they all broke at the same moment. And you know, even though we're all used to seeing computers around, actually we depend on them way more than most people realize. So read on a little to see what could happen if a whole bunch of computers failed in the electricity supply, telephones, police dispatch radios, radio and TV stations, and even cars and trucks:*

Over to one side you become aware of a bigger light. Flames flare up, and the crowd sways as people attempt to scatter. You realize that someone's clothing is on fire. You watch for agonizing seconds, until finally the flames subside. Thank God, you think to yourself, someone nearby was brave enough to smother the fire. Stop drop and roll is tough to do in such a crowd. You wonder how many will be trampled before the crowd clears the Square.

Your host Diane meanwhile has felt her way across the office to her desk and pulled a flashlight from a drawer. She uses it just long enough to rejoin you and the other guests at the window. "Better save the batteries," she says, "there's no knowing how long this might last." Over the continuing noise of the crowd outside, you hear a guest open a beer in the dark, and someone says "Damn!" as they spill hot coffee on a hand. Someone else fiddles with the radio a moment, and pronounces it dead. The batteries are fine, but it stopped working right at midnight.

"Hadn't we better get out of here?" asks a worried-sounding voice.

"Not yet," says the host. "We'd better wait until the crowd has gone, or we'll be trampled as soon as we get out of the building."

"Should someone check out the fire escape?" says another voice.

Diane tries to be reassuring. "All looked after. I checked it out this afternoon, just in case. We shouldn't go out there too soon either, in case other people in the building start to panic. And I don't want to split the group, or we'll never find each other again in the dark!"

You look out the window once more, and you notice a couple of small fires have appeared the other side of the Square. It's impossible to tell if they were deliberate or accidental. As you watch, one of them starts to grow, and you see that a part of the building is burning. The flames climb slowly up the wall, and no one seems to take much notice. People are pushing and shoving, and fighting is breaking out. It's beginning to look like a full-blown riot.

You pick up the phone to call 9-1-1, but there's no dial tone. You put it down, and dig your cell phone out of your jacket. You turn it on and the display lights up, but it's completely blank. Someone else has a cell phone too. Her display works, but all it says is "Looking for service." The phone itself is dead like the others.

By now, the crowd below is beginning to thin. But when you look closely at where the lights are, you become aware that some of them show bodies lying on the ground, with people gathered around them. And as the fire across the Square continues to grow, you break into a cold sweat. All of a sudden this isn't fun any more. It's no longer an adventure. It's all too real, and it looks like there's people dying out there.

The building across the way is well alight, and now a couple more buildings have fires of their own. Why are there only three police cars with lights flashing?

After about 30 minutes of this, the host says it's time to leave. She turns on the precious flashlight for a minute while everyone gathers up their stuff. "Just food and clothing," she says, "because we may have to walk. No beer." The guests all troop out the door behind her and the glowing flashlight.

At the elevators, you press the button and no light comes on. "The fire escape's this way. Follow me," says Diane. You all go slowly down three flights of stairs, the people at the back stumbling in total darkness.

Halfway down, a terrifying sight awaits you. The flashlight picks out a body, lying awkwardly on the stairs. The back of the head is all bloody, the clothes disheveled. After a moment of horror, you stoop and feel for a pulse, but there is none. "What should we do?" asks someone from behind. "Nothing right now," you respond. "The cops can look after him tomorrow. I think they've got their hands pretty full right now."

Eventually you reach the main floor. The lobby is empty, but through a broken window you can hear the noises of the people outside. You try the doors and find they're locked. That explains the broken window. You all step carefully through the hole, onto pavement strewn with broken glass. You stare around in amazement. Why aren't there more police vehicles? Where are the ambulances?

It looks just like there's been a war. There are people, mostly in small groups. Some are milling around, and others walking as if they're going somewhere. There are soldiers and police all over. Here and there are bodies on the ground. Some are alive, and some of those have people helping them. You see a man sitting on the sidewalk with three soldiers around him. Two are holding flashlights, while the third is splinting his broken leg. People are weeping over some of the bodies.

A couple of police cars are the only vehicles moving. Their headlights add to the flickering light of the dozen or so fires. Some other vehicles have had their windows smashed out, and two or three are burning. Some soldiers and firemen are trying to start a firetruck.

A man steps onto the sidewalk and points a handgun at one of your group, demanding money. Before you can think to react, there's a shot from behind you, and the mugger falls. You turn and see a soldier 20 yards away lower his rifle. "We have orders to shoot," he says, and turns and walks away. You look back at the mugger on the sidewalk, and realize you have just watched a man die.

Shocked and numbed, you all follow Diane around the corner. Only one or two vehicles go by, and others are stopped in the middle of the roadway. You pass under the silent, stranded trains. It will be a long, dark walk home.

Sounds far-fetched? I hope it is! But everything that went wrong in the story did so because of a computer failure. Every cell phone has a computer chip in it. Most radios do these days. Vehicles made in the late 1990s typically have from *30 to 50* computer chips built into them, controlling everything from the digital dash to the electronic fuel injection (EFI), electronic ignition, burglar alarm, remote start and keyless entry.

Police radios, elevators, building security systems, train-control systems are all run by computers, and of course so is the electricity supply. The telephone system is really just one giant computer spread across the continent, handling a billion calls a day.

But would they ever *all fail at once?* Normally, that would never happen. But at midnight on December 31, 1999 when we roll over to the new millennium, they might. Some will fail right at that moment, for sure. Some more will fail in the hours before midnight, and many more over the weeks and months following, well into the year 2000.

The big question is, how many? And how badly will they fail? And I can see the other big question forming in your mind – *why?* Why would a whole bunch of computers all break at the same time, just as we're having the biggest party the world has ever known? Is this maybe just some scare plot by a bunch of party-poopers?

I'm afraid not. It's a real problem, and in a moment, as Paul Harvey might say, "You're going to hear *The Rest of the Story.*"

# What Caused the Problem?

## Dates & Storage Space

Software has always had a problem with a lack of storage space for information in the computer. One way that programmers have learned to cope with this is to shorten all the dates recorded in the computer, so the year has only two digits. So 1997 becomes 97, and 1984 is 84, and so on.

Back in 1965 when I began my career as a programmer, computers were expensive. That year, I began working on a mainframe computer that occupied a room the size of an average classroom. It cost a quarter of a million dollars, a whole lot of money back then – worth at least ten times as much today, say about $2 million. Today, I have more processing power in the chip in my $80 Ironman watch. Seriously. I kid you not. More power *and* more memory.

In a computer, the *memory* is the storage space for information, and its size or capacity is measured in "bytes." A byte is enough room to store one letter, or one digit, or one punctuation symbol. We say a byte can store one "character." Mostly we need larger numbers, so we use multiples of a byte:

A kilobyte or "k" is *about* 1000 bytes. Actually, it's 1024 bytes because of the math used in computers, so we can say it's "a bit more than 1000." Just for comparison, a densely-typed page in the book in your hand could hold about 5k, or just over 5000 characters.

(Because "k" stands for "about a thousand," programmers often shorten "Year 2000" to *Y2k.*)

A Megabyte or "Meg" is a little more than a million bytes. (For anyone who might care, it's actually 1024 x 1024, or 1,048,576, but who's counting?)

A Gigabyte or "Gig" is 1024 times that, or a *bit more than a billion* bytes.

And what does all this cost? In 1970, a Megabyte of storage (for those few who had that much) cost $1,320,000US. Nowadays, it's $1.30US. *Cheaper by a factor of a million!*

So in those days programmers used to do all kinds of things to avoid wasting space in the computer memory, and on the disk and tape files. One thing in particular that they all did was to store dates with only two digits for the year. So my birthdate, February 8, 1944 would be recorded in the computer 440208, which we would represent as YYMMDD, or Year-Month-Day.

While this helped to solve the urgent problem of expensive storage, the programmers were fully aware that it could lead to another problem down the road, when we reached Y2k. But they never expected that they or their programs would still be around when it happened!

What is happening is that whenever we say '03' meaning 2003, the software thinks we mean 1903, and it uses 1903 in all its calculations.

For a while in 1996, some credit cards were being issued with expiry dates of '00' or '01.' When these were swiped at the point-of-sale machine, many times they were rejected. The computer chip in the swipe machine added the two digits '19' to the front of the year, and figured the card expired in 1900 or 1901. No wonder it disallowed the sale!

To get around the problem, the credit card companies had to use an expiry year of 99 until the point-of-sale computers could all be updated. This was finished in early 1998, so now we see cards with '00' and '01' all the time. But this little problem shows how the two-digit date can screw us up royally! This was very embarrassing for some people.

The problem gets worse when we start doing calculations on the dates. A lot of software does math on dates as if they were numbers. The answer comes out as a "time interval," measured in days, months and years. Here is a true story that shows the kind of thing that can happen. (If you find this section boring, you can skip ahead a couple of pages to the heading "Finding Them All.")

In the food industry, many products have a limited shelf life, so they come with an expiry date. Some companies, notably Marks and Spencer, have computerized systems that automatically send food products to the garbage if their date expires before they get sold.

A computer handles this by subtracting one date from another, as if they were some strange kind of numbers. The result is a number of days, or months, or years.

For instance, How many months and days was it:
From January 13 to January 27, 1998?

|  |  | yy mm dd |  |
|---|---|---|---|
|  | January 27: | 98 01 27 |  |
| *Minus* | January 13: | 98 01 13 |  |
|  | Gives: | 00 00 14 | The answer is 14 days |

From January 13 to February 15?

|  |  | yy mm dd |  |
|---|---|---|---|
|  | February 15: | 98 02 15 |  |
| *Minus* | January 13: | 98 01 13 |  |
|  | Gives: | 00 01 02 | The answer is 1 month and 2 days. |

Or again, if we subtract my birthday (February 8) from today's date (I'm writing this on the second of September, 1998) it looks like this:

|  |  | yy mm dd |  |
|---|---|---|---|
|  | Today: | 98 09 02 |  |
| *Minus* | My birthday: | 98 02 08 |  |
|  | Gives: | 00 06 25 | The answer is six months and 25 |

days. Use a calendar to check this.

But if the dates are the other way around, then like regular subtraction, we get a negative number of days (or months or years.)

From January 27 to January 13?

|  |  | yy mm dd |
|---|---|---|
|  | January 13: | 98 01 13 |
| *Minus* | January 27: | <u>98 01 27</u> |
|  | Gives: | -00 00 14 |

-00 00 14   The answer is *minus 14* days, a negative number of days.

How about from February 15 to January 13?

|  |  | yy mm dd |
|---|---|---|
|  | January 13: | 98 01 13 |
| *Minus* | February 15: | <u>98 02 15</u> |
|  | Gives: | -00 01 02 |

-00 01 02   The answer is *negative* one month and two days, or **-33** days.

Or again, if we subtract today's date from my birthday, February 8 (I'm writing on the second of September, 1998) it looks like this:

|  |  | yy mm dd |
|---|---|---|
|  | My birthday: | 98 02 08 |
| *Minus* | Today: | <u>98 09 02</u> |
|  | Gives: | -00 06 25 |

-00 06 25   The answer is *negative* six months and 25 days.

Now here's the calculation that the computer program does for the food:

|  |  | yy mm dd |
|---|---|---|
|  | Expiry Date: November 1, 1999 | 99 11 01 |
| *Minus* | Today's Date: November 1, 1998 | <u>98 11 01</u> |
|  | Tells us how long we can keep it: | 01 00 00 |

**We can keep it for *one year*.**

And 12 months plus a day later,

|  |  | yy mm dd |
|---|---|---|
|  | Expiry Date: November 1, 1999 | 99 11 01 |
| *Minus* | Today's Date: November 2, 1999 | <u>99 11 02</u> |
|  | Tells us how long we can keep it: | -00 00 01 |

**This is a negative number of days.**
**This means we're one day *beyond* the expiry date!**

So, whenever the program gets a negative answer to this calculation, it prints out the shipment number on the disposal list, and that shipment gets sent off to the garbage dump.

In this next example, today's date is November 1, 1998, and the food still has two years to go until it expires on November 1, 2000. But watch what happens with the calculations:

|  |  | yy mm dd |
|---|---|---|
|  | Expiry Date: November 1, 2000 | 00 11 01 |
| *Minus* | Today's Date: November 1, 1998 | <u>98 11 01</u> |
|  | Tells us how long we can keep it: | -98 00 00 |

**This is a *very large* negative number!**

The program now thinks we're 98 years beyond the expiry date! So off it goes, and sends this shipment of perfectly good food to the dump. There are companies who have already run into just this problem, and have wasted thousands of dollars of food before the error was noticed and corrected.

And just for variety, there are some programming languages where the minus on the date would simply be lost. The people who decades ago designed these languages assumed that such negatives could never happen.

This would mean that in the example just above, the answer would come out as *positive* 98 years. This would prevent us from sending the food prematurely to the dump, which is nice, but it means the food might stay on the shelf for another 98 years! Hopefully, someone would notice the smell before then.

There have been many other examples of date calculations screwing up on the year '00' like this. We can expect a whole lot more, some no more than a minor annoyance, and some like this one costing a significant amount of money.

The problem is that the program assumed the missing two digits of the year are always '19.' Up until now, almost all software in the world has treated dates this way. But now that some computers are having to deal with dates in the next millennium, the software has to be changed so that it treats the year '00' as being 2000 instead of 1900, '01' as 2001 instead of 1901, and so on.

And any software that deals with people's ages must be able to handle people who were born last century, and who plan on living on into the new Millennium. The *only* way to handle these people is to have four digits for the year, so that 1900 and 2000 are distinct.

If we use only two digits, there's no way for the software to tell which of those two years it has when it sees '00' in somebody's birthdate. Or if it sees '02' it can't tell whether you're two years old or 102!

This is easily fixed, you may say. Just change all the dates so they have four digits for the year! Now that memory is so cheap, we can afford it. And that's just what we're attempting to do, but, as we'll see below and in the next chapter, it's not as simple as you might think.

## Finding Them All

The problem is that software is very, very complex. In fact, finding *all* the places that dates are used in the software is just not possible. We'll do our best to find and fix them all, but we simply won't be able to find every one. Some will get missed during the testing, and they'll show up later when the software is running for real in production, after January 1, 2000.

In his book *"Computer Crisis 2000,"* Michael Fletcher gives an excellent illustration of how such a simple problem can grow so complicated.

> "Imagine you have been asked to change a light bulb. No problem. You take the replacement bulb, unscrew the old one, screw in the new one, and flick the switch. What could be simpler?
>
> Now imagine that you have been asked to change every light bulb in your community. That includes small 60-watt bulbs, large 100-watt bulbs, neon tubes, car headlights, refrigerator lights, traffic signals, desk lamps, flashlights, store signs, and Christmas illuminations. You don't know where they all are and some of the doors to get to them are locked, with no keys. In addition, you know you don't have enough spares, you will have to work in the dark to find some of them, and you must accomplish this entire task in the next two weeks.
>
> THAT is the nature of the year 2000 problem. The challenge is one of location, access, analysis, resources, spares, knowledge, and time. It could have been fixed with no problem if we had started early enough. We didn't and so we have created a monster to conquer in the time remaining."

Let me now spend 3 or 4 pages explaining just what a software program really is, and why it has to be so complicated. And if this gets boring for you, feel free to skip ahead over the page to the heading "Good Companies Getting Bad Data."

## What a Software Program Is

The computer has sometimes been called an "electronic idiot," and that's pretty close. It can do an amazing number of things, but it can't *think*. It always needs to be told what to do, and what to do next, every step of the way. Any so-called "smarts" we think the computer has, are really in the software program, and were put there by a programmer.

It sometimes helps to compare the computer to those old "player pianos," that could play tunes from holes punched in a roll of paper. Or a music box, where the music is in the form of little bumps on a metal cylinder, that twang the tuned metal strips to make the notes. In both cases, you can play any song you wish.

There are literally millions of songs out there that have already been written, and could be played by one of these pianos or music boxes. And there are billions of possible songs that haven't been written yet. You could make the machine play any of these songs, provided someone first punched the holes in the paper, or made the bumps on the metal cylinder.

These machines have zero musical ability. They can play any music ever written, anything at all, provided a "programmer" tells them what to do, every step of the way. And the hardware and software? The piano and paper roll are hardware, and the *music* written in the holes is software.

The same is true for the music box: the box. The cylinder and the wind-up spring to make it go are hardware. Even the little metal bumps on the metal cylinder are hardware. The *music* recorded in the little bumps is the software.

So the music is really a set of instructions for the machine to follow. The program says make this note, then this one, and so on. So it is for the program, or software, for a computer. Here's another example to show why software is so complex.

Let's say your hockey coach or dance instructor is standing in front of you, and tells you to turn your head to your left. Then she says to lift your right arm up from your side until it's horizontal. A pretty simple thing to do, right? Wrong! How many messages were running up and down the nerves in your arm between your muscles and your brain? Hundreds of millions, in just those few seconds.

There are 13 billion cells in your brain, and a billion or so of these are connected to the muscles in your arm. There are hundreds of millions of muscle fibers in the muscles of your arm, and each one has a trail of nerve cells leading to your brain. When your brain says to move your arm, it sends individual messages to each muscle fibre, via connecting nerve cells.

And even though you were looking left and couldn't see your arm, you could still feel where it was the whole time. There are sensors in your arm that feel its weight, and the angle of the elbow, and things like that. As your arm moves, these sensors tell your brain what's going on, again through pathways of nerve cells.

So you see how complex it is to get a simple little thing done with the human body. It's that way for the computer, also. When you click on an icon, or type the name of your favorite game, and watch things start to happen on the screen, there are literally millions of teeny step-by-steps happening behind the scenes. The same when you click on an icon and just drag it across the screen.

The list of steps that the programmers write is kind of like a recipe for the machine to follow to do the job. This list is often called "program code," because it's not written in English, or any other people language. Instead, it's written in a computer programming language, which is really a code that the computer was built to understand, and the programmer had to learn. Each teeny step is then called a "line of code" because it's one instruction, usually typed on one line on a computer screen.

Some of these languages have names like "Java", "C++" (See-plus-plus), "Visual Basic" and "Smalltalk." Then there's "COBOL" and "FORTRAN" which are both out-of-date languages. But there's a lot of software still in use that was written in COBOL and FORTRAN, and must be tested and fixed for the Year 2000 problem.

Some of this old software was written as far back as 30 years ago, and those programmers are now retired or dead, and that doesn't help. We politely call this old software "*legacy software*," and we expect it to be a major problem in Y2k conversion projects.

Everything you do on a computer works this way. And a programmer (or a team of them) had to write down every little step in advance. They do have some assistance. There are "tools" they can use, software programs that do part of the work for them, and they often like to reuse parts of programs that have been pre-written by another programmer.

But still, programmers have a mass of incredibly detailed work to do, and, surprisingly enough, they have this habit of making errors.

These errors are referred to as "bugs," and a normal programmer will spend something like half his or her time finding and correcting bugs. Writing the code is one thing. *Fixing* the bugs once they're found is not usually too difficult. *Finding* them is always the problem. Programmers must test and test and test. But even the best of them can't find *every* bug.

And testing can never *prove* the absence of bugs. If a test finds a bug, then the test has proved the *presence* of bugs. But even if today's test finds no errors, tomorrow's test might find some. We can only spend so much time and money on this, and try to reach an "acceptable" level of errors. And just what is "acceptable?" Well, it depends!

Studies have found that an average programmer, by the time (s)he has finished testing, puts their software into production with about one bug still in it per one hundred lines of code (LOC). Since there can be thousands or millions of LOCs in a software product, this may sound like a lot of bugs.

But just think for a moment – how many people do you know who can write 100 lines of English without a mistake? Even after they've proofread it carefully a couple of times!

By using some very expensive and time-consuming methods, programmers can do better than that. But it's so expensive that this is only done when the extra expense can be justified. Of course, only the best ("*expensive*") programmers are used for this task. For software that looks after human lives or costly property, they can spend the extra time and money.

This means things like software on board an airplane, or in navigation systems, or in hospital equipment, or in a satellite where we can't reach it to fix things. These more expensive programmers can manage about one defect (bug) per 10,000 lines of code, or about 100 times better.

But what about nuclear power plants, nuclear weapons, NORAD and other military applications? By spending even more time and money, those programmers can get down to *one defect per million* lines of code. That's incredibly good, compared to the level I'm used to working at. But when you stop to think that the U.S. military has more than 600 million lines of program code in its software, that means we can still expect maybe 600 bugs.

No one in business can afford, or even find, programmers that good. At least not all the time. There are some geniuses out there, some of them grossly underpaid for what they're capable of. For an example of how *not* to treat your computer programming genius, watch the first Jurassic Park movie. (I haven't seen the second, but I would expect something similar. Maybe I'll have some time when I finish this book . . .)

What this tells us is that when we try to find all the date references in our existing software, we can expect *at least one percent of them* to be missed. Actually, the experts estimate that about 5% will get through. Either way, since we depend so heavily on computers in everything we do these days, you'll see in the rest of this book, that we could be in for a rough time.

And that's what this book is all about. In the chapters still to come, you'll discover what *will* happen, what's likely to happen, and what might happen but probably won't. Then you'll learn what you should be doing to protect yourself, your family, your property and your money, in case the worst should happen.

## Good Companies Getting Bad Data

That 5% estimate is for the good ones. Among companies, governments and software vendors, some are working hard to correct the problem, and others are not. Some don't know about the problem, and some do know but refuse to believe it's serious.

But even if your company (or your employer) goes all out, does everything right, and has all (or almost all) their dates fixed in the software, what about their suppliers and their customers? So much information these days is passed from one company's computer to another's. Orders, invoices, bills, packing slips, paychecks, they all go electronically from one computer to another. This is often called Electronic Data Interchange, or EDI.

What if some of those guys don't get the job done right? They could be sending you data with all kinds of incorrect dates and date-related calculations. And many of these errors would be hidden in such a way that they might not show up on a report or a screen until month-end, or some maybe not until year-end. This could thoroughly screw up *your* business operations as well as theirs.

## Legal Problems

What if you own or manage a company, and you end up sending bad data to some of your customers? Some people might stick their head in the sand and hope that Dave Brown and the Y2k problem will quietly go away. Sorry, I'm real and I'm right here in your face. And so is Y2k. Once you read this book, however, I don't think you'll be one of the ostrich people. But many businesses have just buried their heads.

Or maybe you did everything right, spent the money, started in 1995 while there was still plenty of time, and still had those pesky 5% that got through. And maybe you were just unlucky enough that they were dates that mattered, and cost your customers money when they got screwed up. So now you have customers who have lost money in a big way, and who must now *spend* money to straighten out their billing, or whatever it was that went wrong.

Do you imagine they'll be happy about all this? No way! They'll be on their way to the lawyer's office, and pretty soon you'll be arguing it out in court. Y2k is expected to be the *biggest single source of lawsuits ever*.

There'll be clients suing vendors and banks over bad data, and patients (or their estates) suing hospitals over monitoring equipment that didn't, or automatic machines that gave the wrong dosage of medicine.

Even government agencies and their employees will be sued. There could be airplanes getting lost, or worse, not getting down safely. There'll be all kinds of products and equipment that will stop working, and some of the people affected will be going after the manufacturer to fix it, or pay for it.

And the lawyers will love it! So here's a message for all you young students out there. If you're partway through your legal training and not quite sure whether to continue, get into gear and get it finished!

And if you're just starting out, remember that these cases will drag on for years into the new millennium. So you should have enough time to get your schooling, spend a year as an underpaid legal clerk, and get into the profession while there's still a high demand.

The president of one law society, when he saw an article that said lawyers were "salivating" over the Y2k pickings, responded that "They're not just salivating, they're slobbering!" Lawyers and programmers are going to make a lot of money. But if you don't start right away, pretty soon it'll be too late.

But for the rest of us, we need to try as best we can to protect ourselves. This could be awkward, since insurance companies are starting to get nervous. Many of them are adding a note to their policies, saying they won't cover you against damage or loss arising from a Y2k-related problem. Which says we really don't need this problem. So why don't they just fix it? (Whoever "they" might be.)

# Chapter 2: Why Don't They Just Fix It?

## The Programmers Did It, They Can fix It!

Well, yes they did. But programmers are not the only ones to blame. Way back 30 years ago, or even 20, computer memory was so expensive that something like this had to be done. We couldn't afford to use four-digit years in all the dates in our computer files. And once it was done, we were stuck with it. Then as we began to see the millennium approaching, we realized we would be faced with an expensive conversion project.

The amount of money saved was certainly significant. Some experts figure that the savings over the last 30 years amount to about the same as what it'll cost to fix all the software for Y2k. But that's not good enough. We're still going to come out behind rather than ahead, because of all the indirect costs, all the disasters from the 5% that will get through, and the legal costs, and so on.

On top of all that, the U.S. government made the two-digit year **a *federal and military standard.*** This meant that any software written for the Feds ***must*** do it that way. The programmers had to do it, even though they knew how much trouble it would cause later.

Paul Strassman, former director of U.S. Defense Information under George Bush, says that "the responsibility rests squarely on the shoulders of government and industry leaders." He says they should have been in closer touch with their programmers and computer managers, that it was "carelessness, disregard, dereliction and thoughtlessness."

Part of the problem, he points out, lies in the fact that executives mistrust computer managers. And I agree. It's true. They find it difficult to trust us techies whose jobs and jargon they don't understand. How can a company president feel comfortable making million-dollar decisions on the advice of someone who talks as if he's from another planet?

And how do you convince management they should spend vast sums of money on a project with no return on the investment? We could have just told them the simple truth, that it would allow them to stay in business!

But even a year or two back, most non-computer managers would have laughed at any suggestion that 2-digit dates could put companies out of business. To them it was beyond belief that careers might be destroyed, and lawsuits could cause personal as well as business bankruptcies.

Here are a couple of examples of how this problem is known to some, and not to others. The first is a gentle and rather humorous insight into how most people have heard very little about Y2k. The second is a rather more ominous look at shortsighted management decision-making, trying to save money in the short term.

### Example 1: Melda

My wife Nina and I were talking recently to her sister Melda about our last trip to the Philippines. We remembered how beautiful the Pearl Farm Resort is, and indeed it was just like Fantasy Island, only prettier yet. Melda suggested we ought to spend New Year's Eve there for the Millennium.

She really was quite shocked at my reply. "I don't think I want to go anywhere that night!" I said rather forcefully. "In fact," I told her, "I don't even think I want to drive across the city to your house that night!" She obviously thought I was nuts.

The conversation that followed was Melda's introduction to the Y2k problem. She is an intelligent and aware person, more so than average. After being 30 years a teacher, she is now a director of several companies, and she and her husband Virgilio are the hands-on managers of our family business, Maligaya (Filipino for "Happy") Travel. ( maligaya@oanet.com )

So you can see that non-computer managers are just now becoming aware that there's a Y2k problem. In the travel business this is critical – we should not be booking anybody to fly on the day before or several days after the Y2k midnight rollover. Nor should we book for August 21 or 22 of 1999, because of the GPS satellite system rollover (see Chapter 3).

The other example is more serious, more ominous and more expensive.

### Example 2: Dave Elyk

Dave Elyk is a colleague of mine, and teaches with me at the Northern Alberta Institute of Technology (NAIT). In 1990 Dave led a team on a programming contract for a government department. Anxious to do the right thing by his client, he used four digits for the year in every date in the system.

The client was furious! How dare they squander taxpayers' money by wasting so much storage space?! After Dave had handed over the completed software, the client hired another consultant to go through it and change all the years to two digits!

Now, after spending taxpayers' money to make it wrong, they have to spend a bunch more on a massive cleanup job to make it right again. And they can't just go back to using Dave's original programs, because, as is the way with software, there have been numerous changes made through the years.

So did the taxpayer come out ahead in the end? You be the judge. There's money at stake here.

## $600 Billion – Mankind's Biggest Project Ever!

Capers Jones is a respected software guru, whose work is known around the world in the IT (Information Technology) business. He has written the best book so far for facts, figures and forecasts about the Y2k Problem. (See Appendix, "To Find Out More.")

He comments: ". . . The year 2000 problem is almost unique in human history. There has never been a man-made technical problem that will impact so many businesses, so many government groups, and cause so many problems at a personal level."

I have to agree with him. I think the last time we had problems this big was World War II. This one probably won't cause as many deaths and injuries, and physical damage (we hope), but its economic impact will be right up there. And there *will* be a number of deaths.

According to Jones and others, Y2k will be the most expensive single problem in history. He estimates the computer industry will spend about $600 billion (with a 'b') worldwide to do all the testing and corrections. But here are the other costs that this figure doesn't include:

The Rush Factor
The Cost of Bad Data
The Cost of Breakdowns
Legal Expenses

### The Rush Factor

Since so many companies and government agencies have ignored this problem or procrastinated over it, many will start to panic in 1998 and 1999. But the programmers will all be taken, and the consulting companies and Year 2000 contractors will all be booked up. This will push up the wages and the contract prices.

It'll also mean, in many cases, hiring from the bottom of the barrel, so the work will sometimes be poorly done. This will mean more errors and corrections to add to the expense. And just the extra rush, stress and pressure will cause errors and mistakes.

## The Cost of Bad Data

When things do go wrong – and some will – it'll cost *money*. And the biggest part of this whole problem is that *we just can't tell how many things will go wrong.* Nor can we tell how badly they'll go wrong, how quickly they'll be found, or what all this will cost us.

What if a department store or credit card company overbilled all their clients? If the error was thousands of dollars on each bill, they'd pretty soon hear about it. It would cost them time and money to answer all the angry calls and letters, and for the programmers to find and fix the problem, as well as printing the bills over and mailing them out again.

But what if the overbilling was for about $20 per customer? You might notice, and so would my wife Nina. She always checks this kind of thing. But how many people would just pay the bill and not notice? I probably would. The fact is that thousands would. In this case the error is way more difficult to spot, and by the time it's found, it may have done more damage.

In an extreme case a company might lose their customer records altogether. Gone. Erased or irretrievably damaged. If they lose their Accounts Receivable files, how will they know who owes them money? I have seen this happen a couple of times in the past, and it's costly if you have to rely on the honesty of your customers to pay what they owe you. Some do. Many do not. Businesses can go under when this happens to them.

So what else could go wrong? Pretty well anything *could* go wrong. This is bad data we're talking about here. And whether it's caused by something going wrong in your own software, or it's sent to you by government, school, hospital, insurance company, customer, supplier, employer or whoever, it could cost you and me a bundle. Here is a partial list of ways that your life could be affected by bad data from the Y2k problem:

### Computers Are Used by Businesses and Organizations To Do These Things for You:

| | |
|---|---|
| Sorting your mail | School registration and academic records |
| Your paycheck | Banking and mutual funds |
| Maintenance schedules | Airline reservations |
| Monthly bills | Schedules for trains, buses, boats and planes |
| Credit card processing | Anything you do with the government |

Screw-ups in any of these services could cost money, time and hassle. For you and me, as well as the people who work there and have to straighten it out. For companies, the shareholders could stand to lose a lot of money with reduced profits and dropping share values. And don't forget, one of the shareholders might easily be *your* pension fund or *your* mutual fund. We're all in this together. It's not just the rich who could lose here.

### The Cost of Breakdowns

Computers are used by and hidden in just about everything around us these days. That's not an exaggeration. Here's a list of everyday things that involve computers in one or more ways:

### Computer Chips Are Hidden (Embedded) Inside These Products:

| | | |
|---|---|---|
| TVs and VCRs | Industrial robots | GPS receivers |
| Microwaves | Two-way radios | Artificial limbs |
| Calculators | Radios and stereos | Hospital monitoring equipment |
| Airplanes | Anything with a motor: | Security systems: buildings, vehicles |
| Ships, Radar | -Vehicles (A big one, this!) | Automatic medicine dispensers |
| Bank vaults | -Power boats | Automated Teller Machines (ATMs) |
| Elevators | -Generators | Automatic vending machines |
| Pacemakers | -Lawnmowers | Basically, *automatic anything* |
| Cell phones | -Chainsaws | Anything with a *digital display*, |
| CD players | -Snowblowers | whether LEDs or liquid-crystal |

*Some* of these things will get screwed up. (Remember the 5% of dates that we expect will be missed.) The question is, how many and how badly?

And here are some more things that we depend on, some of them every day. All of these services use computers to keep their systems running. If their computers fail, they may stop supplying us with the things we need to continue living the way we're used to.

In Chapter Three we'll see how a few software failures in the past had serious and potentially disastrous effects. We can expect that *some* software will fail. It's impossible to predict which ones, how badly they'll fail, and for how long. But *some* will have problems, for sure.

### Computers Are Used in the Control Systems That Keep These Systems Running:

| | | |
|---|---|---|
| Electricity supply | Natural gas supply | Traffic lights and traffic control systems |
| Power plants | Air traffic control | Railway locomotives & braking systems |
| Industrial plants | Navigation systems | Railway signals and train control |
| Elevators | Nuclear power plants | (Especially *driverless* **trains!**) |
| Pipelines | TV and Radio stations | Oil refineries and chemical plants |
| Water supply | Building security systems | Assembly lines (Lots of robots.) |
| Satellite anything | Stock markets, stockbrokers | Nuclear submarines and aircraft carriers |
| Currency trading | Heating & air conditioning | Research installations of many kinds, |
| | Commodities markets | including nuclear |

This is a long list of possible failures. Whichever ones fail, there'll be direct costs. If (God help us I hope not!) airplanes, navigation systems and air traffic controllers all lose touch with each other, there could be deadly and expensive crashes.

If the gas and electricity go out anytime in the winter of 1999/2000 where I live in northern Canada, there'll be frozen and burst waterpipes, and other direct costs. Traffic lights, railways, industrial plants, all have the potential to fail and cause dangerous and costly disasters. Bhopal and Chernobyl could happen all over again.

Then there'll be the indirect costs of lost wages, insurance payouts (if the insurance companies survive) and so on. If we had a significant number of such disasters, they could depress the world economy, and cause stock markets to drop or even crash. And then will be all the legal wrangling that takes place after the shouting dies down.

### Legal Expenses

There are several ways that the legal problems could affect you, or the people and businesses you deal with. Perhaps your employer might be affected, which could seriously affect your wages, or whether you still have a job. If your city or local government suffers, you can expect your taxes to go up. And if some of the businesses you deal with have troubles, you might end up having to find new places to shop or to get your car repaired.

Here is a partial list of costs that might be involved in suing or being sued:

Legal Costs
Damages Against You
Time in Court
Damaged Reputation

**Legal Costs** Estimates are that for many companies and government agencies, the lawyers' fees and court costs for Y2k problems could be as high as 30% of annual software budget. That is, for every dollar a company spends on software in an average year, they can expect to spend about 30 cents on Y2k legal fees.

By this I mean a one time only cost, so if a company spends about $1 million each year on computing, then their Y2k legal expenses will probably be close to $300,000 total.

**Damages Against You** But then, what if you lose in court? There's no telling how high the awards might go. Companies may sue for profits lost because of bad data. Personal injury awards might be in tens of millions of dollars per person. And some insurance companies are refusing to cover Y2k.

There's no knowing how many injuries there might be. It may well be that some companies who survive the millennium crunch with reasonably small problems and moderate damage, will find that the lawsuits will drive them into bankruptcy.

**Time in Court** Defending yourself in court could be expensive in lost wages, lost employee time and lost productivity. Going to court to defend yourself doesn't create any goods or services to add to the amount of wealth in the country. Lawsuits don't increase the GDP (Gross Domestic Product), and don't make anyone richer except the lawyers.

**Damaged Reputation** Whether you own a business or work for one, you'll need to think about questions like these: Will your customers still trust you after a big Y2k failure? Will you lose them to a competitor? Will your employer still trust you?

If your employer is forced to downsize after a Y2k disaster, will it be *you* who is still around? Or will it be your co-worker who prepares better for Y2k and saves the boss a bundle?

## Not Me, I Just Work Here!

Many people in high places may think they're off the hook on lawsuits because they're "just an employee." Well the news is that when a company suffers severe losses, or goes under, the shareholders in many cases can sue the managers and directors for not performing their duty. This may even affect managers who know nothing about software or 2-digit dates.

Whatever happens within the company, the managers are always responsible to the shareholders. No one's expected to be perfect, of course. But the courts may well decide that a manager was negligent and not doing his job if he had his head in the sand about Y2k when he should have been checking on his programmers.

This means that there could be personal bankruptcies as a result of Y2k lawsuits. As I mentioned earlier, insurance companies are already getting nervous, so companies and individuals should not expect a lot of help there. If you are one of these people, you need to beware that your personal assets and wealth may be at risk. See your lawyer *now*.

And you might not have to be in top management, or a business owner, for this to happen. Technical and professional people advising top management may also be at risk.

# Not Just a Technical Problem

So you can see that this whole thing is not just for the technoids and geeks to worry about. Business owners and managers should be doing a lot of reading and research. Ordinary people should be preparing just in case. So the advice I give in Chapters 7, 8 and 9 is for the ordinary person, and it's all stuff that would be a good idea even if there's no disaster.

We *know* there'll be problems. We *don't* know how bad they'll be, or how long they'll last. The whole Y2k thing may turn out to be nothing more than a few minor inconveniences. But again it might be a disaster. Most likely it'll be somewhere in between, and I guess we'll all find out around midnight that night.

So here's my key piece of advice, and I'll repeat it later in the book: Whatever you do to prepare and protect yourself and your loved ones, should be things that *would have been a good idea anyway,* even if there's no disaster. Like buying a few flashlights and a couple of fire extinguishers. Like stocking up a bit on some canned food and a few staples like rice, potatoes, flour and milk powder.

## It's Getting Late

By now, governments and businesses should be well into their Y2k software conversion projects. As I write this in early 1998, it's becoming apparent that many are lagging behind. At this point, many businesses and government agencies have not started, or have just started.

In the Fall of 1997, software guru Capers Jones estimated that "About 30% of U.S. software companies with year 2000 problems (had) not yet actually started repairs," but were still looking to see how bad their problem was.

Because of the conflict with the Euro currency problem (see below), Jones suggests that about 50% of companies in Western Europe were ". . . lagging in year 2000 repairs and will begin serious work only in 1998 (if then)." Both the currency problem and the Y2k problem will be competing for a very scarce resource – *programmers*. There are only so many programmers to go around.

You can imagine what this kind of competition will do to wages and unethical hiring practices in the programming industry. Add all this to the fact that Europe is running even later than North America, and we may have an impossible situation.

And worse yet. Some writers have expressed a fear about all the new consulting firms popping up offering Y2k conversion services. With so many new and unknown companies, they're afraid some sneaky programmers will add unauthorized things to the software.

Typically, this might mean the programmer puts a secret code into the software so that he can get back into it months or years later. So after he has done his job, pocketed his fee, and moved on, he could sneak back in without the client knowing! This is called a "back door," and was shown well in the movie "*War Games*."

Hopefully, none of this will happen. Such a back door would give opportunity for later sabotage, espionage, or even blackmail. But with so many new and untried consultants, and so many clients in desperate need close to The Day, it just might happen.

## Manpower, Motivation and Money

*It is imperative that companies and governments plan* in advance *how to attract and then* keep *good programmers.* They must think *in advance* about what incentives they'll offer to bring these people aboard, and then what they'll offer to keep them from jumping ship at the next, more lucrative offer. And the next, and the next, each offer better than the last.

Manpower (personpower?) will be important. Good personnel, working all hours of the day and night, will be critical. Keeping them motivated is a challenge that computer managers can't do alone, they need help from Human Resources ("Personnel" or HR) specialists. But the personnel specialists who help must understand people and motivation in general, and *programmers* in particular.

We're a weird bunch, us programmers. We're used to working all hours in a crunch. But we're also human. Staff simply will not put out at the level that's going to be needed, unless they're treated well. And that means a lot more than just money.

If management have their heads firmly stuck in the sand (or wherever!) and pooh-pooh huge demands for money and resources for an urgent Y2k conversion, the programmers will go elsewhere. The money will be needed for both wages and consultants fees, and the resources needed include software, hardware, office space, programmers and support staff.

Treating these people with respect will be one of the most important things that non-computer managers *and other employees* can do. In our society, high salaries are the beginning of respect, but only the beginning. It's perhaps equally important that the programmers feel their contribution is *sincerely* valued and appreciated by management and staff at all levels.

Programmers will be so mobile during this period, they'll pick and choose the places that are rewarding, and maybe even "nice," to work for. The rest will be left contemplating the bottom of the barrel. If there's any left at all.

## Is It Too Late Yet?

Maybe. As they say in the auto industry, "You can only get so many mechanics under the hood!"

Did you hear about the committee who didn't want to wait nine months for one of their female members to have a baby? So they decided to assign nine women to the task, and have the baby in a month. Doesn't work, does it? And Y2k is something similar. Even if you could find enough good programmers to double and triple and quadruple the team, there are things that will slow them down.

Every time a new member joins the team, someone has to stop work long enough to brief them on the project and the company. Maybe they need to be trained on the particular languages and techniques being used. And as we near the bottom of the barrel, we may need to do more and more training each time we hire somebody.

At the extreme, we may have to take newcomers off the street, or existing employees, and try to turn them into programmers. This just won't work, but for some companies it may be the only option that's open. There's a book by Fred Brooks, entitled "*The Mythical Man-Month*," that explores how it's impossible to rush the solution of a problem simply by throwing more money at it.

Capers Jones figures it should take most organizations around three calendar years to fix all their software, with quite a lot of finishing-up and testing work in the fourth year. This is based on diverting about 15% of the software budget and the programmers to the Y2k project. That way, normal software work could continue.

But to do this would have meant starting in 1995 or 1996. Hardly anybody did! Those few who did are now in a good position, and can expect to be still in business when their competition start having problems, and maybe going out of business.

Peter de Jager ("dee *Yay*-grr) is a Toronto Y2k specialist, who runs an informative website at www.year2000.com. He comments that ". . the awareness in the U.S. is greater than the awareness in Canada. (In) The U.S. and Canada (it) is greater than that in the U.K., which is greater than that in Europe, and there's no real indication at all . . that anything is being done in the Far East."

Something interesting in the Canadian newspapers recently. It seems that while de Jager was addressing a group of our elected representatives in Parliament on the dangers of Y2k, the Prime Minister and his deputy were absent. They were kicking off the millennium celebrations by announcing a $150 million dollar grant! I do hope the lights are still on for the party.

De Jager further comments that "I find it very difficult to believe that . . . we're still talking about this as if some people don't believe it's a real issue. It's very, very strange." Not all that strange, Peter. It's just plain old human procrastination.

Those companies that start late and have to rush during 1999 will be forced to take drastic measures. They'll have to use a lot of "bandaid solutions," temporary fixes and workarounds. They'll need to put most of their regular software projects on hold – Jones estimates 85% – so they can do what they need to stay in business.

Many of these suspended projects will not be restarted until 2002 or 2003 or later, by which time they will have become critically urgent.

But how will they choose which ones to do first, and which to do only partly, and which to leave undone until sometime into the new millennium? This is *triage*.

## Triage

This is a term borrowed from the battlefield paramedics. When a small group of military doctors or paramedics encounter huge numbers of wounded, they must make some difficult decisions. Before they can start saving people, they must sort the wounded into groups.

There are those who must have attention right away, those with serious life-threatening injuries but who can wait a short while, and those who can afford to go to the back of the line. And the most agonizing decision they face is when they must allow one person to die, so that time and resources can be given to someone with a chance of living.

This process is called triage (tree-*ahzh*), with the "ge" pronounced as "zh" because it's a French word. This is exactly what many companies are being forced to do already with their Y2k conversions. To make it into the next century still functioning, any company starting as late as 1998 has only two choices:

**Postpone other software projects** and divert massive resources (up to 85% of programmers and money) to the Y2k project. This will leave 15% of their programmers to do critical maintenance work only, enough to keep the existing software running.

**Perform triage.** They must decide which software systems are mission-critical, that is, without them the company simply can't function. The software that switches telephone calls is mission-critical to the phone company, because without it no one gets to make a phone call. Their billing software is critical too, but not quite as urgent. They must get paid in order to stay in business, but it could wait a little while if necessary.

But software like payroll, internal accounting and warehouse inventory control is not. These things are certainly important – just ask the employees about late or screwed-up paychecks! But they're functions that could be delayed temporarily, or done manually. The company could survive without this software, although with some discomfort.

At the other extreme there's bound to be a certain amount of software that can be thrown out. Either it's no longer being used, or it's nice-to-have but by no means necessary. It's very important to identify this software and dump it before they go wasting time and money fixing it for Y2k.

Many companies will no doubt end up using a combination of these approaches. And for those in Western Europe there's this other problem.

## The Euro Currency Conversion

There's an additional timing problem for Europe. This one is a classic example of management (in this case politicians) making plans in total ignorance of the size and seriousness of Y2k.

The countries of Western Europe are about to adopt a single, international currency. Instead of francs, marks, pounds and guilders, they'll all use something called the EMU (European Monetary Unit), or "Euro." And for a couple of years during the changeover, everybody in Europe will be able to choose either the Euro or the local currency.

This leads to another big software project for all businesses and governments in Europe! For the countries of Europe, the experts are estimating that the Euro currency changeover will be half as big as their Y2k project, and so it'll cost about half as much.

But it all happens at the same time that their programmers are frantically trying to cope with Y2k! And on top of that, Germany is planning to change its capital city right in the middle of all this. Capers Jones suggests seriously that the new currency should be delayed until 2005.

In North America, Jones expects that about 15% of all software will *not* be ready by the time Y2k comes around. Because of the currency change, it's expected that the figure for Europe will be more like 30% that will not be ready, in other words twice as much. Now 15% sounds to me like a lot, but it sounds survivable. But 30% is scary.

*If close to one third of all the software in the second-richest region
of the world is likely to fail, that could cause problems.*

With the "global economy" of today, if Europe starts into a recession with businesses going bankrupt all over, that's going to drag the rest of us down too. And if the North American economy is already struggling with a bunch of business failures and other problems caused by Y2k, add the ripple effect of Europe's problems and it could be serious even this far away.

And after that, it would ripple on around the rest of the world as well, all through Asia, South America and Eastern Europe. But Africa, India and China will be interesting.

Did you know that over half the people in Africa, India and China have never made a telephone call? They don't depend on technology, and computers in particular, like we do. But even if they're insulated from having power and phone go off, and they never fly, they'll still suffer if we end up with a global recession. They could starve because of Y2k failures thousands of miles away in Europe and America.

# Procrastination and Denial

So you'll go in to work tomorrow, and start telling them all about the horrible things that are going to happen. That fellow Brown said so, right? And everybody laughs. "There's no problem!" they say, "Our Year 2000 project team started last month, and they've got it all under control." And they walk off chuckling.

Or, as I did, you ask at an investment seminar, "How are your mutual funds planning to handle the likely response of the stock markets around the end of 1999?" I got a polite brush-off, an assurance "We have the teams working on the conversion," and a quick change of topic.

Of course, I didn't ask about their conversion project. What I wanted to know about was companies that might be getting close to Y2k without completing their conversion. How would the stock market, and my mutual funds in particular, react to problems that these companies might start to have?

## Upper Levels of the US Government

The web site at www.y2ktimebomb.com includes a great deal of serious comments in the "Westergaard Year 2000" section. John Westergaard and a number of columnists report each month. On May 12 they published a letter from a reader who asked to be anonymous to protect his job, and you'll see why when you read his story.

This person markets software and services to the US feds to help with finding the dates in the software. The senior managers that he sells to are not computer people. Listen to some comments that were actually made by these "intelligent" senior federal managers:

> "I won't be here after October 1999, so I don't care."
> "We only support authorized software and hardware on our system. If someone has something that isn't authorized, that's their problem, even if it affects our network."
> "This is more a CYA (*"Cover You're A— "*) problem than an actual operational problem."
> "When it becomes a crisis, then we'll start looking at it."

This writer advises *sensible* government managers and employees to have back-up contingency plans, so they can do their jobs manually without the computers if necessary.

If this is the "head-up-their-CYA" attitude of senior decision-makers in the world's most technologically advanced nation, then I'm afraid we're all in trouble. Other nations are unlikely to be much better.

The columnist, John Yellig, then adds his comments, which I repeat in full:

> "While it is not Westergaard Year 2000's policy to publish material without supplying a source, we felt that the material in this e-mail was too compelling not to share with our readers. The implications contained in this correspondence are frightening, given the amount of power wielded by those who made these statements. We can only hope that these people come around in time to avert the disaster they're currently perpetuating."

I don't really hold out a lot of hope on this one, John. I think they're all hoping to retire before they have to think about these things.

### Problems Won't Wait for Midnight

Problems will start surfacing well before that midnight rollover. The food-dumping problem has already happened. Credit cards with "00" or "01" expiry dates have already been rejected. Any business that has to deal with due dates, maturity dates, spoilage dates, schedules, and so on, can expect problems as soon as these future dates begin taking them into the year 2000.

Those who pretend there's no problem, or choose to ignore it, or refuse to believe it, may be surprised as we approach the Millennium.

In their excellent book *"Time Bomb 2000,"* Ed and Jennifer Yourdon say ***"The typical large business-oriented software project is 100% over budget and one year late."*** (Their italics.) We can't afford to be one year late on the y2k project!

The horrifying statistics on the software industry are that *25% of projects are late*, and *24% are canceled*, abandoned before they're finished.

Y2k is mankind's biggest project ever, software or otherwise. For most companies and government agencies, the Y2k software conversion project will be their largest software project ever. Given the immovable deadline, can we afford it to be their *latest* ever?

There *will* be some problems. I sincerely hope that "All our troubles will be little ones." But governments and corporations around the world are dreadfully unprepared. And remember, even the ones that do a great job of planning and converting are still expected to let 5% of the date errors get through without being corrected. Plus there'll be errors in some of the fixes.

Many of those will cause just little problems, but a few may bring serious disruption to some of the things we have come to depend upon. If we're really lucky, we may make it through into the new Millennium with just a few minor problems. If we're not so lucky, I plan to be prepared, and I would suggest you do too.

# Is This a Bug or a Virus?

Just for the record, you may have heard people referring to the "Year 2000 bug," or the "Year 2000 virus." Well, calling it a "bug" is quite correct. It's an error (or rather a whole bunch of errors) made by programmers, and in need of fixing. But it's not a virus.

Some like to call it a virus because of the fact that passing bad data from one computer to another passes the problem on rather like a virus. However, a virus is something deliberately written to screw up your computer, or at the very least to invade your privacy. This one is truly just a bug that no one intended should be a problem.

But if the people around you insist on calling it a virus, it's not worth an argument. Let them call it what they will – at least they're admitting that there *is* a problem.

# Chapter 3: Will It Really Happen?

## Will The World Fall Apart?

I hope not. But, at the risk of being like Chicken Little in the nursery tale, who ran around announcing that the sky had fallen, I must sound a warning. There are so many things that could go wrong, and so many companies and organizations around the world are unprepared.

And for the ones who are doing something, 5% of errors remaining in the software of millions of companies is 5% of a very large number. Given the track record of the software industry, and the things I've seen with my own eyes, I find it extremely difficult to believe that *nothing* will go wrong.

Maybe our world is strong enough, and our society is resilient enough, to stand a few things failing here and there. But what happens when they *all fail on the same day?* The opening scenario on page one of this book paints a grim picture indeed. I hope I'm totally wrong on this one!

If it should happen that, a few months or a year into the millennium, I'm hailed as a prophet and a forecaster, it'll make me very sad. *I don't want to be proven right.* On the other hand, I would be very pleased to be forced to spend the entire year 2000 looking foolish and saying "Sorry!" to everyone. (If you have egg on your face, make omelette!)

This rather contrary attitude is required for any serious "prophet of doom." To be considered sincere, such a person must believe intensely in what he has to say. And I do. At the same time, if he cares at all about his fellow personkind, that would require that he sincerely hope to be proved wrong! And I'm not the first author to take this stand.

Ed and Jennifer Yourdon had some similar things to say in regard to Y2k in their book, "*Time Bomb 2000.*" Also, James Davidson and Lord William Rees-Mogg take much the same stand in their landmark book, "*The Great Reckoning.*" I have some good things to say about both of these books in later chapters, and in the Appendix, "To Find Out More."

Meantime, I have taken it upon myself to be the "voice crying in the wilderness." I'll stick my neck out and risk looking like a fool, just in case by doing so I might help a few people prepare better. And if a few things do go wrong, and one or two of you out there are a little better off after Y2k is all over, because of my warning, I'll be satisfied.

If as a result of reading this book somebody saves their job, saves their employer from going out of business, or even avoids property damage or personal injury, then I'll be *immensely* satisfied. One such incident will be enough reason and reward for me to stick my neck out and write this.

So what kind of things am I referring to when I say *some* of them will for sure go wrong? As you read this next section, think back to the opening scenario about Times Square, and to my comments that so shocked my sister-in-law Melda.

First, here are some failures that have already occurred because of software problems. I include them here to show what really can go wrong from various causes. The scary thing about Y2k is that everybody in our society, and indeed everyone in the entire world, can expect at least a few failures like these, *all at the same time.*

## Software Failures That Already Happened

### What Does a Software Failure Look Like?

In the next few pages I hope to show you what has already happened even without the pressure of Y2k. I want to show you a few minor software failures, that had major results. We must remember that Y2k will be a much bigger opportunity to screw up than any of these were. And in Y2k failures, any incident will likely involve several failed systems adding their effects together.

One thing you should note in these accounts is *how* the software failed. That is, what did the software *do* when things went wrong? The programmer decides how the software will handle these things when he writes the program code. And the programmers don't always make sensible decisions. (I can say this about programmers because I am one.)

This is often because the programmer doesn't fully understand the circumstances. In the Honda example below, I would take a guess that the programmer was probably *not* a motorcyclist, or at least not a very fast one. It may not have occurred to him/her how dangerous it could be when a bike is laid over for a turn at 120 mph (180 km/h) and the engine stops.

As is true of so much in this world, they didn't ask *me* when they built it! I have always been a great believer in *fail-safe*. I learned the same lessons in stockcar racing, skydiving, motorcycling, wind-surfing and programming: Be ready that things could go wrong, and design them so that when they do, you can still get along.

"Getting along" for a skydiver, for example, includes making it to the ground alive.

Much of the software operating in the world today is not fail-safe. When it fails, it does so in an awkward or even dangerous way. And very many of these potential failures are "exception conditions" that *should* never happen, and missed out on the testing because no-one thought of them at the time. The aluminum smelter described below is a prime example.

Even though software testing is so important, the sad fact is that most software goes into production poorly tested. Remember, the bug rate for normal business software is one bug per hundred lines of code! And a regular PC software product like WordPerfect or Corel Draw can be close to a million lines of code. If it's average-quality software, that would suggest perhaps 10,000 bugs!

Here are some software bugs that have happened already. Some of them are date-related, but not all. All of them are *software failures*, and they'll show you how easily software can cause problems. In these stories, it's not so important why the software failed. What matters is how it failed and what that did to the people who depended on it.

Airline Reservation Systems: The 89/90 Decade Rollover
British Licences – Valid 20 Years
The 1990 Honda 750 EFI.
Phoenix Traffic System.
The New Zealand Aluminum Smelter
Apollo VII Lands In the Wrong Ocean
Home and Desktop Computers Fail Software Tests
Union Pacific Railroad Software Amalgamation

## Airline Reservation Systems: The 89/90 Decade Rollover

During the 1980s, all the world's major airlines brought in their automated, worldwide computerized booking systems. At Maligaya Travel we have used several, and currently we're on the American Airlines "*Sabre*" system.

December 31, 1989 was the first time the airlines ever had to deal with a decade change since those systems came into use. According to accounts I have heard, *it took them 3 or 4 days* to sort out problems and get everything working smoothly again.

*Three or four days!* Imagine how many bookings they normally make in three or four days. Millions! And this was a simple decade rollover. There were no two-digit date formats to change, nothing that complicated. And yet, the software had enough trouble with the change from years that looked like "198x" to years that looked like "199x", that it took 3 or 4 days for the programmers to straighten it all out.

If such a simple rollover change can cause noticeable hassles, what might a year, decade, century and millennium change do when they all happen at the same moment?

And on top of that, we're perhaps *100 times* as dependent on software in today's world than we were in 1990. This last point will come clear as we go through the rest of this chapter.

Other worldwide automated computerized systems have not had the practice that the airlines got when they went through the decade change. Think about the phone system, the Internet, the international credit card systems, the currency markets and stock market trading, the instant worldwide radio and TV broadcasts, military battlefield communications, and *everything* to do with satellites. Every one of these worldwide services has grown out of all recognition since 1990.

So none of these systems has seen a decade change, at least not in its present form. Yet they're about to hit a *millennium* change, with the memory of that 3 to 4-day hassle the airlines went through. And they'll all hit the change at the same time.

## British Licences – Valid 20 Years

Some years ago, Alamo Rent A Car in the US was getting rejections when they keyed in the expiry date of a British driver's licence. These licences are valid 20 years, but Alamo's software was screwing up the validity check for dates like '00' and '01.'

There have been numerous places in our society where similar rejections have occurred over the last decade or so. The number in the news has been slowly growing.

## The 1990 Honda 750 EFI

In 1990 (not related to the airline problem above) Honda brought out Electronic Fuel Injection (EFI) on their four-cylinder 750cc motorcycles. This marvel of modern technology, however, lasted only a year or two, and then they went back to carburetors.

It seems that one or two of the sensors kept failing. These sensors measure various things around the engine, such as fuel flow, air flow, manifold pressure, air temperature, etc.

The problem went something like this: Let's say the suspect sensor was measuring air temperature, and sending the temperature reading back to the computer in the EFI. If the air temperature sensor failed, the software couldn't calculate the proper amount of fuel to mix with the air, so it stopped running.

Now, in business software like Accounts Receivable or Payroll Processing, this is very much the right thing to do. When the software can't get the numbers right, it should stop and tell somebody! But as I mentioned above, it's not a good idea in the middle of a high-speed turn. And that's exactly what was reported in the motorcycling magazines of the day for this model Honda.

What could have been done differently? If I had been the programmer, I probably would have said well, if the air-temperature sensor fails, we don't want the bike to stop. So what I might have done is to assume a midrange value for air temperature, maybe 15 °C (60 °F).

This may well have made the bike run roughly, and lose some power, but it's less likely to be fatal than a full stop in a fast turn. For a motorcyclist, "getting along" would include finishing the turn with your butt still securely planted on the bike!

So this was a small software problem that made the difference between a successful product and a failed one. Not to mention the casualties it might have caused. I must confess I'm unaware of any lawsuits arising from this issue, so it would appear no one was seriously hurt. But I'm sure you see the potential for harm. *And how unpredictable the immediate results of a software failure can be.*

These next two accounts are more obvious and a little more sinister.

## Phoenix Traffic System

In 1994, the traffic people in Phoenix, Arizona, tried keying in a date later than 01/01/2000, just to see what would happen. I have no idea whether they had official permission to do this, or whether they still had jobs at the end. It would appear they didn't take enough backups before they tried it.

The whole system crashed, and it took them three days to get it back up again. They have since spent $63 million US to convert the software for Y2k. This little adventure shows the need to take backups of computer data *before* trying *anything*, no matter how big or little.

## The New Zealand Aluminum Smelter

(Spelled *Aluminium* when you're Down Under)

There's only one aluminum smelter in my home country New Zealand, at Tiwai Point in the South Island. The ore comes from Chile, and is made into pure metal using the cheap hydroelectric power in N.Z. The aluminum metal is then shipped to factories in Japan.

At midnight on December 31, 1996, all 660 process-control computers stopped. All the smelting "potlines" ceased production. Two hours later the same thing happened at an aluminum smelting plant in Tasmania, Australia. They're two hours behind New Zealand's time zone, so they stopped at *their* midnight. Not only that, but the Tasmanian programmers wrote the software!

The problem was eventually traced to the fact that the software didn't know that 1996 was a leap year, and couldn't handle day number 366 of that year. So after day number 365, it stopped with a polite little error message. And when the computers stopped, so did the machines they were monitoring and controlling. This software was running on all 660 computers in the N.Z. plant, and a whole bunch in the Tasmanian plant.

Meanwhile, the staff were running the plant manually, but by the time it was all fixed the next day, damage had been done. Without the computers to look after them, five of the smelting pots had overheated, and had to be replaced. Total replacement cost: *one million dollars!* All because:

(a) The programmer didn't build the leap year factor into the software, and
(b) When the software failed, it was *not fail-safe.*

Such a simple problem, a simple but very expensive mistake. Programmers make a lot of them. Expect a bunch to show up at and around Y2k.

Leap-year errors in the software will start showing up long before February 29, 2000. Some software will have to do calculations that involve that date long before the date itself. Some will screw up on the actual date, and others, like the aluminum smelter, long after the leap-year date.

And expect lawsuits when one guy's software destroys another guy's factory.

## Apollo VII Lands In the Wrong Ocean

The movie "*Apollo 13*" rightfully gained several Oscars, but that wasn't the first Apollo mission to have trouble. As Apollo 7 descended toward the Earth after a successful mission, the usual flotilla awaited them in the splashdown area in the *Pacific* Ocean.

This was off the Western end of the Panama Canal Zone, at that time still controlled by the U.S. There was an aircraft carrier, a swarm of destroyers, a few scuba divers to open the capsule and help them out, and of course a bunch of helicopters to pick them up.

Unfortunately, they missed. The hapless adventurers sailed high over the heads of their welcoming committee, completely cleared the Isthmus of Panama (fortunately), and landed way out in the *Atlantic.* Choppers from the Eastern end of the Canal Zone had to be scrambled to go after them, and these poor guys were left bobbing around in the chill Atlantic waters for twenty minutes or so before they saw a soul.

It turned out that a programmer writing the software to calculate the descending orbit had used the value 22/7 for the constant Pi. You'll no doubt remember from school that Pi is the circumference of any circle divided by its diameter, and its actual value is

3.14159 and many more digits. The value 22/7 is often but perhaps, as it transpired, unwisely, used as a *very rough approximation*. It should certainly never be used for orbital calculations.

Again we have a simple error buried deep in the software, and not brought to light during testing. And again, the consequences were out of all proportion to the "size" of the error. Just a simple mistake . . . 22/7 is close, but not close enough. 365 days in 1996 is close, but not close enough.

What might have happened if more aluminum pots had overheated? Or one blew up when workers were nearby? What if Apollo 7 had come down on land in the middle of Panama? The actual costs were severe, the potential costs horrendous. Yet the mistakes themselves were small, almost trivial.

Remember the 5% of date errors that we expect will sneak through the Y2k conversion projects. Most will be small errors, many trivial. But some could have huge effects, out of all proportion to the "size" of the mistake. These are the ones that scare me.

## Home and Desktop Computers Fail Software Tests

Karl Fielder has a company called Greenwich Mean Time that does Y2k work. They have tested more than 4000 software programs including some that are still for sale in stores (as of early 1998). Here are a few of their findings:

- 4% of the programs tested didn't know that 2000 is a leap year.
- 4% of the programs tested won't run in the 21st century.
- Of the programs that had Y2k problems, *more than a quarter* claimed to be "Year 2000 compliant." I guess they were mistaken.

For the second group, there is a work-around, but it has its own dangers. You could just set the computer's internal clock back to a year like 1972, when all the days of the week were the same as 2000. This works because the calendar repeats every 28 years.

This might be OK for a home computer, but it wouldn't do for business computing. In business we need all the automatic "date-stamps" to be correct, such as the "Creation Date" that DOS and Windows always put on a file. Some software uses these dates to delete outdated files, and this could be a problem. Or a disaster.

And the first group, well they got caught by a little quirk in the calendar. As everyone knows, the Earth's year (time it takes to go around the sun) is 365 1/4 days. So we use the number 365 days in a year, and every four years we add a day to February, so leap years have 366 days. But that still isn't quite right. Actually, it's a little less than 365 1/4 days. Every 100 years we get a bit ahead, so centuries are *not* leap years, even though they divide by four.

But that's still not good enough! That takes us a smidgeon too far the other way, so to get it as close as we're going to come, *every fourth century* is *a leap year*.

The rule is: A leap year is every year that divides by four, **except centuries,**
Unless the century divides by four, then it's a leap year also.
1600 was a leap year, 1700, 1800 and 1900 were not. *But 2000* is *a leap year!*

## Union Pacific Railroad Software Amalgamation

### The Great Union Pacific Fiasco of 1997/1998.

The largest railroad in the U.S. recently bought up a competitor, Southern Pacific Rail. Each railroad had its own software for tracking the whereabouts of its freight cars. When they tried to combine the two, it all fell apart. The Wall Street Journal: "The nation's largest railroad has lost track of hundreds of freight cars."

The problem took three months or more to clean up. Rail traffic was in chaos for that time. This affected their thousands of customers, too. Among those customers were *power plants*, several of which almost ran out of coal and oil.

Not only that, but all the effort that went into fixing this mess has taken resources away from their Y2k project. This event has been a good lesson in how much damage a few software problems can cause.

# Other Failures That Already Happened

Purely by coincidence, there have been a number of mishaps in 1997 and 1998 that could be viewed as a sample of what might go wrong when the lights go out:

The Quebec Ice Storm
The Auckland Power Failure
PanAmSat Galaxy IV

### The Quebec Ice Storm

In November, 1997 there was a severe ice storm that affected mainly the province of Quebec, and also parts of Ontario and some of the Northeastern states of the U.S. Power outages in some areas lasted several weeks. Many farms and rural dwellers had generators, but even these didn't always do the job. We saw a pile of 200 dead pigs on one news broadcast, when a farm generator failed.

Joe Boivin is head of the Global Millennium Foundation, a not-for-profit based in Ottawa. He warns against pregnancy and childbirth in 1999-2000. "Look at the ice storm in Montreal," he says, "Visualize that as six months long. Why would you want to introduce a new child in the midst of something like that?"

I agree with Boivin, and I think six months may turn out to be a conservative figure. It's just possible that a Y2k power outage might last way longer. Even when the power comes back on, there'll be other problems for some time. Other services may be out. Hospital and medical services may be out, or struggling, or overloaded.

### The Auckland Power Failure

Here we have just the opposite. A power outage at the height of the hottest summer in a hundred years of record-keeping. The central business district (CBD) of the city of Auckland, New Zealand has 88,000 residents and a large number of businesses, supplied with electricity by five underground cables. Four of the five cables failed over a period of one week. It took more than six weeks to get the power back up to everybody.

Ross Stewart works in a high-rise building in Auckland, and on his web site at www.year2000.co.nz he told how his building had a generator sitting in the parking lot. But it was only for essential things like fire alarms and electric security doors. No lights, no elevators, no air conditioning. Even the parking lot gates were stuck half open for a month.

Restaurants could not use their fridges and freezers, traffic lights were out, shops and offices were closed. Many businesses moved out to the edge of town, *some permanently*. My nephew Arryn's office started getting power for half-days, so he would go home each afternoon. But restaurants and food stores can't operate on a half-day supply. Businesses lost a lot of money, and many went bankrupt.

Elevators were out all over the city. The local paper ran a story showing a woman with heart problems who had become a prisoner in her 9th-floor apartment because she couldn't climb stairs. Paramedics lost valuable time on many calls, running up multiple flights of stairs to reach patients in high-rise buildings.

*There was no water pressure.* And while this was certainly a major problem and inconvenience for thousands, *it was critical for the firefighters.* Fortunately, there were no major fires in that period. But in a Y2k outage, especially here in the Frozen North, increased use of candles for light, and fires for heating, and propane gas for cooking will lead to an increase in fires. Lack of water could easily turn an accident into a disaster.

Generators were flown into Auckland from Australia, Japan, Korea, the US and other places. One ship was moored at the dock with six huge generators running in its hold, and the power company just ran cables down to it.

But in a Y2k outage, there may be nowhere to buy generators from. Australia, Japan, Korea, and the US will have their own problems. Fortunately, Auckland is now better equipped for an outage than any other city, with the possible exception of Montreal. (But see the problem that Canadian Tire hardware stores had, page 102.)

As the power kept going on and off, voltage spikes in the lines damaged computers, fax machines and electronic equipment. Buy some power bars for your stereo and TV *before* Y2k.

In Chapters 7 and 8 you'll find some advice about stocking up on candles, flashlights, batteries, propane, firewood and everything else you'll need in the event of an extended power outage. And everything you'll see there is something that would be a good idea anyway, even if there is no disaster.

But electricity is not the only thing we depend on for society to run smoothly and safely.

## PanAmSat Galaxy IV Satellite

On Thursday, May 21, 1998, the Galaxy IV satellite owned by PanAmSat died. And so did hundreds of thousands of pagers all across the US. It hit doctors, realtors, service technicians and all those who build their lives and their livelihood around instant communication.

The cause is unknown, but one theory is that it was hit by a sand-grain-sized meteor (see page 28). Or it may have been a solar flare (see page 29). Technicians on the ground were unable to make it behave, and finally had to give up. They were forced to abandon a 100-million dollar piece of space junk. The pager traffic was rerouted to another satellite, and the world is more or less back to normal.

What this incident tells us is just how much we depend on high-tech communications for our society to "run smoothly and safely." This truly is the "Information Age." In the 1970s the OPEC nations crunched the world economy by manipulating the price and disrupting the flow of oil. These days it's the *flow of information* that's our weakest point.

And now that we've seen some things that have already gone wrong, let's look at a few others that will happen before and after Y2k.

# Forewarnings and Follow-Ons

There's good news and there's bad news. The good news is that we get a chance to practice. The bad news is that after Y2k has gone by, we still have a couple more problems coming. Of course, there's always a chance for the good news to turn bad. Our practice opportunities could turn out to be disasters in their own right:

## Forewarnings:

GPS 'Week Counter' Rolls Over August 21, 1999
September 9, 1999: "9/9/99"
Meteor Showers
Solar Flares

First the good news. We get to practice on a software rollover problem that affects only one single area of software:

## GPS Week Counter Rolls Over August 21, 1999

In 1980 the U.S. Navy launched a series of satellites for a navigation system called "Global Positioning System," or GPS for short. By reading signals from several of these satellites, a GPS receiver can tell exactly where it is, anywhere on the face of the Earth, to within a few meters or yards of accuracy.

The military ones can tell where they are within a couple of centimeters, or about an inch. The system is now employed for all kinds of military uses, and for a great many civilian ones as well.

About *ten million* commercial ships and airplanes now rely on GPS units for navigation. Police and rescue services use them extensively, both for finding their way, and for computerized 9-1-1 dispatch systems. Trucking companies, bus and taxi companies, couriers and post offices around the world use them to track vehicles.

Surveyors, mapmakers, oil geologists and all kinds of other "land scientists" use GPS for accurate positioning data. And, something you might not expect: many banks and financial services use GPS units to get *accurate time* from the GPS satellites. The atomic clocks in the satellites are among the most accurate ever made, so these companies often use them for interest calculations involving billions of dollars, sometimes to fractions of a second.

Then there are more millions of hobbyists and sports enthusiasts around the world who have GPS receivers in boats, off-road vehicles and even in backpacks. Yes, you can buy these things for as low as $200 U.S. and they fit in a large pocket.

(I'm still waiting for the $20 one with a cell-phone attached, so I can put one in each suitcase. When my suitcase and I arrive in different airports, I can call it up and it'll tell me where it is!)

Various armed forces around the world have GPS in planes, ships and vehicles. But what may be more critical is their use in weapons guidance systems. A failure here could easily become a disaster. The military are not publishing any numbers, of course, but the U.S. military alone must surely have millions of these things in use.

Every one of these millions upon millions of GPS receiving units has software, and the date and time are an important part of the calculations. The satellites also carry a lot of software, of course. I must confess I have no idea how easy it'll be if the U.S. Navy needs to load new software into their GPS satellites.

When I heard about this, I was hoping they had the foresight to set it up so they can "upload" new software by radio from the ground. It would be very expensive, and difficult to do in the time available, if a shuttle had to visit every one of 20-odd satellites to load new software. However, as you may have seen in news reports, the US Navy is claiming that the satellites *are* ready for Y2k.

But what about the small percentage of dates in the software that we expect they'll miss? For GPS satellite software, the number will be way less than the 5% that Capers Jones forecasts for commercial software. But even if it's a thousand times better, or one date in every 20,000, that could still mean something like 500 ships and aircraft might be at risk, and countless surveyors, hikers, cops and fishermen.

Even the best military software still has about one bug per million lines of code. In GPS, even one bug *could* cost lives.

But what about the millions of GPS *receivers* that the ships, airplanes, surveyors, hikers, cops and fishermen carry?

Software errors here could translate into a lot of ships, planes, four-wheelers and hikers getting lost. Lost ships are survivable, because the world is no longer very large, and they'll find themselves before long. But lost airplanes have limited fuel, and could have a problem getting down safely.

Ships and aircraft have backup navigation systems that are not GPS, so those should work OK for the August rollover (see next paragraph.)

But even if my number estimates are way off base, any failure is one too many for the person it kills.

Lost missiles are another matter entirely. If one in 20,000 of Y2k software date errors might be missed in the GPS software, this is better than we expect in other software. But it could cause a lot of trouble on and around the Y2k date, December 31, 1999.

If there's a war, and who can say what Saddam might do, we could be shooting ourselves in the foot. Literally.

### The August Rollover

But the GPS has another problem. One important piece of the GPS calculation is the *week number*, and the weeks have been counted from January 7, 1980. That was the day that GPS Week Zero began. Week One began on January 13, 1980, week two on the 20th, and so on. The counter in the GPS computers, however, has a limit of 1024 weeks.

After week 1023, the counter will roll over to Week Zero again. Then it'll go on to weeks 1, 2, 3, 4 and so on all over again. This will happen at midnight on **August 21, 1999.**

This is just like the mileage on your car. If there are 5 digits on the odometer (mileage counter), it'll go to 99,999 miles and then roll over to zero. Then it counts 1 mile, 2 miles, 3,4, and so on all over again.

The computer uses *binary math*, where the digits are different, and the magic number in this case turns out to be 1023 instead of 99,999. But it still has only limited room, and after it fills up it goes right back to zero. On the morning of August 22, 1999.

I don't expect too many ships and airplanes to actually get lost on August 22, 1999, because they all have backup navigation systems. But here are some important points to keep in mind:

- Small-time users of GPS usually don't have much else for navigation except map and compass, and the amateurs may not even have those.
- Ships and aircraft have other navigation systems, so they're OK for August 22. But the other systems are all computerized. So on Y2k, they're still at risk.
- I have no idea whether weapons guidance systems built around GPS have backup guidance in case their GPS dies or screws up. I don't expect anyone would tell me if I asked! And how would the missile be able to tell that its GPS had screwed up, and it should be listening to the backup system?

This rollover could cause just as much disruption to the workings of GPS as Y2k is doing to everything else. This is why I recommend you don't fly on August 21 or 22, and perhaps not for a few weeks after that. If you rely on GPS in your job, hobbies or sports, it would be a good idea to avoid using it on or around that date. And test it carefully before you let your life depend on it again.

This is especially true if you need your GPS to keep from getting lost in a Canadian winter at -40° (F or C, it's the same on both scales), or a tropical desert or jungle at +40°C (+ 104°F) or hotter, or a war anywhere, or any such hostile environment.

You'll need to take precautions if you're doing anything where a GPS failure might endanger life or property. You may also want to be careful about where your investment money is over that period.

GPS is our advance warning, then, a chance to practice. It gives us a chance to see whether or not software failures are really likely to bring about disasters. If the GPS rollover goes smoothly, it'll look good for Y2k. But don't get too confident – it doesn't *prove* anything. On the other hand, if GPS *is* a disaster, that says be prepared for even worse on Y2k.

## September 9, 1999: "9/9/99"

This is another one along the lines of Y2k. Way back in the early days of computing, programmers needed a code to put at the end of a file of data to tell the software that it should stop reading the file. Kind of like putting a cover on the back of a book so people know they should stop reading. Remember this machine is an electronic moron.

One code often used was to put all '9s' in the date field of the last record in the file. In other words, '9/9/99' or September 9, 1999. A small amount of that software is still out there, and still running. The first time someone gives it a real date of 9/9/99 it'll stop at that record, and will never finish the file!

As with most software errors, most of these will be trivial annoyances. It stops, we fix it, we move on. But there'll be the occasional one that causes an expensive malfunction, or a critical delay. And, as always, there could be a few that place someone in danger.

Be super wary on that date, especially if you know you're using older software. Around that date, check all your bills, credit card statements, and everything else extra carefully. You never know who might be using an old program for some little thing. It'll be good practice for checking your documents for Y2k.

## Meteor Showers

Several times a year the Earth passes through clouds of space debris. The shooting stars we see every August are pieces of rock, anywhere from the size of a baseball to the size of a house. When they hit the Earth's atmosphere at incredible speeds, they vaporize and burn up in a second or two, giving the short-lived streak of light we see from the ground.

A baseball might last less than a second. A house-sized rock might give a 5-second streak from one side of the sky to the other. These are much more rare. Even rarer are the ones that make it all the way to land. The odd time that a 10 kg (20 lb) or 50 kg (100 lb) meteorite has crashed down to the ground, we can be sure that when it entered the Earth's atmosphere it was bigger than a house!

But all of those are so rare, and outer space is so big, that we've never yet had one hit a satellite. The most common particles are the ones about the size of a grain of sand. These are too small for us to see them burn up. First the glow is too small to see, and it's over in microseconds anyway.

But at the speeds these things are traveling, they have the impact of a rifle bullet. They can easily damage the delicate electronics on a satellite. There already have been two reports of this happening, including the PanAmSat Galaxy IV.

In November 1999 we enter a 33-year peak period for a meteor cloud known as the Leonid, when the Earth passes through the tail of a comet. The last time this happened, in 1966, we didn't even have a hundred satellites up. Now there are more than 500 of them. A few grains of sand scattered among them could bring down a lot more than just pagers. The phones, the Internet, weather forecasting, navigation, TV and everything else in our society uses satellites.

What if a few satellites are disabled just around the time we're trying to cope with Y2k communication blackouts? Add more load and stress to the communications systems around the world. A synergy would take place, multiplying the effects of the troubles already happening. And, ominously, utilities and pipelines use a lot of satellite communications too.

## Solar Flares

Just to add one more straw to the poor old camel's back, 1999-2000 is the peak of the 11-year solar cycle. Sunspots and solar flares send out hordes of cosmic particles. These are protons, neutrons and gamma rays that pour into space from a flare and head toward the Earth. At the peak of the cycle, they can be strong enough to disrupt some radio transmissions, and can disturb the electrical workings within computer chips.

I wouldn't expect computers at ground level to be affected too much, but those in satellites might. And some TV, radio and microwave transmissions might. Not too much, but it's happening *at the same time* as everything else might be going wrong.

Now we've seen the ones that will come before Y2k, here are some more that could cause us problems *after* Y2k.

## Follow-ons

There are a number of other dates after Y2k where we expect similar problems to happen, mostly because of errors in software. Each of these dates is another point where many software programs will hit the same problem at the same moment. Some of these programs will screw up. We don't know how many, or which ones.

Leap-Year 2000
January 1, 2001
UNIX and Year 2038

And this, which is nothing to do with software:
The Planets Aligned on May 5, 2000

## Leap-Year 2000

We've already seen what happened in New Zealand and Tasmania when the software had not been written to handle the leap year. Also, the study by Greenwich Mean Time has shown that even as late as 1997, some 4% of PC software does not know that 2000 is a leap year. As a result, we can expect another rash of failures on and around February 29, 2000.

Many PC users are using old software. In 1997, remember, the number was that 4% of all the software tested was unaware that 2000 is a leap year. Software from before that date could have an even higher percentage.

These failures will not be as numerous or as widespread as the Y2k failures two months earlier, so on the surface we might expect them to be less trouble. But in at least a few of these cases, the leap-year problems will hit companies who are already struggling with their Y2k failures. We can expect that for some companies, this will be the proverbial straw that breaks the camel's back, and some companies will fail because of it.

How many? Your guess is as good as mine. But I do expect *some*. So for you and me, this should be more of the same. Don't relax your preparations and precautions too soon after you make it through Y2k. Make sure you're still prepared, just in case the lights go out all over again, and in case more jobs disappear. All the preparations in Chapters 7 and 8 will still apply, and you should check the list again *before the end of January 2000*, just in case.

And the leap year problem may still have some effect at the *end* of 2000, as you'll see in the next section.

## January 1, 2001

This will be the first year-end after the Y2k fiasco, and I can think of at least two ways that this could cause some software to have problems:

- This is the first time that all the year-end software has been run with '00' in the "old year" of the data. At Y2k itself, we had '00' in the "new year" data field in all the calculations, but we still had '99' in the "old year" field. There are bound to be the usual 5% of date errors in this part of the processing, and they won't be found and fixed before the deadline, so some of the date calculations and financial calculations won't work. And we can expect a whole bunch of other calculations to run into trouble also because of it.

- Think back to the account of the disaster at the New Zealand aluminum smelter. Did you notice the problem didn't occur on February 29 of 1996, but at midnight on December 31, ten months later?! That's because the calculation happened to be based on the day number, which would be in the range 1 to 365, or 1 to 366.

We can expect the same kind of thing to happen with *some* software at the end of the year 2000. Some of the calculations in the software will expect the next day after number 365 to be day one (of the next year, 2001). Of the programs that have this problem, some will fail sensibly, or "safely."

A few will fail *un*safely, like the smelter software did, and like the software in the 1990 Honda fuel injection. (I expect Honda learned a lot from this experience. With luck, they may by now have some of the more resilient software around, that could be *less* likely to fail at Y2k than some of their competitors.)

Hopefully, though, the date problems at the end of the first year of the new Millennium will be somewhat milder than Y2k itself, for a number of reasons:

- By this time we should all have learned from handling Y2k and its results, so we should know better what to watch for, and what to avoid, and how to prepare. Again, it'll be appropriate to review your preparations as the year 2000 comes to a close, and go through Chapters 7 and 8 of this book all over again.

- Companies that survived Y2k will have been working frantically throughout the year to find and correct all the date bugs that got through. By the end of 2000, most of the software in use should be in much better shape than a year before at the Y2k rollover.

So all this tells us we have two conflicting things going on here. Some companies and some software will be stronger and in better shape to handle this one, others will be struggling or weakened. Many of the bugs will have been found by this date, but some new ones are possible. How many? As usual, who knows? Naturally, I expect this rollover to be much less disruptive than Y2k itself. But, as the Boy Scouts have always said, *be prepared.*

## UNIX and Year 2038

Most people have probably never heard the name "UNIX." It's one of the most widely-used software products in the computer industry, but rarely seen on the desktop computers or 'PCs' that we're used to. UNIX is one of a class of software known as "operating systems."

You're more likely to have heard of DOS, Windows and Windows 95/98, which are operating systems for the PC, and you may have these on home or office computers. If you have a Macintosh, your operating system is probably called "Mac OS" or perhaps "System 7."

When you fire up your computer and start using it, you're probably using one of the popular software products such as MS Word, WordPerfect, Excel, Quattro Pro, Acpacc, or your favorite video game. Those we call "application programs" or "application software."

Think of them as *applying* the power of your computer to do something you need. An operating system is software that manages the computer for you, and helps to run your application software.

The popularity of UNIX as an operating system in commercial computers comes from its ability to run on many kinds of computer hardware. It can be used on almost every computer out there today, including the huge "mainframe" computers, that can be connected to thousands of people, all using the computer at the same time.

UNIX is even available for your desktop PC or Macintosh, although this is usually done only for specialized needs, or sometimes when large numbers of PCs need to be connected to a central "server" that carries the databases.

Like any software product, UNIX was written by a team of programmers, primarily Drs Kernigan and Ritchie of AT&T. The programming language they used was called 'C' and has now evolved into a later version called 'C++' (pronounced "See-plus-plus,") C, C++ and UNIX all use a date system that works by counting the seconds from midnight on the morning of January 1, 1970.

Can you see it coming? As usual, the designers of C and UNIX had to allow only limited space to store this number. The space they allowed was four bytes, and because of the binary math used in computers, the largest number of seconds it can hold is 2,147,483,647. One second later, as you must have already figured out, it'll roll over to zero!

This will happen on January 18, 2038. As I write this on February 18, 1998, that's 39 years and 11 months away! No one is paying it much attention because it's so far in the future. But haven't we seen that attitude somewhere before?

If you don't keep a close eye on it, the future has an awesome habit of suddenly becoming the present!

## The Planets Aligned on May 5, 2000

Not too many people have heard about this one. I haven't seen any reports from the astronomers, so I'll not pretend to be an expert. But what I have read is that around May 5, 2000, the natural orbits of the sun and planets come together so that they'll *all line up on one side of the Earth*.

The facts are that the planets will line up around May 5, 2000. I have not yet heard geophysicists, astronomers or other scientists say anything about the effects this will have on our planet. But the *timing* in relation to Y2k is such that any minor effects on the weather or on earthquakes could become a major problem **when added on top of all the Y2k disruptions**.

So I present the following strictly as a reporter, since I consider I'm not qualified to make any kind of judgement on it. But read on to see why I feel you need to hear about it.

The bodies involved will be our own Moon, the Sun itself, along with Mercury, Venus, Mars, Jupiter and Saturn. In other words, all the nearest planetary bodies (Moon, Mercury, Venus, Mars) along with the two biggest (Jupiter and Saturn), and the Sun.

Now we all learned in school that the Sun and the Moon pull on the waters of the oceans on our Earth and cause the tides to go in and out. And when they're both on the same side of our planet, they pull together and give us what are called "spring tides." These are the highest high tides, and the lowest low tides each month.

These are nothing to do with the season of Spring. What happens is that the combined gravity of the Sun and the Moon pulls all the seawater to one side of the Earth. This gives that side a *very* high tide, and the opposite side an extra low tide. This happens about once a month or so, and the strength varies from month to month.

What they didn't say much about in school, but astronomers all know it, is that the planets also have an effect. It's possible for scientists to measure the difference that the planets make to the tides. Their gravity also pulls on the waters and modifies the effect of the Sun and Moon.

There are predictions being made that when they all line up together, along with the Sun and Moon, there'll be trouble. Not only are we likely to have the biggest high tides in history, but other things may happen as well. It's being suggested that this may cause severe weather, and earthquakes.

**High Tides**   These could cause considerable coastal damage if they're very much higher than normal. If they turn out to be perhaps a foot or so above normal spring tides, they'll be mostly an annoyance. But much higher than that could be serious. There could be serious coastal flooding in low-lying areas, with severe damage. At the time of writing (early 1998) I have yet to see any calculations from NASA on all this.

**Weather Problems**   The weather on our planet is caused by heating of the air by the Sun. It's modified by the way the water in the oceans can soak up vast amounts of this heat. Any time a large quantity of water moves from one place to another around the Earth, it carries heat with it, and changes weather patterns.

As I write this, we're still feeling the effects of El Niño. He has given us the warmest and weirdest northern winter (remember Montreal) and hottest southern summer (remember Auckland) that we've seen for decades.

Line up the planets. Spring tides higher and lower than we've ever seen. Huge amounts of warm water sloshing around from one side of the planet to the other. All of this can only mean weather and climate changes.

And at least half of them will be bad. Edmonton saved millions on its snow-clearing budget this year. Quebec lost money, people and pigs in their worst ice storm ever. (It was even worse than the one depicted in one of the hit movies of the winter, "*The Ice Storm!*") Floods and other weather disasters hit countries all over the world.

All thanks to El Niño. What do you suppose we might get when the "Big May 2000 Slosh" happens, who knows, maybe many times the size of little old El Niño?

Then there's the other half of the predictions.

**Earthquakes**  With such a force on the Earth as we've never seen before, predictions are being made that it'll cause flexing in the Earth's crust. This would result in *Earthquakes*. As a scientist, I'm prepared to accept that this will have *some* effect. As usual, the big question in my mind is *how many and how bad*?

I must stress that I have not yet found seismologists, vulcanologists or astronomers shouting this one from the rooftops. No cluster of experts like de Jager, Yourdon, Gary North and Ed Yardeni (you'll meet all these guys later) has turned up yet.

The voice crying in the wilderness about this one is Richard Noone, of The Survival Center. Their website is worth visiting for the survival equipment they sell, whatever your views on the seriousness of the planetary problem. (See Appendix, To Find Out More.)

*But I believe it must be mentioned because of the timing.*

**Hit Us When We're Down**  May 5, 2000 is just five months after Y2k. Depending on how badly Y2k hits us, we might just be getting our society back on its feet around then. Or we might just be hitting the bottom of a trough of economic depression. This along with all the other disruptions that could happen to our world.

Even if Y2k doesn't turn out to be the huge disaster some of us are predicting, we'll still suffer enough that by May of 2000, at best we'll still be in recovery mode. In other words, our economy and all the systems in society will not yet be working at full strength.

Ed Yardeni is Chief Economist for Deutsche Morgan Grenfell, a big Wall Street financial firm. Yardeni's *public* prediction is that we'll have our biggest recession in decades. I hear rumors that privately he thinks it'll be worse than that. And I'm talking about the entire world here, not just the developed countries, but *everybody*. By May 5, I think we might be about halfway through it. Or we might be five months into a really long depression.

Whatever, the last thing the world will be ready to cope with at that time is a rash of natural disasters of any kind. And they'll likely begin well before the actual line-up date, and continue long afterwards. This would cause them to overlap badly with Y2k and the recovery efforts, whatever form those may take.

So be prepared. And stay prepared even after Millennium Day itself becomes history.

That now brings us to the end of the list of things that have *already* gone wrong, and things that are *still* in store for us after we deal with Y2k. Let's take a more thorough look at what that really could go wrong on Y2k, and in the next chapter, how bad they might get.

## Things That *Could* Happen on Y2k

This is a strange topic to write on. Most of what I say in this section probably won't happen. But *any* of it might. And it's just conceivable that *all* of it might. I sure hope not, but I think it's important for each of us to give these things some thought.

You need to think about each possibility that I outline below, and make your own decision about how likely you think it is, and what to do about it. I would dearly love to know exactly what's going to happen, because then I could tell you exactly what to do about it. But it can't be that way.

You will have to take responsibility for your own safety and possibly your survival, and that of your loved ones. I can only bring these things to your attention. The final decisions on what to do are yours, and yours alone. I can tell you what could happen, and show you some options (see Chapters 7 and 8), and you get to decide.

And I hope that none of this happens, and I hope I'm totally embarrassed, but I think that's a vain hope. Let's begin with a couple of factors, *administration* and *synergy*, that will affect all companies in all industries, and then move on to specific industries.

## Administrative Problems In Large Companies

Large organizations use computers, and therefore software, for practically everything. Many of us have lived through the computerization of some new part of the company, or the conversion to a new computerized system to replace the old one.

*These changes never go smoothly*. Information turns out to be wrong. Reports, bills, paychecks and everything else come out late. And then the numbers are still screwed up, and it has to be rerun and go out even later.

Customers get upset. And of course they don't pay until they finally get a bill. Suppliers are even more upset because they get paid late, or not enough. Employees must have their paychecks on time. Of all the tasks done by computers these days, paychecks have traditionally been the number one priority, the one job that must go out on time, otherwise we could have a strike on our hands!

Y2k will be just like this. Any major software change is like this when it first goes into production. One of the major differences for Y2k, however, is that *everybody will be doing it*! Every business and government organization *in the world* will be going through the same stuff, *all at the same time*.

## Synergy

This rather strange word can be very important when things like this occur. It's one thing to have one company or government department late and in trouble over their computer processing. But it probably won't have much effect on how the rest of society functions. But what if they're not alone?

Let's say the Treasury Department is having problems getting money out to the other government departments. That means the Highways Department won't be able to pay their contractors. And the Welfare department will have hungry people on its doorstep. And so on, as all the other departments feel the impact of a computer problem they didn't cause.

If two or more departments have this kind of trouble, there'll be some places where the problems in one department make the problems worse for another one. So twice as many computer failures will cause *more than twice as many* problems!

This is *synergy*, where we say "The whole is more than the sum of the parts." So if we had six departments with software failures, we would expect way more than six times as many problems, and they would take more than six times as much time, people and money to fix.

But it goes way beyond just government departments. Think about that 5% figure for Y2k bugs that go unfixed. This suggests that, while all companies and governments are going to have troubles with those 5%, some will have *serious* problems.

Out of the Fortune 1000, the largest companies in America as rated by "*Fortune*" magazine, at least a small percentage will have serious problems. But since these are the largest companies in the U. S., these problems are likely to be quite extensive.

Capers Jones has some significant estimates of the number of Y2k business failures we can expect in North America. I would expect the figures for the rest of the world will be as bad or worse. Jones forecasts that about 1% of Fortune 500 large companies may go under because of Y2k problems, and a few more may declare bankruptcy to avoid being sued.

Among medium-sized companies of 1000 to 10,000 employees, Jones sounds very pessimistic about their ability to handle Y2k at all well. He suggests that while companies in this group use a lot of software, they mostly don't manage it well.

He expects these businesses will start late, underestimate the cost and time, will not hire skilled contractors with automated methods. What's more, most will not have any contingency (backup) plans for doing things manually when some of their software doesn't get fixed.

Jones expects that between 5% and 7% of these medium-sized companies will go under because of Y2k. He puts a 3% estimate on small companies under 1000 employees.

So that gives us 1% of large companies, 5 to 7% of medium companies, and 3% of small companies that will close their doors in the days and weeks following Y2k. Plus a number of government agencies will be struggling, and the Yourdons suggest that quite a few of those may close their doors too.

With the synergy that will take place, we may see a ripple effect through our society and our economy. Over the days and weeks, struggling businesses and government offices will have their plight worsened by the struggles or closure of companies and government agencies that they have always depended on.

As this causes more to close, there's always a chance that we could see a runaway chain reaction that gets worse the further it goes.

We'll talk more about synergy in Chapter 4, "How Bad Could It Get?" Here now is a list of possible problems that could hit all parts of our economy and our society:

Electric Power
Other Utilities
Natural Gas
Water
Communications
Telephone
Cable and Satellite TV
The Internet
Police and Military Communications
Billing, Banking and Government:
   Screwed-Up Bills and Payments
   Late Mailings
   Will there be Mail Anyway?
   Forecasting in Government and Business
Embedded Systems
Critical Systems

## Electric Power

Electric utility companies use as many computers as any other large organization, so they can expect as many problems and failures. So we'll likely find our power bills are late, maybe by a few days, maybe a few weeks or even months. And of course we can expect that when the bill eventually does arrive, it'll be all wrong! Having read this book, you'll be ready for this; you and I will politely point out the errors, and pay the corrected bill when it comes.

But this is not where it ends. Like all modern industries, the electrical generating and distributing system uses hundreds of thousands of computers to control the power itself. Computers in generating plants keep the turbines whirring at a constant speed, keep the voltage steady, and look after any variations in the load.

This last is important. One of my students, an engineer with Trans-Alta Utilities, told me that they saw the readings change on their meters here in northern Alberta when the July 1996 California/Idaho power failure put all the western states out.

Computers all throughout the power distribution system keep the loads balanced, so no part of the network gets overloaded – most of the time. The problem is that when a failure happens somewhere in the system, as it did in California that time, the computers transfer the load to other parts of the system.

But if that overloads another piece of the system, there's two things that could happen. Something could fail, as it did in Auckland, and stop the flow of current. Or the computers over there may sense the overload and shut the line down to prevent damage.

Either way, that load now has to be transferred to other lines in the network. If they overload too, then the process repeats itself. In this way, the failure can begin to ripple out across the countryside.

It works just like the fuses or circuit-breakers you have in your house and car. If too much current flows, enough to be dangerous, the fuse or circuit-breaker cuts off the power. This can be very inconvenient at times, but it saves damage and saves lives. The trouble is that in the power system, every time a circuit-breaker trips, it puts an extra load on somewhere else. This can cause another circuit to cut off, and this can cause overloads in yet other places.

In this way, a single failure (like the 1996 California one) can ripple through the system, shutting down power to city after city, and state after state. Because all of North America is in one combined power grid, borders offer no obstacle.

Canada and Mexico can cause a problem in the US, or suffer from one caused in the U.S. The southern parts of the Canadian provinces of British Columbia and Alberta went out that time in 1996, along with most of California, Oregon, Washington and five other states.

A similar power failure happened earlier in 1977 in the state of New York, plunging the entire eastern seaboard of the U.S. into darkness, and parts of Canada too. That time there was a small amount of rioting and some looting. People were advised to stay indoors for the night, and within about 24 hours power was restored. In those days, very few people had battery-operated TVs.

It's interesting to note that nine months and one week later the papers reported a major 3-day surge in the number of babies born in those states! I have some serious advice later on about pregnancy and childbirth in case Y2k causes problems with hospitals and medical equipment.

I have seen claims by engineers in the power industry that they have improved the system since all this happened. And I'm sure they have. The California failure was not as widespread as the earlier New York one.

Each time something like this happens they learn a bunch, and improve things. So a single failure in the control software somewhere in the power system probably would not put out as many lights as last time. But read on . . .

There are about 10,000 generating stations across North America. There are about twice as many major transformer substations spread throughout the grid. If 5% of the software errors are expected to sneak through, that might mean that 5% of the power plants have bugs. That would be perhaps 1500 software errors. And suppose perhaps one in ten caused a problem, that would mean about 50 generating stations and 100 transformer stations with problems.

Not too bad; 150 out of perhaps 30,000 power plants, you might say. But think of this. The system can deal with one failure, and stabilize itself with a certain area of the continent left in the dark for a while. That's what happened around Chicago in 1965, New York in 1977, and California and the West in 1996.

But two failures? What about 20 or 30 failures? What happens if 50 or more dark patches ripple out across the continent and start running into each other? That's when the ripple effect and synergy effect could get out of control and darken an entire continent.

And don't forget that these things will happen worldwide. Even if North America manages to avoid total darkness, what about Europe, Asia, Africa, Australia and even little New Zealand? The developed nations may have new and sophisticated control systems and software. I'm guessing they'll *probably* get most of their software converted in time. *Maybe*.

But even North America is vulnerable, and so is everyone else. Second and Third-World countries have older electrical distribution systems, and are even more prone to this kind of failure. And as of early 1998, most Third-World countries have not even started their Y2k fixes, in the power system or anywhere else.

The first country to see the sun each day is the Kingdom of Tonga, in the South Pacific, directly North of New Zealand and a little West of Fiji. The Tonga Islands have a population of around 100,000 and they're 13 hours ahead of GMT, the "zero" of time zones.

After that, New Zealand is next, so these things will be happening for the Kiwis. Then it's the Aussies' turn. Then New Guinea and Japan, Indonesia, the Philippines, Hong Kong and the rest of Asia. The rest of us will be watching closely on that day.

And if the power goes off, will we be able to see by gaslight? Maybe not.

## Other Utilities

Hospitals, TV stations and telephone exchanges all have emergency backup power generators. Provided they start (see "Embedded Systems" below), these places will be able to continue working. But both water and sewage systems use electric pumps. And the pumping stations mostly don't have emergency generators. Or if they do, will they start on that fateful morning? No power, no pumps, no pressure.

And even the pumping stations that do have backup power, and if the motors do start, how long will the fuel supply last? If things get really bad for an extended time, the pumps may stop one by one as the backup generators run out of fuel.

**Natural Gas** The first thing we need to say about the gas supply is that it's pretty much independent of the electric power supply, because most of the compressors that pump the gas are themselves powered by natural gas. Which would only make sense.

However, all pipeline systems, including natural gas, are controlled by computers and software. So this means that, with the expected 5% of date errors that sneak through, there's still a chance that the gas might shut off.

For every house that's heated by piped-in natural gas, there's an unbroken line of connected pipes all the way from your house to the well-head. There are storage tanks in the system, but they'll empty in days in the midst of a cold winter when the gas goes off.

Home furnaces are run by electricity, and mostly controlled by computers. Enough said.

**Water** Some cities may have real problems with water. I have seen reports in the past that New York, for example, has been working its water supply to the limit for decades. The system was stretched to where a failure in any one part of it would have caused severe problems. They do have a huge new supply line under construction, to be done before Y2k.

But even so, one or two failures in their computerized control systems could cut off a lot of people. Add to this the likelihood of losing electric power, and I'm sure you can see the possibilities for synergy and ripple effects.

Then again, what about firefighting? We'll have an increased risk of fires just because we'll be celebrating with the biggest worldwide party ever known. We've seen on the news what can happen when sports fans celebrate a victory, or riot after a loss or a disagreement with the referee. This time around, probably half the population of the world will be celebrating, or about three billion of us.

There'll be fireworks, which are a fruitful source of small fires. And small fires become big ones when there's no water. Even if there is water.

If the lights go out there'll be candles, and if the gas goes off there'll be fireplaces pressed into service, and a certain number of people burning themselves, and kids falling into fires or onto candles. Just check the statistics for a summer of camping and camp-fires around your province or state for those last two.

And if the lights and other utilities go off, permanently or off and on, we may have some rioting in the streets. If the problems last for more than a week or two, there's also a chance of riots fueled by missing welfare checks or other such things in the poor districts of some cities. Riots always mean fires, both vehicles and buildings.

*Firefighters need water.* Pure and simple. Some cities, big or small, could have problems.

**Home Heating Oil** This is delivered at the end of a long supply chain. If one link in the chain doesn't work, no oil, no heat. And most of the furnaces these days are computer-controlled, and electrically-operated.

## Communications

We're in the "Information Age." That's not just an empty phrase. There's more information flying around the world than anyone would have thought possible at the beginning of this century. At the turn of this century, the ultimate in technology was the telephone. That and the telegraph had linked far-flung parts of the world, but only by wire. There was no radio (or "wireless" as it used to be known). In about 100 years, we have gone from that to satellites, cell phones and the Internet.

Imagine trying to explain the Internet to Alexander Graham Bell, inventor of the telephone. The man was a genius, to be sure, and he would no doubt love what you had to say, but even he would struggle to understand it. Things have changed since his day, and now we depend on sending information all over this world in moments.

We had the Gulf War by radio from Baghdad in real time. We had instant TV shots of smart bombs, pictures that traveled all over the world in seconds. As I write this, the Nagano Winter Olympics are live in the other room. Cell-phones, e-mail and the world wide web are the latest tools for our businesses.

What happens to us if it all stops? Or a big chunk of it does?

**Telephone** This is one of the most intensively computerized services in the world. Prior to the 1980s, there had been some incredible advances. But still, as of that time and except for a relatively few microwave links, there had to be an unbroken trail of copper wire from your phone, all the way from your mouth to your friend's ear on the other side of the world.

This is no longer true. Nowadays, as soon as your voice signal travels down the wire to your local switching center (also called "telephone exchange" or "central office"), it's digitized. That means that instead of an electrical image ("analog") of your voice, the system now has a string of numbers (digits) that *describe* the shape of your original speech waves.

These numbers are then passed through from one computer to the next. Sometimes they're stored for a time until the next channel has free capacity to take them forward on another leg of this incredible journey.

At the other end, the numbers are used to recreate an image of your voice, and this "artificial copy" of your voice is what your friend hears. All this happens in a fraction of a second, so the two of you think you're actually holding a conversation.

There's a lot of computers in this picture, with millions and millions of lines of program code. Across the world, or across the city. Five percent, or even one percent, of such a large number is still a large number.

Also, like the power system, the telephones are linked in a network. The system adjusts to a failure in one area by redirecting traffic elsewhere. As with the electric power grid, this works great for one, or perhaps a couple of failures. But a multitude of failures *all at the same time* could jam everything.

My good friend Ravi Ravindra, a noted computer consultant with DMR/Amdahl, was in a hotel room in Los Angeles for one of their larger earthquakes. He reached for the phone immediately, and called his wife in Alberta. After telling her he was OK, he attempted to dial his Edmonton office. No luck. He was unable to get long distance *anywhere* for 48 hours.

In those first few seconds, the phone system was still operating normally. By a minute or so after the quake, the load on the phone system had risen to a point of total overload. It took two days to return to somewhere near normal.

When I was in High school, I worked part-time as a telephone operator, on a manual switchboard for a small town. On New Year's Eve, we doubled the staff by adding me to the midnight shift. The night man and I were handling about one call every five minutes.

The radio said "Happy New Year!" We shook hands – and the switchboard lit up like a Christmas tree! We could only handle about 10% of the calls, but we did our best, and it was like that for an hour or so.

When the Edmonton tornado hit our city on Friday, July 31, 1987, it killed 27 people and destroyed $300 million in property, all in 30 minutes. From Calgary, 300km (180 mi) to the south, I couldn't get a call into Edmonton. Nor could I call my father in Hawaii. He had flown out of Edmonton the night before on his way home to New Zealand. I could call anywhere else within Alberta, but not to Edmonton or out of the province.

Telephone systems have a strictly limited capacity. Overload them, which these days happens very rarely, and they begin to behave unpredictably. New Year's Eve is one of the busiest times of all, especially *that* New Year's Eve. And in this day and age there'll be millions of people trying to make local and international calls, ***all at the same time***.

Add a few software failures here and there, sounds to me like a recipe for chaos.

And what was it we said earlier about firefighting? If you can't get through to the Fire Department or 9-1-1, it probably won't matter whether you have water or not! My eighty-year-old mother-in-law wears a radio button that allows her to call for help via the phone from anywhere in the house. It won't be much help that night.

The elderly, and anyone else who might be in need of urgent help, usually depend on the phone. You'll need to make other arrangements for any elderly or infirm among your family and friends. Like being sure someone is with them for that night.

So we have two problems at the same time with the phones. The busiest night of the century, and the possibility of software failures. Together, these two problems could ripple across the continent too, along with the electrical failures.

One other thing I find intriguing about the world's phone systems. It has been estimated that close to half the population of the world have never made a phone call. Many third-world countries are still using the older analog switchgear. Some of this is old enough to be electro-mechanical, with physical switches choosing wires to route the calls. Some places have newer, but still out of date, electronic switches, but many of these are analog, not digital.

Analog electronics don't have a Y2k problem! Neither do the electro-mechanical switches, of course. So it could be that many people in the third world will find they still have telephone service, while those of us in the so-called "developed world" have none! Of course, cell-phones are such a new technology, that they're all digitally switched, even the older analog cell phones, so *all* cell phones are Y2k vulnerable, even in the third world.

**Cable and Satellite TV** All of this high-tech stuff is just riddled with computers and software. TV and radio are no exception. There are computers all throughout any broadcast studio, its transmitters, the cable TV system, the satellite uplink and downlink stations, and the satellites themselves. Private dish receivers too. All computerized. All vulnerable to software failures.

We'll have a very important need for radio and TV on Millennium Day. As the Millennium Midnight traverses the surface of the Earth, we all need to be watching. The instant news we have all become accustomed to will show us the celebrations as midnight strikes around the world. And maybe it'll show us the odd disaster here and there.

# The Internet

Right from its beginning in the 1960s, when it was called ARPANET and used solely for research, the Internet has been designed to be fail-safe, and resilient to failures. This is great news, and I wish more of our society had been designed this way. It happened because the project was started by the U.S. military, and they work all the time with life-and-death situations. They understand how important "fail-safe" can be.

Even so, the Internet has never had the kind of test it'll get with the coming of the Millennium. As we approach The Day, traffic on the 'Net will increase. On and around The Day it'll be very busy, with New Year and Millennium greetings going around the world to friends and loved ones. It's a lot cheaper than an international phone call. There are about 200 million end-users on the Internet, and the number is growing daily. The 'Net itself consists of hundreds of thousands of computers all linked together.

The Internet is the ultimate in computerization. It was built from the ground up as a network of computers talking to computers. The entire 'Net is Y2k vulnerable. 5% of a very large number . . .

Many businesses now depend on the Internet. Hundreds of thousands use the world wide web for sales and advertising. *All* large organizations, along with literally millions of medium and small businesses, use e-mail every day of the week. Tens of millions of private individuals use e-mail regularly. I really expect the whole thing to come to a grinding halt. I can't even speculate about how long it'll take to fix. Maybe days, could be months, perhaps a year.

If problems develop, there'll be a lot of panic and emergency traffic. All of us with relatives in New Zealand will want to check on them in the first hour or so of the Millennium, when they're into it already and we're still waiting. Then those with family in Australia will get their turn, then Japan and the Philippines, and progressively through Asia and around the world. Expect the traffic to grow throughout Millennium Day and beyond.

All this will be stretching the 'Net to capacity. And in the midst of all this traffic, what if some of the computers that form the 'Net itself have problems? If one goes down, the 'Net has been designed to transfer the traffic to alternative routes. As the "packets" of data that make up your message go skipping from one computer to another around the world, they'll be rerouted around the dead computer.

As with the power lines in Auckland, and as in any network, this will place a heavier load on the surrounding computers and links. At best, it'll merely slow them down. At worst, some of these could overload and die, *passing more load onto the ones that are left.*

Depending how many computers this happens to, we can expect the entire world-wide 'Net to slow down. Remember it'll be fully loaded or overloaded already before the failures start. Messages normally go in a few seconds or minutes from Canada to New Zealand, or from Britain to India, Holland to Surinam, or anywhere. They might take hours. Who knows, they might take days. If they get there at all. At that point the 'Net is basically unuseable.

All this assumes that your PC is working, and I think it probably will be. I'm not so sure about the phone system, so I hope you're able to dial in to the 'Net that Day and at least try to send messages.

**Police and Military Communications**  I see a couple of potential problems here. One that will be visible to us civilians is their field radios. On that New Year's Eve, we would expect the police to be out in force, and the soldiers too. Even if there's no software disaster, as you and I both fervently hope, we'll still need more manpower than our police forces can provide.

This will be the biggest celebration/party/fireworks display/riot/whatever that the world has ever seen. It's the first party ever to go *right around the world.* Sure, that happens every New Year to some extent, but most years most people go to bed not too long after midnight. This time more will stay up, and more will want to watch the festivities around the world. (There's that instant communication again!)

Governments everywhere will need to have all kinds of trained manpower, i.e., soldiers and police, on hand for crowd control, and just in case of trouble. But communications are the key to such operations. If they're using modern portable two-way radios, those things all have computers in them! They would be safest to have each person carry an old-fashioned radio as backup, that is if they have any still around.

The other problem I see concerns the heavy-duty military communications. I mean the voice messages and computer signals going between military bases, ships, aircraft, satellites, and so on. Some military commanders have expressed fears about Y2k.

If their systems are in some state of disarray, terrorists or spies could break into the networks unnoticed under cover of all the confusion. I must say that if I were one of these people, I would certainly see this as a golden opportunity to attack the US and others.

## Billing, Banking and Government

When banks handle checks or other transactions, they depend on computers to tell if there's enough money in the account. When you use an Automated Teller Machine (ATM), it uses a communications network to call up your bank account from a database. The database can be in a computer thousands of miles from where you are, but the ATM uses it to check your balance before it does the job for you.

Communications networks like this are totally computerized. All the databases with account balances and all the other information are on computers. Every record in the database has dates recorded with it. All the banks are connected together by networks from one bank's computers to another bank's computers.

Everything that happens at a bank, or between banks, is at risk for Y2k failures.

And when you find you can't use the ATM, and you line up for a teller, guess what? Even if they can still get information from their computers, *there won't be enough tellers!*

Since the banks introduced ATMs, telephone banking, touch-tone banking and on-line banking, the need for tellers has declined. There weren't any massive layoffs like some other industries. They just quietly didn't hire as many as the years went by.

If the computers die, we're going to be very short of personpower behind the counters of the banks. I have not heard of any banks beginning a campaign to train more tellers. Even if they did, there might not be time.

**Screwed-Up Bills and Payments** So much of our society is built around numbers on sheets of paper, sent through the mails. We get stacks of bills in the mailbox each day, and the lucky ones receive the occasional check as well. It's all done with computers. So what we can expect is that many of the numbers will be wrong.

This will cause havoc! We're likely to get wrong information on what we owe our creditors, and what the government expects from us. Our whole system of business and commerce depends on these numbers. If only 5% are wrong, but we have no way to tell which 5%, then we can't trust any of them! You just can't run an economy this way.

Just imagine for a moment what it would be like if every number that came through your door was wrong. I'm sure you wouldn't want to pay any of your bills until you and the creditor could agree on how much you owed.

If you're a student, and your fall semester grades are supposed to come in the mail in early January, you could end up having some arguments with your school. Missing your loan payments or insurance premiums can cause all kinds of problems, sometimes expensive ones. Missing payment on a traffic fine might even land you in jail.

But even if only 1% of these numbers are wrong, *we won't know which ones to trust*, so it'll be almost as bad as having all of them wrong! And in countries where the tax year ends on December 31, as it does in Canada, or October 31 in the U.S., we'll all be struggling with our tax returns right when Y2k hits.

**Bank Runs** There are many things that can cause large numbers of people to want their money out of a bank, all at the same time. It's usually a mixture of fear, rumor and just enough fact that does it. But here's more.

A bank never has all of your money in its vault. They lend it out to earn interest, and then pay some of that interest to you. In the U.S., among other countries, certain kinds of bank accounts are strictly controlled by law as to the percentage of your money they can lend out, and what percentage they must actually have in the vault.

The purpose is to reduce the chance of a "run" on the bank. When one of those happens, everybody wants their money at once, and of course there isn't enough on hand to pay them. Panic ensues, and banks can shut down, and then no one gets any money.

These are the kinds of accounts where people make regular deposits and write checks and so on. Other types of accounts are less easy to move money into and out of, so they're not as tightly controlled. The bank is allowed to keep a smaller fraction of the actual money on hand in these accounts, and lend out a bigger fraction.

U.S. law allows banks to "sweep" some of your money from the controlled accounts into uncontrolled accounts. This reduces the percentage of our money they have to have in the vault! It also reduces the amount of protection against a run on the bank, and increases the chance that you and I might lose our money if there is one.

Governments have over the decades set up mechanisms to protect our money. The U.S. has the Federal Deposit Insurance Corporation (FDIC). Canada has the CDIC. But these are *insurance* programs. They depend on having a *percentage* of the money available, and never having more than a few banks in trouble.

Y2k could cause massive panic. Banks may be in trouble across the continent and all around the world. Rumors and fears would be rife. A recipe for a banking disaster.

The FDIC and the CDIC could very quickly both go broke. Don't depend on them.

In Chapter 7, you'll see my advice on money and investments. The big thing is not to panic, *because it might not even happen!* You will need to have a portion of your money in cash, enough to live on for a month or two in case the banks have problems. Get it out early, in case there's a run on the banks later. And there are one or two other places to put some of it. *But not all of it.*

And *see your financial adviser first, before you do anything.*

**Late Mailings** Because of software that fails unpredictably, and because of having to rerun print jobs that were screwed up, a lot of the numbers will go out late. Even if the numbers are right, many of them will arrive late enough to cause problems.

Late bills mean late payments. Screwed-up bills mean missed payments, or none at all while people argue. Late or missing government checks would certainly place an extra load on the phone system as everyone tried to find out what happened, when will they come, and how do we buy food in the meantime?

In the extreme, it could mean social unrest. Sometimes people in poorer parts of our cities have been known to riot when they feel mistreated by governments or police forces. Hungry people can become very angry, very quickly.

**Will there be Mail Anyway?** All of this assumes the mail will be there, even if perhaps a little late. But post offices and courier companies all over the world use computers for everything too. Tracking mail or shipments, sorting it on its way, and billing for it when it finally arrives. All computerized. All vulnerable.

And if the Post Office or one of the courier companies gets stuck, all the customers will move off to the competition. And guess what? Overload! The ones that are still able to function may have to shoulder the load their competitors can no longer handle. But mostly their systems can't handle more than a moderate overload, so here's yet another service in our society that might collapse on us.

If we lose much of the capacity of the mails, it would mean that commerce and society could slow down considerably, with possibly serious economic effects. Add this to everything else, and a depression begins to look more and more likely.

**Forecasting in Government and Business**  Many businesses must try to predict the future demand for their products and services. That way, they can estimate how much to spend on factories, warehouses, offices, and everything else they need to do their business.

About the only way to do this is to calculate from the past. By keeping records of sales over the past months and years, businesses can use complex statistical formulas to estimate the demand in the next month or two, or for several years. By using census results and so on, governments can predict such things as population growth, and the need for education, welfare, or other services.

All of this is done by computer, that is, by software. People could never do these complex calculations fast enough, or accurately enough. Before we had computers, forecasting was a very rough process. Now, with the aid of these incredible (but stupid) machines, it has become a sophisticated and very necessary part of running any large organization. And everything in it is date sensitive.

Need I say more? Businesses and governments are likely to make some very expensive mistakes in planning for the first few years of the new Millennium. Factories may be built that were not needed. Warehouses and other facilities may turn out to be too small, and get overloaded, because our forecasts were on the light side. If some of these mistakes mean we'll have inadequate medical and old age services, or undersized highways, there could even be some deaths caused by this problem.

## Embedded Systems

At risk of sounding repetitive, practically *everything* has a computer in it these days. Let me repeat the list from Chapter 2. Remember, this is not a complete list. Can you think of more?

### Why would embedded software need dates?

By December 1999, there will be *25 billion* computer chips embedded in other products around the world. Let me say that number again:

### That's B̲illion, with a 'B̲'

### Computer Chips Are Hidden (Embedded) Inside These Products:

**Office Equipment**
Faxes, printers, copiers, etc.
Calculators, Computers

**Security**
Security systems: buildings
Security systems: vehicles
Video cameras
Bank, business and home alarm systems
Generators

**Communications**
Telephones
Cell phones
Telephone switching centers
PBXs
Cell towers
Two-way radios

**Entertainment**
TVs and VCRs
TV and radio stations
Camcorders
Radios and Stereos
CD players

**Medical**
Pacemakers
Hospital monitoring equipment
Automatic medicine dispensers
Artificial limbs

**Buildings**
Security systems
Elevators
Environment control systems
Heating/Air conditioning
Greenhouse systems

**Transportation**
Airplanes
Ships, Radar, GPS receivers

Traffic control systems
Almost anything with a gas motor:
    Vehicles, Power boats

**Manufacturing**
Assembly lines
Industrial robots

**Business and Commerce**
Cash registers
Bank vaults
Automatic vending machines
Automatic teller Machines (ATM)
Anything with a *digital display*, whether
    LEDs or liquid-crystal
Basically, *automatic anything!*

**Home Appliances**
Chainsaws, lawnmowers, snowblowers
Microwaves
Watches and clocks

The Gartner Group figures it'll be closer to 50 billion, but let's be conservative and work with the smaller number. There's always a chance the picture is worse than I'm painting.

If your car or your VCR doesn't run, how much will that affect your life? We could all do without a VCR or a microwave for a few weeks or months. Could you do without your car? Maybe you could, as long as the buses or trains were running.

But what if your car failed at night on the highway? That would be more difficult to deal with. Or what if it wasn't your own vehicle that failed, but the ambulance that was rushing to take you or a loved one to Emergency?

But, you may well say, I understand that the timer in my VCR uses the date, so it might go wrong on Y2k. But my toaster and the engine of my car don't. Why would the Electronic Fuel Injection (EFI) on my car need to worry about the date? Or the spark timing, or the ABS brakes? Why would my microwave or toaster care about the date?

All that the EFI computer in your car has to do is read all the sensors for air temperature and air flow and such, figure out exactly the right mixture of gasoline and air, and set the nozzles to make it. It takes a computer to do this because it has to be done thousands of times a second to keep the engine working at its best.

That's how the computer improves the power, economy and emissions from your engine all at the same time. The old-fashioned carburetor was a mechanical device to do the same job, but it could not get the mixture exactly right, just somewhere close. It worked to a very rough estimate compared with the accuracy of computerized EFI.

The computer chips ("microprocessors") that run the ignition timing and the Antiskid Braking System (ABS) work much the same. We say they run in "real-time," receiving data from sensors, calculating what should be done about it, and sending signals to change the spark plug timing, or ease off the brake pressure when one of the wheels tries to lock up and skid.

Why would dates be involved in any of this? Three possibilities:

- There may be dates in there that we weren't expecting. When you take your car in for servicing, the first thing the "service technician" does is to plug in the computer. This is a larger computer built especially to plug into the "onboard" computers in your car and check to see what's going on. One of the figures that appears on the screens of most of these workshop computers is the time since the last service! That involves *dates*.

I don't pretend to know the ins and outs of these workshop computers and their software. I know just enough to be suspicious when the car manufacturers say "There's no date references in our onboard software! What could possibly go wrong with our beautiful late models?"

I'd rather trust their early models, like 1980 perhaps. BC models – *Before Chips*. There are enough embedded chips out there that even one percent of one percent is still a large number!

- Programmers think weirdly. I've said this before, and I repeat it here, and I know it's true because I am one. The sheer numbers involved tell us that a small percentage of weird errors is still a large number.

  Each of those 25 billion embedded microprocessor chips has thousands of parts inside it. Every chip has somewhere between 100,000 and several million hardware components inside. Each one also has from 1000 to 20,000 or more lines of program code (LOC) built in. (Remember what those are?)

  In all this complexity, and knowing the error rates that programmers work with, we know there'll be places where a programmer used a date here and there in the software, ***even when he didn't really need to!*** *Perhaps* even in your toaster or waffle iron.

  These may well be calculations that could have been done *without* a date reference. And most programmers would do them that way. But here and there we'll find an inappropriate date-based calculation where it was not necessary. A small percent of a small percent could still be a lot of failures.

- These chips are so complex that no engineer ever designs one from scratch. When an engineer needs a little bit of memory to add to the chip (s)he is building, (s)he borrows the design from a chip that has already been built. Much like, if you were designing a new lawnmower, you wouldn't bother designing wheels or a motor. You would use "off-the-shelf" designs for those parts.

  When a chip designer is working on a new chip, (s)he might borrow part of a design, and that borrowed "component" may have dates in it that this project doesn't need. But they're there. And they just might cause a problem, in a *small percent* of cases. And we know that when some of them fail, a few of these will *not* fail safe. So we're vulnerable.

It's perhaps significant that not one major automobile manufacturer has stated publicly that *all* their vehicles are guaranteed to start on January 1, 2000. Most have said nothing at all, and no news is bad news! However, as of early 1998, just two companies have promised that their 97 to 99 models will run . . .

## Hiding the Truth

Now here is some chilling news about how chip makers are treating the problems they have found. Peter de Jager reports that several executives from manufacturers talked to him.

One said he had found problems in some of the microchips his company produces. The ***marketing department***, of all people, was given the task of deciding ***not when, but*** if they were going to tell the customers. It seems the customers still don't know

Another executive found problems in his company's chips, and said nothing on the advice of his lawyers. De Jager calls this "irresponsible advice" from the lawyers, and I totally agree. He says " . . . to know that something will break and choose to ignore it" is "unconscionable."

This action could expose some of those customers to failures, loss of business, closure of business, property damage, and even injuries or deaths.

But it's happening. Stories like this get me worried. What they tell me is that many chips will fail around the world *unnecessarily*. These are failures that could be prevented. But instead, they'll be allowed to happen because of fear of lawsuits if the customers were told in advance. I have a feeling there may be more and bigger lawsuits if these chips happen to fail at an awkward moment.

Then there are the out-of-date chips. If they fail, where will we get replacements? Many are no longer made, and some makers have gone out of business. More chip manufacturers may fail as a result of their Y2k problems. So where does that leave their customers? Up the creek with neither a paddle nor a replacement chip.

In these cases, the chip can't be replaced, except for a few cases where someone else makes one that will do. So the customer may have to scrap an entire machine. Hundreds of thousands of dollars worth of equipment could become useless for want of a $20 chip!

One option would be to wait and hope that another company makes a replacement, but that would only happen if they have a chance to sell several hundreds or thousands. Or if you paid a high enough price each, for a small number of chips.

Another would be to reprogram the chip. This may be possible in a few cases, provided the programming language that was used is still around, along with a programmer who knows it. Many chips use languages that are just for that chip, or that maker, and only a very few programmers ever knew how to use the language in the first place.

Or the equipment could be redesigned to use a more modern chip. This would be very time-consuming and expensive, and would require the right kind of engineers and maybe programmers as well. If you can find them. Whatever option a company chooses, it'll mean down time and lost production for weeks or months, on top of the costs of fixing the problem. Some companies will go broke, for sure.

How many embedded chips will fail? As usual, *who knows?* Many, I'm quite sure. Enough to be a problem. Some will be in the critical systems described in the next section. When all this happens, would you want to be hooked up to a computerized hospital machine that has been given the job of keeping you alive? Or monitoring you to see if you're alive? I won't say it *will* fail, obviously. But some of them very well might.

## Critical Systems

As I have suggested a number of times in this book, some of the software we depend on in this world is in critically important places. As we saw in the N.Z. aluminum smelter account, some software can cause serious damage if it fails. Luckily, no one was hurt or killed in that case, but I'm sure you see that in other cases injuries and even deaths might easily happen.

There are many other places in our society where we depend on computers and software for our very lives. With things like airline reservation systems and maintenance schedules, we're depending on regular software running on computers in offices.

This is what we in the IT (Information Technology) world call "MIS software." That stands for "Management Information Systems," and it includes everything from bills, tax processing, personnel records, to paychecks, schedules of all kinds, and so on.

Where MIS software becomes critical, is in things like train and airplane schedules (avoiding collisions, for example). What about shift schedules for the technicians at a nuclear power plant? The software had better make darn sure there are the right number of people, and the right kind of people, in charge at any time.

But some of these critical systems are in embedded software. There are embedded processors guarding your life in the ABS in your car, and getting your airplane safely up and bringing it down again. They're hidden in medical equipment, and all over. Here is the usual somewhat incomplete list:

Electric Power
Nuclear Power
Hospitals and Medical Equipment
Building Systems
Airplanes:
    Reservation Systems
    Flight and Crew Scheduling
    Maintenance Schedules
    Airport Operations and Administration
    Communications and Air Traffic Control
    Navigation and GPS
    Onboard Control Systems
Ships
Railroads
    Driverless Trains
Industrial Processes and Assembly Lines
Vehicles
Weapons Systems

Let's take a more detailed look at each of these.

## Electric Power

We have seen above how this might be a problem. There are computers embedded in every part of the supply chain. They control the fuel flow, and steam temperature and pressure for steam-powered plants, and the water pressure for hydro plants.

The chips are in charge of keeping the generators spinning at the correct speed, even when the electrical load on them changes. This keeps the voltage and the frequency stable.

They're found in all the thousands of control stations and transformer substations between the generating plants and us, the end users. And we use electricity for so many things. Do you have backup power for your home security system? For any medical machinery in your house that's electric?

Even clocks, if there's a diabetic or someone like that in your family who must have food and medicine *on time*. Does your place of work have backup power for anything? Elevators? Important computers? Entrance security systems? Or any equipment that could be dangerous if it stopped. Check what happened in Montreal and Auckland.

## Nuclear Power

The major fear for all of us here is the Big Bang. Three Mile Island and Chernobyl showed us what can go wrong. Chernobyl was a case of old and outdated equipment, poorly maintained and used. Three Mile Island, on the other hand, was entirely preventable. As reported in the papers at the time, it appeared to be a case of the software reporting the problems correctly, and people not bothering to take notice.

What if the software didn't notice? The software in nuclear plants is high quality, like military software. But like the military stuff, *it's not perfect*. One error per million lines of code (LOC), but there's an awful lot of code, and there's a lot of nuclear facilities.

So we'd better make sure we have the best people on duty on Millennium Day, and after that date as well. We'd better print the schedules in advance of The Day, too!

## Hospitals and Medical Equipment

This is a scary one, because it touches ordinary people and our loved ones. So much equipment in Intensive Care Units (ICUs) is computer-controlled. And these are the serious and critical patients who can least afford to have a machine screw up their medication, or their breathing, or pacemaker, or whatever. Or have a machine fail to call the staff for help when their blood pressure rises or drops, or the heart races. Or stops.

Those hospitals that have started checking are finding themselves "wrestling with vendors" to find out which equipment is and isn't compliant. And how do they go about testing it, anyway? In an April 1998 article on www.plesman.com Howard Solomon quotes Adrian Tiganila of the Toronto Sick Children's Hospital: "Getting straight answers on Y2k compliance from medical equipment vendors is a problem."

They share this problem with all users of embedded chips, in other words, *everybody*. You'll see I have a lot to say about chips in medical equipment later, in Chapter 4.

And on top of that, a hospital needs electric power. They all have backup generators; let's hope they start (see "Vehicles" below). We need gas to heat the hospital, or electricity to cool it, for patients whose bodies have limited tolerance for extremes of heat and cold.

We need phones and transportation systems, to get the staff shifts to the hospital, and in the days following Y2k those systems may be malfunctioning, overloaded or completely out. And we need to get food to the hospital, and be able to cook it, to feed patients and staff.

Hospitals are dependent on many of the systems in our society that in turn depend on software. They also depend on the embedded software in their own equipment.

In these days of funding cuts and downsizing there's a problem. Hospital boards and administrators focus on the immediate needs of the hospital. Funds to stay open, mergers and other political things, serve to distract attention from Y2k and its hospital impact.

Again, this effect is not limited to hospitals. Other parts of our society are falling into the same traps, all over the place. But I believe that for hospitals it's particularly dangerous. Not only do I see hospitals as more sensitive to Y2k problems, but the consequences of a screw-up could more easily be fatal, and for a large number of people.

And hospitals will also suffer the same problems as other buildings.

## Building Systems

A number of thermostat manufacturers have tested their products and found that perhaps one third of these devices will fail completely on Millennium Day. Finding and replacing them will be a job for a skilled technician. This is serious because it'll happen will occur in the middle of winter, during the biggest party the world has ever seen, on the Friday night of a busy three-day holiday weekend. The busiest *ever*.

The technicians may want to join the party. There may not be any technicians working that weekend. And they may not be able to get any replacement chips. Many buildings and people could freeze, pipes could burst, much damage could be done.

Ford Motor Co. tested one of their factory buildings. The software crashed, and locked some people out, and others inside. Their building management people were horrified.

Another sensitive and possibly fatal area is airplanes.

## Airplanes

There's a whole raft of software systems that must be there to make air travel happen at all, let alone happen safely. As in hospitals, some of these are MIS software, like reservation systems and scheduling. And some of the most critical and dangerous are embedded in the airplane itself, and in other systems that are outside the airplane, but it needs them to be there in order to fly safely.

**Reservation Systems**      These are MIS systems, and they won't directly cause any airplane crashes. But if they screw up, they could make the scheduling problems for flights and crews a whole lot worse (see below). Plus, it'll be extremely inconvenient for millions of travelers, and we could end up with people stranded in airports here and there, or perhaps everywhere. While this is inconvenient for most travelers, it could be expensive for some.

**Flight and Crew Scheduling**     Getting the right airplane to the right place at the right time is a huge task for any sizable airline. Add to that the complexities of getting the right crew to right airplane at the right time at the right airport. Then hope the reservation system (see above) doesn't have too many passengers waiting. What if the reservations screwed up so there was nobody waiting to fly? What do we do with the crew and the airplane?

Scheduling the airplanes and the crews is a complex task, and in most airlines it's done with the aid of computers. There are some very important things that the schedulers have to keep track of. Airline laws in most countries require them to make sure none of the aircrew work too many hours straight, or more than a certain limit out of every 24 hours, and no more than so many hours a week. This is for the passengers' safety.

Like anyone else, pilots make more mistakes when they're overtired.

**Maintenance Schedules**     This is another complex task, with serious results if it's not done right. Flying is the most difficult thing mankind has ever made our machines do for us. That's why it didn't happen until the final century of the millennium. We've had trains for 250 years, cars since the 1880s, and airplanes only since 1910. These marvelous flying machines must work very close to their physical limits to make flying happen at all.

For example, does anyone insist on weighing your bags when you get on a train, ship, bus, or even into a car? No, because those machines are built with plenty of extra strength and power, to handle such things. But we've all read how airplanes have crashed from being overloaded. How a little thing like the weight of some ice on the wings can kill.

Actually, it's also the fact that the ice changes the shape of the wing, changing the airflow over it, and reducing the amount of lift it can create. When did you ever have to check that your car or bike was the right *shape* so it could go safely out on the street?

A friend once told me how his father was a civil engineer before the Second World War. He designed bridges and highways and such. During the war they put him to work in an aircraft factory. He knew all the math and the design principles; he just needed to convert himself from building one kind of equipment to another kind. From bridges to airplanes.

What he found the most difficult was that for bridges, if he calculated that a certain beam must support 30 tons, he would normally make strong enough for 90 tons. Three times what he figured was needed. This was 200% more than needed. In other words, his "safety factor," or extra strength in case of problems, was 200%.

In the airplane business, he was shocked to learn that he could only use a 20% to 30% safety factor. That is, once he calculated how strong something had to be, he was allowed to add only one-fifth to about one-third extra strength! The problem is that if an airplane is three times as heavy as necessary, it simply won't get off the ground.

So airplanes are very sensitive to a slight lack of performance. Poorly-tuned engines can cost extra in fuel, and in icy or severe weather may not have enough power to get off the ground. Parts weaken with age, and late fixes could cause something to break in flight.

I cannot specifically blame maintenance for the Boeing 737 that lost part of its roof (and killed one flight attendant) in Hawaii in the late 1980s. But that's an example of what can happen when airplanes get old or are not looked after well enough.

What all this is saying is that aircraft maintenance **must happen**, and must happen on time, or people can die. Y2k errors in the scheduling software might cause a few immediate problems, but could also give us problems that might stay hidden and not be found until months or years later. Sometimes, perhaps too late.

**Airport Operations and Administration**     An airport is a collection of both MIS and embedded software. There are the usual administrative MIS systems that we depend on to keep the people and the airport functioning. Without them, many things around the airport will become disorganized, understaffed, inconvenient, and some of them dangerous.

And don't forget all the security systems. Door access systems, luggage scanning and security systems, passenger gate access, all are vulnerable to software screw-ups. This could be just the time for terrorists to make their hijack attempts.

### Don't fly on 2kY

**Communications and Air Traffic Control**     Then there's the critical air traffic control software. There is software for the displays, the radar, the radio communication, and the navigation and guidance systems, instrument landing systems, and so on. If any of these fail, our crowded skies could become very dangerous indeed.

In the extreme, we possibly could end up with something like Bruce Willis's movie, "*Die Hard II*." In that movie terrorists scramble signals, with disastrous results, although the casualties are limited by the skill and daring of the hero, a vacationing L.A. cop.

Expect no such hero on January 1, 2000. And who would he fight, anyway? This is something we've done to ourselves, without the help of any terrorists. We might do better with the 12-year-old girl UNIX expert who saved the day in "*Jurassic Park.*"

### Don't fly on 2kY.

But just think again about terrorists. Wouldn't it be a wonderful opportunity, if you were a terrorist, if the airports are all having trouble with computers? If x-ray baggage scanners broke, if planes disappear off radar screens, or pilots can't talk to controllers on the radio. If terrorist groups see a chance to catch us with our electronic pants down, *they'll do it.*

The U.S. Federal Aviation Authority has some extremely old and out-of-date computers. Some are models that IBM stopped supporting a decade ago. *IBM has stated that both the hardware and the operating system software* **will fail** *in the year 2000,* and they won't fix it.

The Yourdons estimate that completely replacing these systems could take 3 to 7 years. Can we fly thousands of flights a day by hand? Will air traffic controllers be able to handle modern traffic volumes with binoculars and stopwatches? I don't think so!

This could conceivably bring airline traffic in North America to a grinding halt. And you can bet the rest of the world won't be any better off. What would a few days or weeks or months of that do to the world's economy?

**Navigation and GPS**     Earlier we saw how the Global Positioning System (GPS) is used by "Trains and Boats and Planes" (apologies to Roger Williams.) Computers are used for calculations in practically every piece of navigational equipment these days. Lost planes can fly into mountains, or run out of fuel. Functioning airports might be few and far between, and be overcrowded and partly impaired. Don't fly on 2kY.

**Onboard Control Systems**     Everything that happens on a large aircraft is computerized. The instruments, the controls, the engines and their monitoring gauges, the hydraulic systems, everything. Like the computers in your car, they mostly shouldn't have dates in their calculations. But, as we saw earlier, there are one or two ways that dates might just slip into the calculations, with pilots, flight engineers and mechanics unaware.

It's interesting that the control system on the Boeing 777 is a UNIX network. Be very cautious flying on one in January of 2038. And don't fly on 2kY.

## Ships

Airplanes have the most dangerous failure mode of all. When they go wrong, they sometimes fall out of the sky. Ships, on the other hand, go much slower, and don't automatically sink when they run out of fuel. But a lost ship is still in danger. There are enough pieces of rock and other ships around to make survival depend heavily on being able to navigate. Radar, sonar and control systems on a ship these days are as heavily computerized as airplanes.

## Railroads

From the engines and controls on board a locomotive, to the signals and the radio communication systems, modern trains too are run by software. And as with ships and aircraft, much of this software is such that if it fails it could bring about disaster. Or, in many cases, it could cause a disaster because the programmer didn't arrange for it to fail *safely*.

MIS software is used to schedule trains and crews. If it screws up and puts two trains on the same piece of track, and if the fail-safe systems don't do too well, we could have serious accidents. One of the problems with trains is that they can sometimes carry thousands of people on one train.

And in Europe and Japan they do it, *totally* computerized, at up to *500 km/h (300 m.p.h.)!* Don't *Chunnel* on 2kY either.

Train collisions happen a few times a year in the U.S., and most other countries would have at least one a year. That's in good times. I have visions of trains running into one another, engines refusing to throttle back and slow down, braking systems not working, even crossing lights and bells that refuse to operate.

My brother Warren and his wife Diane know what railway brake failures look like. Walking on the Wellington N.Z. railway station one afternoon, Warren heard a long horn blast. He looked around and saw an electric locomotive hurtling straight at him with a train behind it, and showers of sparks from its wheels. Pushing his 8-month pregnant wife in one direction, he had to dive the other way.

The 100-ton engine hit the concrete stopping block and rolled it out of the ground. The engine rose 5 meters (15 ft) into the air and crashed into the steel and concrete station roof. Luckily, the train was empty, the driver saved himself by hitting the floor, and my brother and his wife were clear.

But they ended up on opposite sides of the mess, and poor Diane had no way of knowing whether her husband had made it out of the way. She had to go clear out into the station concourse, pregnant, through rushing crowds, before she finally found him.

It might be a good idea not to go by train that day either. And there's one group of railways that are particularly exposed to software failures:

## Driverless Trains

San Francisco has BART, "Bay Area Rapid Transit." Vancouver BC has their "Skytrain." SeaTac and other airports have little driverless commuter trains. The computers do a great job of running these systems, with a lower accident rate than regular trains. Usually.

But when it was first built around 1980, BART had a couple of trains go off the end of the tracks, luckily without serious injury. It may have been software failure or maybe hardware. It doesn't matter which; it was an incorrect answer from a computer that did it. This time, we can expect the hardware to be in great shape. I'm not so sure about software.

Because human lives are at stake, this is one of those areas where we can justify the extra expense of higher-quality software. So expect one error per million lines of program code (LOC), rather than the MIS average of one error per hundred LOC, or Capers Jones's estimate of 5% of dates going unfixed. But railroad scheduling and control systems do have a lot of dates. And even one train off the end would be one too many.

## Industrial Processes and Assembly Lines

When Henry Ford invented the assembly line, it was a mechanical gadget that moved a product from man to man. Nowadays, it's software controlled, monitored by a technician, and (s)he makes sure all the products go along from robot to robot. One set of software controls the line itself. More software is in each of the thousands of robots on a big assembly line. And MIS software makes sure the parts arrive at the right point on the line when needed.

This last is called "Just-In-Time" or JIT delivery. This style of working has become very popular with big manufacturing companies over the last decade or so. It has the advantage of cutting down on the amount of inventory the company has to keep on hand, by placing the onus on the supplier to make sure things arrive on time.

Good luck! The likely effects of Y2k would be to disrupt many assembly lines and industrial processes by delivering the wrong product and/or at the wrong time. Too early is bad enough, but too late shuts us down.

We've all seen how disruptive it can be to an industry when factories close for strikes or whatever reason. We've seen how the effect snowballs through the economy of those cities as suppliers are forced to close down. And then retailers suffer also because no one in town has money to buy things. We've seen whole towns go broke.

What if this happened to many plants, in many industries, all over the world, all at the same time? Add in all the other things that we've discussed that could go wrong, and it starts to look a bit like an economic recession.

## Vehicles

This is another area where many people refuse to believe that anything could go wrong. But, as I have explained above, there are ways that date processing might cause vehicles to fail.

Given there are close to a billion vehicles in the world, with the number of chips in them by the time Y2k comes around, that's a lot of software. And with the number of weird ways to do things that programmers can dream up, *some* of these chips will fail. The problem is figuring out how many, and which ones.

## Weapons Systems

This is scary. Some modern weapons have software in their targeting systems. Even though this is mostly high-quality software, there's still a small but finite number of errors will get through. Like Apollo VII, these may land in the wrong ocean – or the wrong back yard.

But not all weapons have high-quality targeting software. A lot depends on where it was made, and who the software was written by. Not all countries and armies have the same standards of software quality that some of the more advanced nations have. Terrorist groups and gangster-type governments may even have among their members a few geek hackers who have done some of their own targeting software. This is not a video game, where a software crash means reboot and lose all your points. This is real, and real people may die.

## Weather Forecasting

So much of what we do depends on the weather. For most of us, bringing the wrong weather gear means inconvenience. But there are times and places where it can mean serious problems, or even death. For example, when I hiked into the Grand Canyon, the signs exhorted us to carry one gallon (4 liter) of water per person. For good reason.

In the 1970s one time, my 4-wheel-drive club decided to go out on a Sunday to cut Christmas trees. We happily drove off about 120 km (80 miles) from Edmonton on icy roads, at about -20°C (-4°F) or so, up the first part of the Alaska Highway.

I remember one downhill stretch where I came over the rise at about 60 km/h (40 mph) and found myself sliding back and forth all over the road. It was glare ice, just like a skating rink, and I had to work to keep the truck out of the snow-filled roadside ditches.

On our way back, at that very spot, we found a large car about 30m (100 ft) off the road, almost completely buried in the snow. It belonged to a lady in her sixties who had never driven in snow and ice in her life.

She was from Texas, on her way to spend Christmas with her sister in Alaska! Her only source of heat was a big black dog. She had absolutely nothing that we Albertans would have considered winter clothing.

In Alberta, skidding off a winter highway into a snow-filled ditch is something that everybody has done at least once. We're used to these conditions, and *carry the gear*. What she didn't realize was that had she pulled the same stunt on the main Alaska Highway, she would have died before morning. Traffic would have been light, and they may or may not have noticed how new her skid marks were.

As it was, we winched her out, and sent her on her way with a shopping list for clothes, candles, winter tires, tirechains and so on, and instructions to buy them at the very next town. In Chapters 7 and 8 you'll see my thoughts on preparing your vehicle for emergencies that might happen around Y2k.

Weather can kill. If you know what the weather will be, you can be prepared for it. If we have a lot of things going wrong on Y2k, we could have many people attempting to travel, or perhaps just survive, with marginal equipment. Airplanes need constant weather information. Bad weather has been the cause of many air crashes in the past.

And the forecasters use computers. Some of the most powerful supercomputers in the world are employed in weather forecasting. There are several million weather recording stations around the world, each with one or more computers or chips.

One of the most important sources of weather data these days is weather satellites. Like everything in orbit, they're computer-controlled, and were launched by computers also. Records kept by time and date, are fundamental to the forecasting process. We're vulnerable.

But then we need radio and other communications to gather the information and get it to the computers, and then get the results out to those who need them. Communications systems will be highly vulnerable to Y2k, and to meteor showers and solar flares as well.

And there is one little thing we're doing wrong, and I think we could have made it easier on ourselves if we had done it right:

## The Millennium is When?

Did you know that we're actually celebrating the millennium on the wrong New Year? Strictly speaking, the Third Millennium doesn't begin until January 1, 2001. This is because the First Millennium began on January 1, Year 1, and not Year Zero.

This means that the year 2000 is actually the last year of the Second Millennium, and 2001 is the first year of the Third Millennium. Not that it really matters.

But think of this. If we moved all the celebrations to January 1, 2001, what a load it would take off everybody, especially our police, military and other security forces. This would separate the Y2k problems and possible disasters from the Millennium celebrations, with their possible riots and other problems.

I've commented in a number of places how things will be made worse by the fact that the world may be falling apart right in the midst of the biggest party ever. It might also have given us time to cancel the party if the world was not together again in time. But it's not to be. The world is celebrating Y2k on January 1, 2000 whether we like it or not, and our software will fail on that very same day, like it or not.

# Chapter 4: How Bad Could It Get?

It could be really bad, or it could be nothing at all. I sincerely hope it's nothing. But I feel I would be doing you and your family a disservice, and all my own loved ones as well, if I simply ignored the whole thing. So in this chapter I give my *opinion* on how bad I think it'll be. If you've read this far, you must by now be forming your own opinions on this. The most important thing you must do after reading this chapter, is come to your own conclusions.

You must make up your mind about how bad this might be, based on what you read both here and elsewhere. And I strongly encourage you to read other books after this one, and to check some of the websites. (See Appendix "To Find Out More.")

Especially, you should read Ed and Jennifer Yourdon's book *"Time Bomb 2000"* and visit their website at www.yourdon.com for another viewpoint on what's coming. Ed Yardeni, Chief Economist at the Wall Street firm of Deutsche, Morgan Grenfell, is also a must at www.yardeni.com

The Gartner Group is an organization that does research in the IT industry. At their website, www.gartner.com , you must register first (for free), and then you can search for documents. Some documents are free, and some you must pay for. I did a search on "year 2000" and turned up 200. They were all the kind you pay for, but just scanning the brief abstracts was pretty scary!

*You* are responsible for your own safety and that of your loved ones. So only you can make these decisions. I can't make them for you. All I'm able to do is place the facts before you, along with my interpretations and opinions, and leave you to make the final choices. So here are some more facts and opinions.

I just don't see how we could get away with no problems at all. There's just too many things that could go wrong, and too many computers in the world. Every country in the world is late with Y2k software conversion.

We have close to 300 million computers in the world, **25 *Billion*** embedded chips, and an army of sometimes normal programmers with an alarming habit of writing fail-unsafe program code. A small percent of a small percent is still a very large number.

**Opinion:** I seriously expect *real* problems for a few months, and perhaps for as much as a year or two.

And I believe we'll have at least the one-year recession forecast by Dr Yardeni. It very likely could be double or triple that. After that, I expect we'll be back on our feet again as a society, but there'll be a mammoth clean-up job that will take *several years or perhaps more than a decade* to complete.

But I could be seriously wrong in *either* direction.

I fully expect there'll be severe economic results. The direct costs will be the Y2k fixup project expenses at somewhere between $US600 Billion and one Trillion. Then there's losses from failed software, and lawsuits will be at least another Trillion.

Then, with stock market problems, and personal and business bankruptcies, we'll be extremely lucky if we can avoid a long depression. After we discuss all the other problems, at the end of this chapter we'll look in detail at the effects on the economy, and the possibility of a depression.

Now here are my predictions (opinions, remember) for the various parts of our society. We'll look at:

| | |
|---|---|
| Electric Power | Critical Systems |
| Other Utilities | Riots and Civil Disturbance |
| Oil and Gasoline | Emergency Communications |
| Communications | Weapons Systems |
| Billing, Banking and Government | Medical |
| Embedded Systems | Fire and other Emergency Services |

# Electric Power

I've focused on this utility for a number of reasons:

- It's *highly computerized*
- It's a network that has in the past had *severe ripple effects*
- *So much of our society is built around electricity.*

The engineers tell us that their grid system is highly resilient. That is, it can have all kinds of things go wrong, and it'll still work. Which it certainly does. There are many things that *do* go wrong throughout the power system on any given day, and each failure is dealt with locally. The grid keeps on delivering power across the continent.

The system survives many failures day after day without serious problems. The history shows that widespread outages have happened very rarely. In recent decades, we have 1965, 1977 and 1996, gaps of roughly 10 and then 20 years between outages. Other grid systems in developed countries around the world have similar records.

But if a few generating plants and transformer substations were to suffer shutdowns or breakdowns because of software, the way the N.Z. aluminum smelter did, it would be a whole new ball game. The grid system has never before had to deal with a large number of serious failures across the continent, *all at the same time*. Each failure in the past was an opportunity to learn, and they learned. Engineers have steadily improved the systems over the decades.

But since the grid system has never been tested with *multiple* major powerplants or substations down at one time, its behavior under those conditions cannot be accurately predicted. Y2k could be the first time ever that things collapse in many places at once.

The engineers also claim that dates can't possibly be involved in their control software. They point out that you can't store electricity, so it's generated *right now* and used the very same moment it's made.

We say that the system is "generating for a real-time load." There are no past or future references, it simply satisfies the immediate demand. They claim there are no date references anywhere in the control software.

But we heard that argument about vehicles, toasters and microwaves. And we know that:

(a) Programmers are weird
(b) There are bound to be a few date references that have slipped into the program code in one or two places, and no one remembers they're there. And in many cases the programmers who did it are dead and/or gone.

Many power companies are already planning to have staff working all night on that New Year's Eve. This is excellent planning, and I applaud those managers who arranged it. One of their main jobs will be to try and turn the power back on manually when it does go off. Good luck – some of you might need it!

In Britain, London Electricity is planning to issue bicycles to its engineers in case the traffic lights fail and the streets become gridlocked. Also, they've stockpiled enough fuel for their generators to last for a month. But I don't think that's anywhere near enough.

Note, by the way, that railroads like the **Union Pacific** carry the coal and oil for a number of electricity generating stations. Further on in this book you'll see what I have to say about the Great Union Pacific Fiasco of 1997/1998.

## Other Utilities

Although they're perhaps a little less likely to have trouble, natural gas and water are still essential to our way of life. However, neither of them is organized in a grid like the electric supply, so a continental outage is practically impossible. But I fully expect there'll be local and regional problems in many places. The closer the failure is to the wells, the larger the geographical area it will affect.

Electrical failure will cut off water and sewage pumps. Many of these pumps don't have backup power. The Auckland power outage was a fine example of this, and then after a week or so they had another scare: Legionnaires' Disease!

Once the water flow has stopped for a couple of weeks, there's a danger of Legionnaires' Disease growing in the pipes. You must *flush the pipes thoroughly* before you drink when the water does come back on, to eliminate this danger.

Sewer backup is another danger, with the possibility of the spread of diseases. Many septic tanks use an electric pump. If it stops, you may have raw sewage in your back yard.

My wife Nina and I were stuck three days in the Philippine city of Baguio (Bag-ee-oh) after the 1990 earthquake. People were using bushes for a toilet, because the buildings were all far too dangerous.

And they were drinking from the streams, which just made it worse! Since it was the wet season, the untreated sewage was washing into the streams in the daily tropical rains, polluting the water to dangerous levels. Our group lived for three days on Pepsi and a heavy, protein-rich Filipino dessert known as *"hopia."*

*In a prolonged electrical failure, clean water will be a problem, especially in cities.*

An electrical outage will have little effect on natural gas supplies, since the pumps are gas-powered. But in cold climates (the "Snow Belt") we all have automatic gas or oil furnaces, with electric controls, electric thermostats and electric fan motors.

But the most difficult thing will be the automatic electric shutoff valve. This uses a "thermocouple" to sense when the pilot light goes out, and *shuts off the gas* for safety. The high-tech alternative is an electronic "zapper" to relight the gas any time it goes out, but *that too is electric*!

Not only that, but modern furnaces and thermostats have computer chips in them, and so they may be at risk even if the electricity and the gas are still on. And that also applies to oil-burning furnaces.

Oil-burning furnaces will not be much better off. Like the gas ones, they're electrically controlled, and so they could be affected by a power outage. But if the power stays on, and the furnace and thermostat still work, will the truck be there with more oil when you run out?

Like every other commodity in this modern world, heating oil is delivered by a long chain of people and equipment, and a Y2k failure of one or more links in the chain will mean no oil comes to your house. And it could mean no gasoline to your local filling station either.

## Oil and Gasoline

In countries with their own oil supply, such as Canada and the U.S., pipelines will be a problem, and so will refineries. There'll certainly be a number of shutdowns because of software failures. Just how many remains to be seen on The Day. And as with household appliances, a wrong result from a software calculation could cause a dangerous malfunction.

In an environment of flammable and poisonous products, this could mean fires, explosions or leakages that could injure or kill employees or neighbors. Remember the Union Carbide leakage at Bhopal in India that killed thousands. It *could* happen here.

Outside North America and other oil-producing regions, I expect the other big problem will be tankers. Even if the refineries manage to keep going, or to restart in a day or so, and not blow anything up, they need a constant flow of crude oil to work with. But there have been reports that some of the major oil tanker fleets have no hope of fixing their shipboard software before Y2k.

The results of this *could* be:

- Lost or grounded tankers.
- Disabled and possibly drifting tankers.
- Tankers on fire.
- Tankers taken out of service by laws that don't allow them to operate unsafely.
- Major oil spills.

Any or all of these events will interrupt the flow of crude to make gasoline to feed the gas pumps in your neighborhood. The specter of the Exxon Valdese rears its head, too. Multiple huge oil spills are not what we need when the rest of the world is already grappling with Y2k problems.

Are you old enough to remember the gasoline lineups in the 1970s when the U.S. last had shortages? Not only were they inconvenient and wasteful, but there were accidents, fights and assaults in the panic. There was even gunfire and an occasional death in the lineups. And then people were storing the gasoline in unsafe containers, which caused a number of house and apartment fires. Don't rely on the Fire Department on Y2k.

Nina and I saw lineups like this in Baguio in the days after the earthquake. Tempers were flaring in a city cut off from all food and supplies. Watch out for angry people whenever there's a widespread problem of this nature. Especially if you think they may have a gun. Angry people are more likely to actually *use* the guns they may be carrying.

# Communications

It's an unfortunate thing is that communications is the key to almost anything we do. That includes handling the problems and dangers and riots or whatever that may happen on Y2k. Crowd control, emergency response, or the President or Prime Minister addressing the nation, all require our modern *computerized* communications systems. Our software-dependent radio, TV and telephone systems.

## Telephone

Local systems I expect will be spotty. Some will work. Others may not. If the problems are at all severe, it won't take too much to make the long-distance network unusable. If there are power blackouts, or riots, or any such problems, people will try to make calls, which will only tie the system up worse. Add to that the extreme demand on any New Year's Eve, and don't expect to call outside your own area. Maybe not within your own area either.

Especially at risk are the little telephone switches used by businesses to handle phone calls within the company. These are referred to as "Private Branch Exchanges" or PBXs for short. Surveys and checks so far have shown that many are susceptible to Y2k problems.

Many have actually *failed Y2k testing*. Many are old, and are likely to be "orphaned" by their manufacturers. That is, the manufacturers will decide not to support certain older models, and not to go to the trouble of creating fixes for them.

Companies who have these particular models will have no option but to replace their switches. This is an expense they were not planning on. Larger companies are probably more up-to-date, either with compliant switches, or models that will have their software updated.

Those affected are mostly smaller companies who can only afford the older models, and these are also the companies who can least afford the extra expense of upgrading or replacing their PBX. I doubt that many businesses will be driven into bankruptcy by this one factor, but it could be the last straw for a company that was only just managing to stay afloat.

## Cable and Satellite Broadcasting

I'm expecting a real shambles. If parts of the cable and satellite systems manage to stay up, we may find many of the stations are down. Or if your local station is up, its cable feed may be down, so you can only get it by broadcast – via the trusty old rabbit's ears, or the antenna on the roof. Or maybe all we'll get is a radio station or two.

It's that chain idea again. To get a signal from a camera or microphone all the way to your TV set, there are sometimes hundreds of computers involved. Studios are totally run by computers, in the cameras, the mixing and editing equipment, the transmitters and everything else. Cable and satellite systems are totally computerized. So is your local cable company, and even your own TV and VCR.

A chain is only as strong as its weakest link. An old, old saying, and a true one, never truer than for Y2k. One Y2k failure anywhere in that long, complex chain could mean no picture on your screen. And New Year's Eve that year is when we're going to need the picture more than ever before.

Remember Murphy's law? "Whatever possibly *can* go wrong, eventually *will*." And the corollary is that when it does go wrong, it'll choose to do so at the worst possible moment.

On that day we'll all need to watch the festivities in New Zealand. Wherever you are in the world, you need to know what happens as first Tonga and then N.Z. hit the midnight mark and head into the New Millennium.

If there are no problems with N.Z., and our picture is still working, we can start to feel confident that Y2k is going to blow over without too much hassle. But what if the picture from New Zealand suddenly disappears as we watch from our cosy homes in Europe or North America? Beware! Expect trouble.

Television and radio will be critically important if it happens that we have a major disaster of *any* kind. Keeping them on the air must be a priority, and it'll take more than just a generator or two. There is not much of the old, non-computerized equipment around, so in the worst case we might end up with only a few little rural stations left broadcasting.

## Amateur ("Ham") Radio and Citizens Band (CB)

One of the major functions of ham radio operators has always been to provide emergency communications. They have regular competitions and exercises, and often volunteer their time and equipment at sports events and other large gatherings. CB clubs and groups do a lot of the same, although they're not as suited to worldwide working. CB radios are neither designed nor legal for long-distance communication. However, in a major disaster we may need to rely on them as well.

Many times throughout this century, the hams have been the only link into an area hit by an earthquake or other disaster. When the Edmonton tornado hit our city in 1987, killing 27 people, the city's disaster plan included making a room available at City Hall for the hams to set up their portable gear. They spent more than a week on 24-hour shifts, responding to enquiries from around the world, people checking on relatives and friends.

If serious problems arise, we may have to depend on these guys yet again, and this time *all over the world*. But there's the usual problem: all the modern ham and CB radios are computerized! I expect that many, and hopefully most, will still operate in January 2000, but we must recognize that they're at risk, like so much of our modern technology. Guys, start testing! Now, please. We may need you.

# The Internet

Right from its beginning in the 1960s, when it was called ARPANET and used solely for research, the Internet has been designed to be fail-safe, and resilient to failures. This is great news, and I wish more of our society had been designed this way. It happened because the project was started by the U.S. military, and they work all the time with life-and-death situations. They understand how important "fail-safe" can be.

Even so, the Internet has never had the kind of test it'll get with the coming of the Millennium. As we approach the Day, traffic on the 'Net will increase. On and around the Day it'll be very busy, with New Year and Millennium greetings going around the world to friends and loved ones. It's a lot cheaper than an international phone call. There are about 200 million end-users on the Internet, and the number is growing daily. The 'Net itself consists of hundreds of thousands of computers all linked together.

If problems develop, there'll be a lot of panic and emergency traffic. All of us with relatives in New Zealand will want to check on them in the first hour or so of the Millennium, when they're into it already and we're still waiting. Then those with family in Australia will get their turn, then Japan and the Philippines, and progressively through Asia and around the world. Expect the traffic to grow throughout Millennium Day and beyond.

All this will be stretching the 'Net to capacity. And in the midst of all this traffic, what if some of the computers that form the 'Net itself have problems? If one goes down, the 'Net has been designed to transfer the traffic to alternative routes. As the "packets" of data that make up your message go skipping from one computer to another around the world, they'll be rerouted around the dead computer.

As with the power lines in Auckland, and as in any network, this will place a heavier load on the surrounding computers and links. At best, it'll merely slow them down. At worst, some of these could overload and die, *passing more load onto the ones that are left.*

Depending how many computers this happens to, we can expect the entire worldwide 'Net to slow down. Remember it'll be fully loaded or overloaded already before the failures start. Messages normally go in a few seconds or minutes from Canada to New Zealand, or from Britain to India, Holland to Surinam, or anywhere. They might take hours. Who knows, they might take days. If they get there at all. At that point the 'Net is basically unuseable.

All this assumes that your PC is working, and I think it probably will be. I'm not so sure about the phone system, so I hope you're able to dial in to the 'Net that Day and at least *try* to send messages.

## Police and the Military

Our military and paramilitary agencies have some wonderful high-tech equipment with which to carry out their sworn duty, to "Serve and Protect." They have all kinds of radio and satellite communications. They have GPS navigation aids, high-tech weapons, laser scopes, night snooper-scopes – *all computer-driven.*

Windsor, Ontario and Edmonton, Alberta were the first two cities to get the current state-of-the-art 9-1-1 system. I believe about 30 cities now have it. Edmonton has 17 stations, 8 call-takers and 9 dispatchers, each with two humungous 27-inch screens. You used to be able to catch a glimpse of stations like these sometimes on William Shatner's *"Rescue, Nine-One-One"* TV re-enactment program.

When a citizen calls 9-1-1, the call-taker sees on the right-hand screen a map, centered on the caller's house, and showing icons (little pictures) where all the police cars are in that part of the city. On the left screen (s)he types in the details of the call, and brings up any related earlier calls, or motor vehicle records, criminal records, or whatever.

To send a police car, the dispatcher just takes the mouse and clicks on the icon on the screen. The icon changes color, and the cops in the car see the same map, and the details. They press a button on top of their unit, and off they go. On the dispatcher's screen they change color again. In some cases, the entire call can be handled without the voice radio.

This marvelous system uses graphic software borrowed from Microstation drafting software, and uses the Oracle database, one of the most widely-used databases in the world. It gets its street maps from Edmonton's Geo-Based Information System (GBIS), arguably the world's largest graphical municipal database.

But doesn't this sound like computers? The entire thing is built around computers and software, in the cars as well as at the dispatch center. And some cities are using GPS to track the cars on similar 9-1-1 systems. That gives them even more chances for something to fail!

I read in the Edmonton Journal on May 28, 1998, that this magnificent system **will not work in Y2K,** *and the fixes had only just got under way.* The Edmonton Police Service is saying that there's no money to fix it, so they're having to spend money from next year's policing budget. I hope they get it done in time, but I have my doubts. And we may be in dire need of 9-1-1 service in the days and weeks after Millennium Day.

And remember those pesky 5% of date errors that are likely to get through. Add to that the extra calls because of the Millennium celebrations, and your city's 9-1-1 system may end up being heavily overloaded. Add a few telephone failures, traffic light failures, a riot or two, and we *could* have a mess.

If you're able to find a phone that works to call 9-1-1, the operators may not be able to get to your call, and if they do they may not be able to call a police car. If they can call one, the car may not start, or may not be able to get to you. And there might be no water pressure for fires. And hospitals will be *a whole 'nother* set of problems if you're injured.

Don't count on a lot of help from the police, fire and other emergency services on Millennium Day, nor on the days following. I have no doubt they'll be doing their utmost to *Serve and Protect*, but they're only human. Their equipment is only computerized. Even with all kinds of help from the military, they may have more than they can handle.

## Canada's Military Preparations – *"Operation Abacus"*

In October of 1998 the Canadian Armed Forces announced just what I believe military forces around the world need to do. Labeled *"Operation Abacus,"* it is a plan to deploy troops where they will be most needed for Millennium Day, and during any problems afterwards. Right now it's in the planning stage, and this is early enough that it will be done in time.

But that's all about regular people. What about all those who are locked up?

## Prisons

This could be a little tense. What if the lights go out in the prisons on Millennium Day, or the food supply stops a few days later? Often the reaction to things like this in the prisons is a riot. And when it happens, as the saying goes, "Who ya gonna call?" (Y2k-Busters?)

There may not *be* anyone to call. We usually rely on the police and the military to back up the prison guards at such times, but they may already be busy elsewhere. Or they may not get the call, or they may not be able to get to the prison through gridlocked streets, or they may have trouble with their weapons.

How could we prevent the problem? We could lock all prisoners in their cells on The Day, or perhaps a day or two in advance. But that action might cause a riot all by itself! And what if a fire starts? It's a common occurrence in prison riots. How do we get the locked-up people out safely, *and still in custody?*

I have sometimes wondered if piped-in anaesthetic gas would solve the problem of prison riots. Nitrous oxide, sometimes called laughing gas, or whatever. Something the medics think is safe might help to prevent riots by putting them all safely to sleep. Guards and civilian staff taken hostage could then be quietly and safely freed while they and their captors are fast asleep.

But such an idea would never survive the human-rights challenges!

One way or another, though, our prison authorities must have plans in place to prevent and/or to deal with riots on The Day and the days afterwards. If you live near a prison, you may wish to check with the warden about her/his plans and preparations.

Remember, the people in our prisons are mostly there because of *anti-social behavior*. The reasons and causes lie buried in abuse and abandonment during childhood. In a later book on child rearing and the First Seven Years of Life, I shall have much to say about causes and prevention. Whatever the reasons and causes, the fact is that these people *don't care*. That's what "anti-social" is all about.

"Not caring" means they won't sit meekly in their cells, cooperating because we have our hands full with other problems. Mostly they simply *don't care* about you and me and our police and military forces. The thing they want is *out*. Failing that, they'll do whatever they can to cause us problems. Expect riots, and expect escape attempts in the confusion. ***We must be careful not to present them with any hostage opportunities.***

And what if the food supply fails? Or the water supply? Are we going to leave these people in their cells to starve? Suppose we're all struggling to find enough food, and the prison guards want to go home and look after their own families. How are we going to keep some semblance of order, and feed the prisoners?

But what if we let them out? Now, not every prison inmate is a serial sex killer. Some are. But virtually every one of them is guilty of *some form of antisocial behavior*. Do we want to unleash these on citizens already in trouble? Do we have the right to risk the lives and property of ordinary citizens in this way?

Do we have the right to risk starving the inmates if things get bad? I believe we do. Apart from the inevitable few who were jailed though innocent, I believe they made this choice and took this chance when they decided to break the law.

But I'm not the only voter in this country. ***This is an ethical issue that needs to be decided in advance.*** Whatever we decide to do about this, ***January 2, 2000 is not the day to decide!*** These decisions need to be made by senior (read, "*federal*") levels of representative government, not by individual prison wardens with a crisis happening right in their faces.

And they'll need weapons that actually work.

## Weapons

All of our military and paramilitary forces will be depending on their weapons. Small arms such as handguns, rifles and shotguns will be unaffected. Laser scopes are computerized, so they may be at risk.

Larger weapons are mostly computerized in some way. If it becomes necessary to use laser-guided rockets, heat-seeking missiles, or any such weapons with high-tech guidance systems, we may have a problem. Airplanes and vehicles to deliver these weapons are computerized, so they may also be a problem.

In all the confusion, we must expect that those who wish to exploit or harm us will take advantage of our temporary disabilities. Anything *might* happen: prison riots, hostage-takings, airplane hijackings, terrorist acts, or even war with Saddam or someone equally likeable.

We'll need the utmost security we can manage, just at the time when we're stretched thin in every possible way. All the people and equipment that could be used for extra security are likely to be busy elsewhere.

It may be necessary to use serious weaponry. It may not work quite as well as it did in the Gulf War. There's a chance it may not work at all. Or worse, computerized targeting systems may be way off, like Apollo 7, or shut down in mid-flight, like the Honda 750 EFI.

*a rocket*
"I shot ~~an arrow~~ into the air,
It fell to Earth I know not where . . ."

Once a rocket is on its way, malfunctioning guidance software could make it impossible to tell where, and on whom, it may land and blow up.

One thing the Military will have to do in the early days of the new Millennium, is to take every kind of weapon out to the test-firing range and check them out. But we're likely to need them from perhaps December 30 or 25 on. If there are disturbances, riots, prison riots, terrorist acts, acts of war, etc., etc., we may well be responding with un-tested weapons!

And as Ed Yardeni points out in his "Web-Book" on his web-site, ***testing one of each kind is not enough.*** When testing some industrial equipment, it has been found that one unit is fine for Y2k, but another one fails. Same microprocessor chip, same model number and everything. Turns out the manufacturer sourced that chip type from several suppliers. Some were Y2k compliant, and others were not.

So Yardeni points out that we must test each individual unit; "type-testing" where we test one of each kind, will not do. But how do we test *every single individual unit* of a given type of rocket weapon? These things are strictly one-time use. They blow up at the end of it.

So no matter how much testing they do, the military can never be absolutely 100% sure of their weapons after Y2k. And, as the saying goes, "*Close* only counts in horse-shoes, hand grenades and nuclear weapons." Where weapons and human lives are at stake, "near enough" testing will not be good enough. And all this will happen just when we need them the most.

## The Danger of War

Will all these failures also happen to Saddam and his ilk? I think so. But you can also expect that such a man will find ways to use the problems to his own advantage. Most likely he will be less concerned with the safety and livelihood of his own people, and more with hurting or embarrassing the West.

In any disaster that might occur, the focus of all reasonable and humane govern-ments will be public safety and preserving society. But there are terrorists, totalitarian governments, religious extremists and dictatorships out there. These people will behave more selfishly, and that could well include attacking the western nations.

## Armed Assault:
### The attack could be an actual armed assault with weapons.

I sincerely hope not. I don't think it's too likely. But I don't trust people like this, and I believe we must be prepared. The penalties for being *un*prepared could be terrible.

And if the guidance systems don't work too well, why would they care? "Surgical Bombing" was a term used in the Gulf War to describe super-accurate guidance of a kind that had never before been seen in war. Rockets and bombs landed right on target, de-stroying the military objective with minimal civilian casualties. If we *must* have war, I guess this is the best way to do it.

But if the guidance systems don't work too well, and Saddam destroys a few hun-dred thousand British, American, Dutch or French civilians, will he care? Even if some of his misguided missiles killed his own people, that would probably be a small sacrifice as far as he was concerned.

Remember, this is a man who is known to have personally executed his brother-in-law for opposing him. This is a man who, we have reason to believe, is trying to build arsenals of anthrax and nuclear weapons. *And would be prepared to use them.* Neither of those could be termed "surgical." Does he care?

And of course Saddam or someone like him may have his own plans for a nuclear disaster while we're all busy trying to survive. There are still many Soviet nuclear war-heads unaccounted for.

As I write this in October 1998, Saddam is escalating his refusals to cooperate with the UN inspectors. This worries me. I suspect he's got something up his sleeve for a

Millennium Day celebration that just might ruin our party. This makes my *Worst-Case Scenario #5* (see Chapter 9) that much less unlikely.

What if he marches again into Kuwait, relying on non-computerized small arms and machine guns in the hands of a million men? No laser sights. How will any of us stop him with our house in disarray, and all our high-tech weapons either grounded or under suspicion?

So just at the moment when our own weapons might give all kinds of problems, we could be attacked by one or more aggressors whose weapons are in even worse shape than our own. At the time of writing, Y2k still has not become an issue in most third-world countries. Governments run by despots for their own personal aggrandizement are the least likely to divert resources to something like Y2k.

While our armies are busy helping our civilians to survive, we can fully expect these warlike "leaders" to sacrifice large numbers of their own people. It's been done before. If they see a chance, expect them to send their armies to war against us, rather than deploy them helping their own population. Saddam and his ilk are like Hitler and Idi Amin. They don't care, except about themselves.

The long term effects could be disastrous. There is potential for them to inflict heavy damage on their neighbors and the western nations. We'll be in a weakened state, and least able to resist, or to deal with the damage. Meanwhile their own society at home will fall apart also because no one has prepared for Y2k. Their own society at home will be in total disarray, worse than ours.

What I have to say in Chapter 6 about First World and Third World countries preparing for Y2k also applies here, but remember that these warlords are a minority. Fortunately for us as well as for their own people, most third-world governments *are* responsible, and *are* concerned with the well-being of their own population. They'll be scrambling as much as any of us to preserve their own society.

It might even be possible that both societies may founder if war breaks out, both aggressor and defenders. Then this could be yet another straw on the back of the economic camel, plunging us into a worldwide depression. As Peter de Jager has said of businesses, it's also true of countries, that "Survival is a competitive advantage."

## Communication Systems

*The attack could be an infiltration into computerized communication systems.*

This style of attack is perhaps more likely. It would be easier to hide, and more difficult to trace and prove. Compared to a full frontal assault, it would be practically invisible.

A US Senate committee (as it happens, on the very day that the Galaxy IV satellite failed) heard from a group of experienced hackers who claimed that they could cut the entire US off from the Internet in a half-hour or so. They have many times got around the security on military and other government computers.

If a foreign aggressor was able to find similar skills at a good price, he could do disastrous damage to our databases and communications, both military and civilian. And while we were in an awkward and over-stressed state around Y2k, we would be a perfect target for this kind of attack.

## Combination

*The attack could be a combination of both.*

If there is a full frontal assault, you can be sure it'll also include an attack on our communications. It would only make sense. Mind you, who can predict the attitude of a man who believes he owns a country and its people? There's a bit of a paradox here:

If such a ruler is aware of Y2k, and our weakness as a result, surely he would also be aware of its possible effects on his own nation. But does he see the bigger picture? Or does he see our weakness, but is he blind to that of his own people?

We could second-guess for the next year and a half, and still never know. This is why the boys and girls in the CIA get the big bucks. We really have little choice but to let the experts do the guessing, while we *"Prepare for the worst, and hope for the best."*

## Will The Attack Happen?

I don't know. I hope not. It could, it might. It probably won't – I hope. The big question for the U.S. and other western nations, and even for the United Nations, is how much military power will we need to have out there keeping an eye on Saddam and Moammar and co., when our soldiers might be needed to help at home. We're going to be spread awfully thin!

And many nations, including Canada, are in the process of *reducing* their military forces. Not a good idea right now.

I quote Bryce Ragland (See Appendix, "To Find Out More"), who heads a U.S. Air Force Year 2000 team, "There's a real risk that some wacko . . . might decide to launch an attack against the U.S. a few seconds after midnight just to see if our defenses can handle it."

And perhaps the scariest part is that they could *all* strike when we're kind of down, and spread so thin. With everything else that might be going wrong, military and civilian, Y2k will be a perfect time for terrorists, too. It could be they'll all strike at the same time, and just spread us thinner and thinner. Can we handle it? We need to be totally sure about the answer to that one.

I don't have the answers. All you and I can do is ask the questions, and make sure the people running our nations are working on the answers. I find it significant that the two most senior people in the U.S. military in charge of information systems, and thus also in charge of year 2000 fixes, *both retired in May 1997.* They have been followed by others . . .

# Billing, Banking and Government

## The U.S. Feds

The United States has the most industry and the most powerful government in the world. It manages the richest economy in the world, and this was the first country in history to come into existence with a constitution guaranteeing human rights. Its citizens are among the freest in the world, and perhaps might actually *be* the freest. *Whatever the U.S. federal government does will affect every other country and their citizens.*

But according to Ed Yardeni (himself a U.S. citizen), "Big Brother" is in a "Big Mess." The U.S. Treasury is beginning to panic, and looking to outside contractors to help. But there are 62 million lines of code to correct in the IRS alone, and experts are saying *it can't be done in the time that's left.*

It's even being suggested that the U.S. may be forced to go to a **flat-rate income tax**, where everyone pays the same percentage of their income. Doing away with the current sliding scale would simplify things enough to allow them to get the tax demands out and the returns back in.

And just as the icing on the cake, the U.S. government has seen fit to change its tax laws for 1998 and again in 1999. As I mentioned in an earlier chapter, this and the Euro currency conversion just add to the load on the limited supply of programmers, just when we need them the most.

For the U.S. Feds, the General Accounting Office (GAO) is the watchdog agency that keeps an eye on the rest of the federal government. Canada has its Auditor-General, and most nations, including *all* the developed nations, have a similar office or agency. It may be worth your while to get hold of whatever your county's watchdogs are saying about your government's approach to Y2k.

In the U.S., the GAO has said that, contrary to what the federal departments are sometimes claiming, the U.S. federal government are way behind in their conversion. The GAO complained that not enough time is being left for testing. Some plans are proposing to finish in October or November of 1999. This leaves a ludicrous *one month* for testing! Such major systems undergoing such major changes *need a year* of various levels of testing. It's not going to happen.

Here are some comments from U.S. Congressman Stephen Horn (December 1997):

- More than half of the federal government's major agencies will *not* fix their most important software in time. (my italics)
- Their current work on Y2k is "unacceptable and potentially dangerous."
- Serious risk of a massive electronic breakdown on Y2k.
- The air traffic control system could become gridlocked.
- Computerized records could be lost or damaged.
- At best, a major headache, at worst an electronic disaster.

And Horn goes on to show how ludicrous some of the planning is, and this in the world's best-managed society. Here is when 14 of their 24 major agencies are planning to have the Year 2000 job done:

- Energy and Labor Departments:                                    2019
- Defense Department                                               2012
- Transportation Department and Office of Personnel Management     2010
- Agriculture Department                                           2005
- Treasury Department                                              2004
- General Services Administration                                  2002
- Justice Department and Health and Human Services Department      2001
- Education Department, Agency for International Development,
  Federal Emergency Management Agency (FEMA)              Mid-2000
- NASA                                                        Early 2000

I find it interesting that the emergency people (FEMA) have said they'll be ready for the disaster six months after it has occurred. The two EdY's (Yourdon and Yardeni) think all of this is too optimistic. I agree, and I think these problems will keep us busy, and soak up resources, and slow down the economy. *This may last for perhaps two to three decades* into the new Millennium.

And here's what may be the ultimate irony, and, I'm sure, the most crushing disappointment for those who thought they had done it all the right way. The U.S. Social Security Administration has been widely touted as the way to go. In 1989 they had a Y2k problem, so they got started on a well-planned conversion.

As of now, it's pretty close – except that they still have to coordinate with all the software in the individual states. As late as 1997 they discovered that even though 42 of the 54 state agencies involved used only two different software products, each state has modified it over the years. Now these have grown into 42 different software products to check and fix.

Yardeni asks the obvious question: "If it took 10 years to fix the first 32 million lines of code, how are they going to repair the latest 33 million lines in less than two years?"

Government agencies around the world face another serious problem. One of the things that could screw up in date-related calculations is when to start someone's payments. If a 101-year-old does not receive his or her old age pension and other payments in January or February 2000, that's a problem. But you can bet someone will pretty soon tell the government it's happening. (Once the phones are working, that is.)

But what if the computer mistakes a 4-year-old for a 104-year old, and starts sending out regular checks? Or welfare and social security and unemployment checks are going out to people who are not supposed to get them yet? Is the government likely to notice? When the whole world is in a shambles, many of these things will go unnoticed.

And when (if) they're noticed, try and get the money back! Good luck! Welfare recipients mostly live from check to check, so each one is spent in a day or so. Typically, these people have no assets or resources, so paying it back later would mean starving the kids. It won't happen.

My prediction is that when errors like this occur, governments will be forced to write that money off. And this at a time when they'll be starved for revenue. All these things will mean some serious government and economic problems. In Chapter 5 we'll see how all this could lead to a severe economic recession.

## Other Governments

Once the U.S. manages to light a fire under its feds, it still has 50 state governments and half-a-dozen territorial governments to worry about. And this is the richest and arguably the most organized country in the world. The scary part is that other countries are reporting similar things. There is much being reported about the lack of progress in the U.K. and other major industrial countries.

Here in Canada we have our share of news reports about late starts and inadequate preparations. In November 1997 the (Canadian) feds sent out a "Request for Proposal," asking companies to submit bids for the federal Y2k conversion. At a billion dollars, the project is too big for any one company operating in Canada, so consulting companies formed into teams to apply. There's barely enough time. *Testing is always the main casualty of the rush job.* Errors and software failures will be the likely outcome.

## Late Mails

We saw in Chapter 2 how the mails and the courier companies could be affected. Looking at the chain idea, you can see that it takes many computers to handle a piece of mail. As it passes through various sorting stations on its way, each one is run by a number of computers.

Computers assign employees to jobs and shifts, and process the payroll. Computers are used to schedule mail pickups and deliveries. And pickup, transport and delivery of the mail depend on trains, boats, planes and trucks.

The courier companies even use computers to track individual packages. You can use your computer, and the Internet, to go to the Federal Express website (which runs on one of their many computers), type in your code number, and the computers will find your package and tell you where it has got to.

If one link in this chain goes out, the whole chain stops. If the posties are not on the job at the right time and place, or if a few sorting stations grind to a halt, the mail will not get through. The Millennium Bug may do what *"rain nor sleet"* have never been able to do: *stop the mails!* Or at least slow them somewhat. Or lose a bunch of mail, perhaps permanently.

Remember, the Post Office in every country depends on the railroads and the airlines. Many courier companies have their own airplanes. And, as you'll read below, the International Air Travel Association (IATA) and the International Federation of Airline Pilots (IFAP) have threatened not to fly into any airport where Y2k safety is at all doubtful.

The railroads will have their problems too. In later chapters you'll read about the incredible mess that happened at Union Pacific, the largest railroad in the US, when their software lost track of thousands of freight cars.

Airplanes, railroads, trucks. Each of these is another link in the chain. Another link that's *likely* to fail.

I don't think the mails will cease altogether. They might stop completely for a few days or a few weeks. What I'm quite sure will happen is that the mails will have a bunch of problems, so there'll be delays, and a number of items will go missing. Some will turn up later, and we can expect that a few will disappear for ever.

So use the mails as little as possible in the first part of the new Millennium. This will reduce the load on the system, and probably speed its recovery. Anything you do send by mail or courier in the early weeks of the year 2000 will need to be followed up – by phone, fax, e-mail or whatever is working. Perhaps we should learn Morse code and use the heliograph!

### US Social Security: $32 Billion per Month

One of the heaviest users of the mails in every country is the government. In the U.S. the monthly total of social security and welfare checks is more than $32 billion. Other countries have other numbers, but it's a big number in most countries.

Then there are many other kinds of checks that go through the mails from the government to the people. In any country, government payouts are a significant chunk of the total amount of money changing hands each month.

Another big problem is money flowing in the other direction – from the people to the government. (I know – this has always been a problem, so let's just not do it any more!) But seriously, if a government runs out of money, and can't pay its operating expenses, can't meet its payroll, and can't make its debt repayments, there's trouble.

In recent years we've seen this happen even in the world's richest nation. Both the City of New York and the State of California have had this experience. Fortunately, both received some help from senior levels of government, and both survived.

In 1996, the US federal government was shut down by simply running out of budget money. They got stuck by an argument in Congress over providing extra funds. During this period, economists could see the effect on the businesses in the US. *Economic activity dropped sharply when a whole lot of government checks simply didn't arrive in the mails.*

But what if many governments were having this problem, at all levels, in many countries, *all at the same time?*

# "Who ya gonna call?"

This is the theme echoing throughout so much of this book. If we're all in trouble at the same time, there'll be no one to turn to for help! If we ever made a movie from this book (!) I think I'd like to rent the Ghostbusters theme song and write some new lyrics for it:

## "Who ya gonna call? *Nobody!*"

Problems in the mails will reduce the flow of money both inward *to* the government and back *out* to the people. Governments will have problems, and so will the people who depend on government money. The effects could be many and varied. We could have hungry people; might this mean soup kitchens like in the 1930s?

Shortages of welfare money could cause an increase in many crimes. This could range from thefts of food, people stealing to eat, to muggings and break-ins as an attempt to replace the missing money. Car-jackings may become very fashionable. An increase in muggings and robberies will mean more assaults and murders, as crimes go wrong, or citizens resist.

As things worsen, and crimes increase, the possibility of riots increases, and looting along with them. Once tempers are strained, any little incident could spark a major riot, much as happened in Los Angeles. If it happens, the only safe course of action is to stay out of it. Listen to your radio (hopefully it works) whenever you drive, and catch any news reports.

Prepare yourself, practice taking extreme care, and remember that no amount of money or face-saving is worth dying for.

## The Private Sector

But what about the non-government parts of the economy? The commerce of our society depends on the mails for payment of everything from credit card bills to university tuition to loan repayments. Invoices and statements go out requesting payment, and payment (usually) comes by return mail. Stop the mails, you stop the payments. And if the ATMs are down too, *everyone starves.*

This time it's not about welfare recipients and such. Now we're talking about the middle class, people who have jobs, business owners, white-collar workers, professionals, and such like. These people are used to a high standard of living, but mostly don't have a lot of reserves to carry them through a difficult time.

In most developed nations, the middle class have a savings ratio of around 3 to 5 percent. That is, they typically save about 3 to 5 percent of their income. But much of it is in retirement savings, and much of that is locked in by the retirement savings laws of their country. All the developed nations have some form of tax-free or tax-deferred retirement savings plan, but the money in it is not available before you actually retire.

Most middle-class families in these nations have very little in the way of cash reserves or liquid investments that they can use to ride out a break in their regular income. We only have to look at the downsizing and outsourcing and so on that has become fashionable in the last couple of decades. Many people have suffered difficult and frightening times, and in some cases real hardship, because of sudden layoffs.

If the economy slows down, we could be faced with many layoffs. Some will be temporary, but in some cases the employer will go out of business, making the layoffs pretty well permanent. You'll remember Capers Jones's figures. He predicts that 1% of Fortune 500 large companies, 3% of small companies, and 5 to 7% of middle-sized companies will go under. Then he suggests an equal number may declare bankruptcy to avoid lawsuits.

Canada seems to be typical of many countries. Figures from a Cutter Consortium study quoted in ComputerWorld magazine in December 1997 show that:

- 90% of Canadian companies are aware of the Y2k problem
- 50% have done nothing about it!
- 13% are checking out their partners (i.e., customers and suppliers) (Statistics Canada)
- 93% of U.S. organizations have not yet figured the direct costs of Y2k.
- 53% of firms worldwide have made public announcements about Y2k commitments.

## Screwed-Up Bills and Payments

Even if the mails are working in a useable state, there are other potential problems. Y2k problems in billing software will cause a lot of bills to go out with incorrect figures. This will be especially bad towards the end of January 2000, as companies hit their first billing date in the new Millennium.

Human nature is a funny thing. You just watch! Many otherwise honest people, faced with a drastically undervalued bill, will pay it as presented, hoping the shortfall will go unnoticed. On the other hand, if the bill is too much they'll complain right now. The phone lines will be tied up, adding yet more to the overload on the struggling phone system.

Another problem with incorrect bills will be incorrect penalties. If your loan payment or mortgage or credit card bill is overdue, in many companies the computer automatically assesses penalties against you and sends out a nasty little note.

If a Y2k error makes the software think you're late, you could be in trouble through no fault of your own. If 5% of the date errors in the software are going to be missed, maybe 5% of us will get nasty little notes.

What if the same thing happened with your utilities? Will the software automatically cut off your electricity, gas, phone or cable TV? This is an interesting question. In this day and age of automation, it would seem likely that at least some utility companies would do it this way. This might cause problems for their customers if the software malfunctioned on Y2k.

Does your utility company do it this way? Or do they have a warm body in the loop to make the final decision? How can you tell? In cold climates like Alberta, where a normal winter goes down to -40º, to cut off the gas or electricity deliberately is out of the question. Water pipes would freeze and burst, and all kinds of expensive damage would result.

Once, when we had a question about service to a rental property we own, it wasn't hard for my wife Nina to get an answer. She found that indeed there *is* a person to make the final decision, at least in our fair and somewhat frigid city.

The Yourdons report, however, that they had a very different experience in New York. After a number of phone calls and some rather frustrating conversations, they were still unable to find anyone who could understand the question! Let alone answer it sensibly. They suggest, and I agree, that it's a worthwhile exercise for each of us to query our local utility companies on this one. Then at least we know what to watch out for.

Then there begins the long process of finding and correcting the errors. This will be an expensive job, with a lot of overtime for some, although programmers are not normally paid for any overtime. Then the bills must be reprinted, and mailed out again.

And then you can bet some customers will be unhappy at having their bills corrected, when it means they have to pay some more. They'll complain, even though the other bill was wrong in the first place. Expect more phone calls and unpleasantness.

Businesses will face problems with collecting money owed to them, because of the mails, as well as all the other things that might go wrong, *all at the same time*. When we add these factors to what Capers Jones has said, I think we might find him to be very conservative with his thinking. I think it could get a lot worse than he thinks.

## The Union Pacific Fiasco

In 1997 the largest railroad in the United States bought out one of its competitors. Nothing very new or remarkable about that, it happens all the time in every industry. But each railroad had its own separate software for keeping track of freight cars and where they are.

When they tried to meld together the two software systems, they were completely incompatible. Everything screwed up on them, and they lost the records of thousands of freight cars. Many went to the wrong place, and others just sat on sidings for weeks.

It took three months or more to clean up, affecting thousands of their customers, some of whom were power stations that almost ran out of oil and coal! So if the power stations do manage to keep going after Y2k, it looks like the railroads may shut a few of them down anyway!

All kinds of business and industrial customers were affected. Factories ran out of raw materials, and warehouses ran out of products. All this slows the economy a little more, and it's one more thing to help us along into a recession.

This is a classic and ominous example of just how much mess a few software problems can cause. And what if it's not just one railroad? Y2k problems will hit everybody, *all at the same time*. We could have several railroads in this kind of trouble, *all at the same time*. Even if all the others are still running, they'll have their problems. None will escape completely.

And then we could have a bunch of airlines with similar problems. And bus lines, and trucking companies, and factories, and warehouses, and power plants, and, and, and . . .

# All at the same time!

This railroad schmozzle has been a good lesson in just how much damage a few software problems can cause. But a business also needs a steady flow of *money* to and from its bank.

## Banking and Finance

Besides the usual problems of trying to fix their systems on time, banks all around the world face the daunting task of trying to make sure all the other banks they deal with are OK. The banking systems in all the developed countries depend on computerized links between banks. There are many links in each chain here, and no single bank has control over the entire chain. Each bank is at the mercy of all the other banks, and the links the other banks control.

Just recently, the U.S. Federal Deposit Insurance Corporation (FDIC) has told all its insured banks to be ready by June 30, 1999. They must have all their software corrected by then, which will give them the remaining *six months* for two critical parts of the project:

- *Testing* between banks to make sure there are no bugs in the transfer process. This is way more complex, difficult and time-consuming than the internal testing each bank does on its own converted software.
- *Overruns*. The software industry is famous for them. We simply don't bring projects in on time. Almost never. Ask any programmer when she last worked on a project that came in on time, never mind on budget.

Six months is *half* what the computer industry experts are recommending. Everybody, banks included, should be planning to test for a whole year.

But if your bank goes broke, you may think you're OK because you're insured. Don't count on the FDIC (US) or CDIC (Canada) or any other bank insurance program. They won't have enough to pay everyone who loses money! In addition, you may have to line up with a million other people to get a small fraction of your money back.

That's if they pay anyone at all. What's to stop a government from changing the rules? They did with gold in the US. They can just decide in Congress or Parliament that no one gets paid, because it's an emergency. Too bad, so sad!

## Loan Guarantees

John Dale Davidson and Lord William Rees-Mogg in *"The Great Reckoning"* (see Appendix, "To Find Out More"), tell of a variety of problems that could cause a world-wide recession or even a depression. One of the more significant, that I have not seen other Y2k authors address, is the issue of *government loan guarantees*.

Many governments in the industrialized nations – in particular the U.S. Federal government – have guaranteed a whole bunch of loans that various banks have made to large businesses. This has often been done, as in the case of Chrysler Corporation, to persuade the banks to lend to a company to keep it from going under. In Chrysler's case it worked, and they're now doing very nicely, thank you.

The way it works is that if the company for any reason can't pay off the loan, the government guarantees to pay it off for them. No money changes hands until this happens.

The problem is that these loan guarantees are not reported anywhere in the balance sheets or any of the financial reports published by these governments. They're not figured into the national debt, since they are *not yet debts*, just promises. But for many countries the total is about the same size as the national debt. *This includes the U.S. and Canada.*

These things will suddenly become debts if some of these companies fail, and are unable to pay off the banks. The banks can then claim the money from the government. Overnight, a whole slew of these become actual debts instead of just promises. All of a sudden the government has an additional drain on its finances that it had never planned on. All of a sudden they could double the debt.

All the forecasters in the Y2k arena are predicting that numerous companies will go under because of Y2k. They're predicting recession even without considering this problem. And when some of these companies die, the governments will be faced with a whole lot of additional debt, just when they're struggling to collect tax revenues and keep going.

It would be like demanding loan repayments from a family already on the brink of starvation. Would they survive? Will governments survive?

Davidson and Rees-Mogg have predicted that a major depression could be caused by the intricate web of debts owed from bank to bank, and these government loan guarantees. They also discuss how the developed nations, the U.S. in particular, hold debt owed to them by developing nations, debts that can be canceled any time by the debtor nation.

It's been known to happen before. They can simply nationalize U.S.-owned companies and other property, or pass laws canceling the debt. It's all within their own borders and perfectly legal. They make the laws. And some of the U.S. companies went into these nations with guarantees from the U.S. government.

If we have a rash of companies and countries going bankrupt over Y2k, the U.S. and other wealthy countries will end up footing the bill. Just when they're having financial troubles of their own all over the place.

## Asian Banks

There's some disquieting news coming out of Asia. Four or five years ago Asia was the hottest investment opportunity. Asian nations were growing rapidly. Suddenly, they have a crisis, and most Asian nations are in trouble. Asia is no longer an investor's paradise.

Articles in the Wall Street Journal have suggested that dealing with their financial crisis is taking the attention of Asian businesses away from Y2k. This is causing them to start too late, and many simply will not be ready. Business writers are suggesting that Asian banks and other businesses start work on contingency plans for when their systems fail on Y2k.

And another thing. It seems many Asian banks (and South American as well) are using a software product that came from IBM in the 1970s. It's called, ironically enough, "System for Advanced Financial Environment" or SAFE. It's still in widespread use in these places, even though IBM stopped supporting it several years ago.

And since it has been modified and customized over the years, there are now a hundred or so different versions in use. Each one is different, and has to be checked and repaired individually. It simply won't get done. To make it worse, the awareness of Y2k among third-world businesses is even more abysmal than in the U.S. and Canada, and we're bad enough.

So they couldn't do it if they tried, and most don't even know they should be trying. Whatever goes wrong with Y2k in the developed nations, expect the Third World to be several times worse.

Then there's Japan, the most highly-developed nation in Asia. There we find that because of the problems they've been having, Japanese banks don't want to lend money to small businesses so they can fix their Y2k problems. This problem by itself has potential to drive many smaller Japanese businesses under.

One major Wall Street financial services firm has reported that they found Japanese government offices, central bankers and such people to be terribly ignorant of the seriousness of the Y2k problem.

## Asian Businesses

Companies in Asia have been slow to recognize the Y2k problem and begin work on correcting their software. In particular, they've been slow at hiring the skilled programmers they need for the task. These guys were already in short supply in the developed Asian nations, such as Japan, Korea and Taiwan, and have been moving off to much higher-paid jobs in America.

Some western observers have found that a lot of Japanese companies seem to have hit a form of "Analysis Paralysis." The programmers are spending all their time analyzing the problem, and not enough actually making the repairs. The opinion I have seen expressed is that this relates to a problem in the Japanese culture over dealing with failure.

Traditionally, a Japanese warrior brought disgrace upon his family and nation if he was captured. He was supposed to win or die, nothing in the middle. If captured, he was expected to commit hara-kiri, a gruesome suicide by stabbing himself in the stomach. The longer the cut and the more the pain, the more honor he regained by his death.

This tradition lives on (in a reduced form, luckily) in a cultural aversion to failure. It shows in this case as a reluctance to put the job to the test. To test something is to risk that it may fail. In software, this is a *very* necessary procedure. Software *always* fails its first few tests. So these programmers procrastinate, and the clock ticks toward Y2k in Japan.

Or does it?

## Asia: No Millennium, No Problem!

A number of nations in Asia, notably Japan, Korea, Taiwan and Thailand, use their own calendars. Japan's calendar counts years from the reign of the current emperor, Thailand's from the birth of the Buddha. So 1998 is year Heisei 10 in Japan, and year 2541 in Thailand. Many people in these countries believe they can't possibly have a problem with Y2k.

But what they're forgetting is that most of their computers were designed in the West, and use chips like the Intel Pentium II – designed in California. So were the operating systems, such as Windows '95 from Microsoft in the State of Washington.

These are the same hardware and operating systems used in all the Western countries, so they're about as likely to fail in Asia as anywhere else. Also, in Asia they use a lot of western software, such as WordPerfect and Lotus, the same stuff we use. Much of their home-grown software that uses the local date format will be safe from those problems, but it must still run on western operating systems and hardware.

But not all commerce in Japan is done on the Heisei date. Much is done using the western date system, measured from the (approximate) birth of Jesus. This is especially true of commerce that involves American or other western trading partners.

So Asia *does* have a problem. So does Europe.

## European Business

In Europe, we're facing what Yardeni calls a "Shockingly unhurried attitude of European bureaucrats, mirrored by the business community." The statistics show them to be well behind North America both in awareness of the problem, and in doing something about it. And we're not doing that great ourselves!

British Prime Minister Tony Blair has been reported "shocked" at the "widespread ignorance" of the problem in Europe and the U.K. And the 1999 date chosen for the Euro currency conversion certainly bears that out. Only governments who were "widely ignorant" of the problem would have pulled that one.

## The Third World

About 40% of the world's production (GDP, see below) is from third-world countries, including Asia. Certain countries are the main suppliers of some materials that we in the developed nations need. Manganese, helium, and insulin are each produced from a limited number of nations, and primarily from one nation. Coffee is grown in a number of regions, but mainly in South America.

The developing nations depend less on computers than the richer nations do. But they have more of the older ones, with a lot of non-compliant software. And many of these people have not yet heard that they'll have a problem. So they won't be immune.

But they may well be *unaware of what's coming*. The Third World is a place of poverty, struggle, corruption and unrest. The governments have many economic, political and social issues to deal with. They're so busy with all those things that they have neither the time nor money to stop for a little while and plan for the Millennium.

Much information about Y2k and how to deal with it is available – in English. With a few exceptions, such as Mexico, India, and the Philippines, English is not a language of choice in the Third World. This makes it very difficult for them.

And just to make it worse, their programmers are all leaving for America.

Problems in the Third World could have a significant impact on the world's GDP.

## GDP and the Velocity of Money

The figure most often used to measure a country's economy is its Gross Domestic Product, or GDP. This is the total cash value of all the goods and services produced in that country for a year. It's a measure of how much work everyone did, and how much they produced. The average standard of living for the people is often estimated by dividing the GDP by the number of people, giving the GDP per capita.

The economic health of a country depends heavily on how much money people spend. In western countries we look at the sales figures for the Christmas period as an indicator of how well the economy is doing. I have heard one economist suggest that if we all spent 107% of our income we would never have another recession. 107 percent? Nice try!

There's a definite ripple effect to spending. When you spend a dollar in my store, I get to take some of it home, and my employees do too. Some of it goes to my suppliers, and they and their employees get to take some of that home.

Some of it goes to the government, too. They send some home with their employees, and spend some on welfare or education or defense or whatever. And all those people get to take home some small percentage of your original dollar.

When tiny fractions of your original dollar find their way into so many homes, guess what? Those people go out and spend it on something. And the process begins again. And now teeny pieces of your dollar go into many more homes, and those guys go out and spend it again. The process repeats and repeats. Even saving it in a bank doesn't interfere with the process, since the bank lends it back out into the economy for someone to spend.

So your original dollar actually gets spent over and over again. In theory, this process looks like it might go on forever, but obviously that's not what happens. If it did, every dollar would multiply forever and become millions of dollars, by being spent millions of times. Not unlike a chain letter (or at least, how a chain letter promises it will be.)

In reality, it has been observed that the process is weakened a little with every repeat, and eventually it sort of "washes out." Kind of like the waves in a pond when you drop in a pebble. They ripple on out across the pond, smaller and smaller, and finally disappear.

Some economists have said that a dollar spent this way is spent seven times over. That is, spending one dollar and letting it ripple through the economy, is really like spending $7. Or another way to say it is that this ripple effect multiplies the spending power of every dollar by seven. We say the *effective* purchasing power of a dollar in the economy is seven dollars.

So what this says is that if someone does an extra dollar's worth of work, or creates an extra dollar's worth of products, *he will add not one dollar, but* **seven dollars,** *to the GDP.*

The other side of this, if we take a dollar out of the economy, it's really more like removing seven dollars. So *in normal times* putting your money under the mattress is not the thing to do. Every dollar you take out of circulation this way reduces the GDP by $7. But as you'll see in Chapters 7 and 8, these are not normal times, and a little money under the mattress for Y2k will be a good thing.

The next question is, how long will it take for this dollar to be spent seven times over? What happens is that when everyone is feeling good and making good money, they spend it faster. Literally. Then it takes less time for the dollar to multiply seven times over. If each person in the chain spends it on an average of half a day after he gets it, then the dollar has made its trip though the economy in 3 days.

But if *everyone* hangs onto their money and spends it very cautiously, after perhaps three days of waiting and thinking, it'll take maybe 21 days for the dollar to do its multiplying act. We describe this by talking about the "velocity" of money through the economy. The "faster" it goes through, the more the economy (and the GDP) will grow. But at that 21-day level, if the economy won't be growing at all, it'll be dying.

The effect of the problems with the mails and the screwed-up bills will be to *reduce the velocity of money* through the system. This could well cause us to begin an economic decline, into a recession.

## Will We Have a Recession?

Think for a moment about US Social Security payments. The U.S. federal government mails out $32 billion per month in social security checks. What would happen if their computers didn't print the checks? Or if the Post Office couldn't deliver them? Times seven, that's a huge sum to take out of the U.S. economy.

Whenever spending slows down, we have all kinds of ripple effects. We see it when there's a major strike, and people who are not on strike are out of work anyway. This happens because the company where the strike is stops buying from their suppliers, who in turn have to start laying people off. And they stop buying from *their* suppliers. And so on.

The same way, if the welfare and social security checks don't arrive, not only do the recipients go hungry, but the stores where they usually shop will also feel it. Multiply by seven every dollar *not* spent.

Here's another illustration of how Y2k can reduce the money and wealth being earned:

When a town is in danger of being flooded by a nearby river, we've all seen on TV how the people get out there in the rain filling and stacking sandbags, to build a wall to keep out the water. And some of you have done it for real. When this happens, businesses are closed, and **no one is working at anything that makes money.** Highly-trained , expensive doctors, lawyers, shopkeepers, engineers and kindergarten teachers are out there stacking sandbags.

So if this lasts a week, say, the people in the town stand to lose a lot of money besides the actual cost of the damage. The loss of business and earnings could easily be more than the physical damage. And it's multiplied by seven. The only benefit they gain from all that hard work and danger is that the town will probably still be there at the end of the week.

Probably.

Y2k is working just like this. So many programmers and other expensive professionals are working on Y2k repairs, instead of writing software that would earn or save money. The only benefit is that the company will probably still be there in the year 2000. Probably.

All this money being "wasted" on a "non-productive" project reduces the company profits, and the dividends paid to shareholders. This reduces the amount they have to spend, and the storekeepers begin to feel it too. Multiply by seven.

As the company's operations slow down, they as well as the storekeepers may have to lay off staff. And this is for a company that does the repairs right, and goes into the Millennium with their software in good shape.

But as Peter de Jager puts it so well, *survival is a definite competitive advantage*. The ones who *don't* do it right and get their software fixed will be even worse off! Business failures because of Y2k are likely to mean layoffs and bankruptcies, and all this will mean less and less spending. *Multiplied by seven.*

So what would it be like if these things happen, not just in a few cities like a strike might, or a few towns like a flood would? What if there were delays in delivering social security checks? It would no doubt happen all across the country if it happened.There'll be reduced company profits and maybe layoffs because of the Y2k project. All over the world.

Many businesses are already showing the effects of all the spending on Y2k fixes. In 1997, New Zealand Telecom showed a 19% drop in profits because of the money they spent on Y2k. Then add in the effect of the business closures because of Y2k, and maybe lawsuits as well, and we're starting to talk about a lot of damage.

## Lines of Credit

Most businesses in the developed world operate with a loan from the bank, referred to as a "line of credit." It's a variable loan, where the amount goes up and down daily as they need cash to operate.

But most of these loans are structured so that the bank can "call the loan" anytime, and demand that it be paid off. Or, with a few days notice, they can just cancel the loan. Either way, the business is suddenly without this flexible and much-needed operating money.

For most businesses, suddenly losing their line of credit would put a huge strain on the business, and its owners and staff. Such a move would force many businesses to close down. *Banks tend to do this as soon as the bank itself feels some strain or financial difficulty.*

If the economy begins to get into trouble over Y2k, and if stock markets drop, crash or become unstable, expect banks to start calling all kinds of loans. Expect businesses to close as a result. All this will help to fuel the depression.

## Business Interruption Insurance

This is an insurance that many companies think they can rely on. If a business has any of these problems, or if they can't run the business because their suppliers can't supply them, or whatever, they may think they're covered. And normally they would be.

But Y2k is a predictable event. Many policies are limited to things that are "unavoidable" or "beyond their control" or "not reasonably foreseeable." Y2k doesn't fit any of these. So insurance won't be any help at all.

Directors of a company will also find they're not protected against Y2k by their director's liability insurance. And many insurance companies are specifically excluding Y2k from all kinds of policies. This says there'll be a lot of personal bankruptcies to add to the business ones, and further slow the economy.

Ed Yardeni is right now (early 1998) upgrading his prediction from a 40% chance to a 60% chance that we'll have a recession. Will he reach 100% by the end of 1999? Will his predicted recession turn out to be a full-blown depression? I think it might.

Yardeni figures this recession will be at least as bad as the one in the 1970s when the OPEC nations raised the price of oil. Back then, cheap oil was the biggest single factor driving the growth of the developed nations' economies. Screw up the oil supply and you screwed up the world economy.

Nowadays it's information that does that. Cut our industries and businesses off from their information sources, or worse, render them unreliable and untrustworthy, and we fall apart.

My beliefs are right in line with Ed Yardeni's predictions. Except I think he's too conservative. I think we'll have a recession, and it'll be a bad one. In Chapter 7 you'll see my plans for what I intend to do about that. You'll need to do some things to protect your pension and other investments.

My feeling is that we *will* have an economic decline. I believe it'll last for at least a year or two. But I believe another 1929-style crash and 1930s-type depression can't be completely ruled out. Maybe for a decade or two. The difference here is that we know when it's going to happen, and we can prepare.

But prepare early, because the effects may well begin long before Millennium Day itself.

## Forecasting in Business and Government

More bad news. Governments and businesses must work with strictly limited resources. There's only so much money, and so many people, for them to get the job done. So they must do a lot of serious *planning and forecasting* to make sure money is spent in the best places.

They need to be able to estimate for several years into the future what money will be coming in, and how many people will need their products or services. They must predict where people will live, how they'll live, housing needs, land needs, transportation needs and everything else. Population trends, especially how long people will live, will affect planning for medical and seniors' services. Expected future birthrates and income levels determine educational needs.

You can't run a business or a government without good planning, which requires good forecasting, which in turn requires good information. When Y2k screws up a lot of our data, it could hurt our ability to forecast. The result will be less-than-perfect (i.e., "sub-optimal") allocation of money to projects or to business activities.

Some will be over-funded, and others will not get enough to operate properly. Money will be wasted on some projects, while others struggle or die for lack of funding. The "fat" projects, the ones with too much money, will become inefficient and wasteful. The starving projects will just dump more bodies on the layoff heap.

All of this will add to the chaos. Expect that some businesses will go under as a result of these unfortunate planning errors. Others will struggle, and maybe lay off a few workers. Either way this will remove more dollars from the economy. Multiplied by seven.

But these things won't come to light until several years after the initial difficulties, well into the Millennium. As the Millennium proceeds, we can expect a steady trickle of these inaccurately-estimated projects in both business and government.

It could take years before we clean up this part of the mess. This will tend to slow any economic recovery that's trying to get going, and could help to prolong the recession, perhaps for a decade or two.

Don't take my word for it. Check me out by reading Jones, the Yourdons and Yardeni, de Jager, Gary North and any others you can find. (See Appendix: "To Find Out More.")

# Stock Markets

One of the big problems with stock markets is that nowadays most of us are involved. Government and company pension plans, along with mutual funds, own a major chunk of all the shares traded on the stock markets of the world. Most of us have our tax-sheltered retirement savings in mutual funds, and so we're all in the stock market. What happens to it could seriously affect your future and mine.

The Bre-X gold fiasco was a prime example. The Bre-X stock shot way up when the big "find" was announced, and dropped even quicker when it was discovered to be a scam. Many individuals, mutual funds and pension plans lost money. Those who had been astute enough or lucky enough to sell before the crash made money.

There are four major ways that Y2k will affect stock markets:

- Stock prices of individual companies dropping because they're not ready for Y2k,
- Y2k errors in market forecasting software,
- General market declines as fear of Y2k spreads,
- Procrastination.

## Stock Prices of Individual Companies

Already we're seeing the share prices of some companies drop when it's announced that they can't possibly complete their Y2k conversion on time. Given the numbers reported in recent surveys, we can expect to see more such announcements. And more share prices dropping.

## Y2k Errors in Market Forecasting Software

Over the past couple of decades, many software programs have been written that will follow the prices of selected stocks and recommend when to sell or buy. The problems are:

- Many of these programs all use basically the same calculation rules and when-to-buy rules ("algorithms"). And for every well-marketed product that's widely accepted, there are *hundreds of copies* of the software out there. They're running on home computers, in stockbrokers' offices, banks, and mutual fund managers' offices.

- From time to time, when the market drops a bit ( a "correction" the insiders call it), these programs will suddenly all kick in together, saying to sell. And some of them generate the sell orders automatically. So thousands of sell orders take place, pushing the stock prices down even further.

  In 1987 and again in 1997, we saw this happen. These two record one-day drops were partly fueled by this process. Fortunately, most of the software has since been improved, and the stock market rules have been tightened up. So it's now much more difficult for this to happen. But not impossible, especially if everything else is going wrong *all at the same time.*

- If there are errors, and hundreds of copies of each error, this could cause some of these programs to issue incorrect sell orders, and start a downturn in the prices, or perhaps a serious crash. Or incorrect buy orders, which could cause a sharp rise in prices. That in turn would cause prices to drop badly when it's discovered that the rise was a false one! Many people could be hurt, including your company pension plan.

### General Market Declines

Stock markets generally reflect the level of confidence the investment community has in the economy. As we approach Y2k, expect that share prices will drop, just because of fear and worry. Whenever investors are uncertain about what's going to happen, they stop buying, and the markets drop. It works like this even if it's good news that's coming. But it's worse when they expect the news to be bad.

But then, if businesses start to struggle and go under after the Millennium Day, this will drive the markets even lower. I could be wrong about all this. Y2k might just be a little bump in the economies of the world, with very few serious effects. But I don't think so. I believe this will be the biggest shock this century for the businesses, governments and stock markets of the world. And it'll happen all over the world, *all at the same time*.

### Procrastination and Ignorance

I'm doing my bit about the ignorance part by writing this book. It seems that at the time I'm writing this, many stockbrokers and investment fund managers are not even giving Y2k a thought. Wouldn't it seem just common sense that when investing your money and mine, our fund managers should be checking on the Y2k status of these companies? Should they be investing our money in firms that might not even be there by January 3rd?

Yet that's what has been happening. Hopefully, as Y2k awareness spreads, they'll wise up. Don't hesitate to talk to your financial adviser about the safety of your money in Y2k. And even talk directly to your mutual fund managers to see what notice they've been taking.

## Market Forecasts

Dennis Grabow, in an April 1998 article published on www.Y2ktimebomb.com notes that most economic forecasters are predicting continued growth for the world economy, and its stock markets, through 1998 and into 1999. While the markets may be a little less bullish, and grow a little slower, than the last few years, they say it'll all be up, and up some more.

High current levels of economic activity, with low interest rates, unemployment, and inflation, they say, will drive "relatively strong market advances." As long as nothing unexpected happens, that is.

Grabow doesn't think so. Neither do I. We think the "unexpected" is here. Y2k. The costs of Y2k will lower the profits of many, many companies. Maybe all companies. Share prices will start dropping as companies announce reduced earnings. Some shares will drop even before these announcements, when investors realize that problems are surfacing in a company.

All this will not wait until Millennium Day. Many companies, such as the US banks, are working to government deadlines. It'll become apparent fairly early when a company is going to miss such a deadline. Financial analysts have already started including Y2k compliance as a factor in their decisions, and they'll be researching the Y2k readiness of a great many companies. And publishing what they find.

Non-compliant companies will find their shares dropping in price. This will affect their credit rating, and make it difficult to borrow capital. This will further slow their growth, and push the share prices down some more. Spiral on down. Vicious circle.

On the other hand, Grabow points out that companies who do get things fixed and working early will gain market share, and will be operating with more efficient processes. This will push their shares up, making it easier to borrow or get credit. Spiral up. The trick will be figuring out reliably which companies are which.

These things are going to begin happening by the end of 1998. Since savvy investors look a few months ahead, the time to be thinking about this is late 1998.

Putting off the inevitable only makes it worse. In Chapter 7 you'll find my thoughts on protecting your investments through Y2k, including your locked-in retirement nest-egg.

# Drivers Licences and Other Things

Now what about other ways that we interact with our governments? We have to have drivers' licences, marriage licences, dog licences, business licences, building permits, you name it. There are dozens of ways that each of us deals with government or big business day in and day out. Most of these could be affected by Y2k software errors.

In the next few paragraphs, let's take a look at some of the things that could go wrong with your drivers licence. It's a good example because it has a legal requirement. You must have one, otherwise if you drive you may end up in jail. A driver's licence is one of those critical little things that we must have in order to live comfortably in modern society.

Here are a few things that might go wrong:

In many states and countries, you get a renewal notice in the mail when your licence is about to expire. We do in Alberta, every five years on your birthday. What if it didn't arrive? Or maybe it did, and you mailed in your check, but it didn't get there. The mails are vulnerable to Y2k. You could easily end up driving without a valid licence. I don't check the expiry date on my licence every time I get behind the wheel, do you?

In Alberta that's a $1000 fine. Could be less or maybe more where you live. It's serious money, anyway. And hassle. In most countries, no licence means no insurance. Ever think of that? It's not too difficult for a normal law-abiding citizen to make a mistake driving and end up with six burned bodies in the ditch. It doesn't happen to everyone, but it happens to *someone* every day. If your insurance company says "nix" because your licence expired, could you cover multi-million-dollar lawsuits without selling your house? And everything else?

And if everything is going wrong in our society because of Y2k, driving might well be more dangerous than it normally is, when times are good. More accidents, more crimes, more road rage. In good times an insurance company might be a little lenient on a licence a few days overdue. Or a policy renewal that's "in the mail."

But if they've been paying out millions already because the world is in trouble, they'll take advantage of every little thing they can to keep their payouts down.

They may have to, otherwise they'll be in danger of going out of business. The whole concept of insurance works on percentages. They expect that everyone will pay premiums, but only a small percentage will make claims. Y2k could screw that up for them.

What if your insurance company goes under, with or without your help? Good luck trying to get a refund on your premium! In places like Alberta and most developed nations, where you're required to have insurance, you'll then have a big problem buying more, so that you're allowed to drive. Either that or you place everything you own at risk of a lawsuit every time you get behind the wheel. Sound like a no-win situation?

Maybe you had a couple of speeding tickets or something. And you paid them off pretty quick to get them off your record as soon as possible. What if the dates get all screwed up, and the software thinks they're still outstanding? Or maybe the checks really do get lost in the mail. Or lost in the interbank clearing system, which is totally computerized.

One way or another, these fines might still show on your record on the computer. When you try to renew your licence, they may not let you! Remember, no licence, no insurance, no protection, no drive.

Maybe the software goes as far as automatically canceling your licence for these imaginary overdue fines. Here's another of those little challenges. See if you can find someone in your government's traffic agency who understands the question, and find out whether there's a person in the loop to check on the computerized decisions about canceling licences.

So that's a sample of things that *could* go wrong with drivers licences when Y2k comes. I'm sure there's more that I haven't thought of. I'm equally sure some of you, unfortunately, will discover them in those first few weeks and months. Be careful; be prepared.

And then there's all the other government rules, regulations, licences, permits and stuff. They're just as likely to screw up as drivers licences, so in the first few months of the year 2000 we could all be battling these problems on many different fronts *all at the same time.*

I hope that only a few of these things actually do go wrong. Here I've painted a fairly dismal picture, but we do need to think about the worst-case scenario. In fact, I think that all of us will meet at least a few of these problems. Some of us may meet more and worse.

We need to be prepared that the worst just might happen, and it might be bad. Make sure all your paper documentation is complete and up-to-date, and it's where you can find it. In Chapters 7 and 8 you'll find some more good advice about your paper records.

And if your drivers' licence is one of the new "smart cards" with a chip embedded in it, then you're also likely to run into problems with the software embedded within it.

# Embedded Systems

### Type Testing Won't Do

Embedded chips are really going to be a problem. Perhaps more than all the MIS problems we've already talked about. And the biggest problem is that we'll have to test every single one. It would be nice if we could test one product or one chip of each type, and then be confident that all the others like it would be OK. But we can't "type test" them.

As we have seen, some manufacturers buy their chips from a variety of sources. Then they include them in the coffee-maker, or microwave, telephone, pacemaker, or whatever it is that you and I end up buying. So six apparently identical products will have chips in them that bear the same type number, but are very different inside the chip.

While all these chips do the job and make your appliance work, there's no easy way for us to tell which variety of the chip it contains. We could go and ask the manufacturer, but there are a couple of problems with that idea.

First, they may not even bother keeping records at that level of detail. They simply may not have bothered recording which variety of the chip went into each individual appliance. When your TV or VCR was built a few years ago, it probably didn't even occur to them that anyone would ever ask!

And second, they'll never be able to handle that many enquiries from all their old customers. Remember, there will be

# 25 BILLION!
## Embedded Microprocessor Chips

That's five embedded chips for every man, woman and child on the face of the Earth! And since more than half the people in this world don't have any, that's *10 or so per person* in the wealthier half. A small percent of these will fail. We have no way of guaranteeing which ones will and which won't. And a small percent of a small percent is still a very large number! One percent of one percent of 25 billion is still *2 million*.

About 5% of these chips do use dates in their working. The chip in your VCR does, but the one in your microwave doesn't. Or at least, shouldn't need to. So how many of those will still be working in the new Millennium?

Your microwave does however use a *time* reference. In some percentage of the chips out there that have a time reference, the circuitry that handles it will have been borrowed from another chip design. Some percentage of these will use dates in a calculation that really only needs time. We can have no idea which ones. This kind of secret bug can only be found by testing, and we know we can't type-test.

And we certainly can't test every one of the 25 billion chips. We couldn't even find them all, let alone test them all in time. And it would cost enough that it would drive many companies out of business. This problem leads to companies waiting for something to fail before they fix it. This gives rise to a very scary deal called the "WFITFAFIT" method, which we'll talk about on page 81.

### Appliances
Capers Jones tells of his neighbor who almost lost his house when the software in his microwave malfunctioned and it caught fire. There are many other household appliances and industrial equipment that could cause fires and worse.

On January 1, 2000 we could have a million or so failures around the world, on top of everything else that might be going wrong that day. Don't expect a rapid response from your local fire department or ambulance service.

9-1-1 (*Nine-One-One*) may not be an option. The phones may be down or overloaded, and the same could be true of all the emergency services that we have come to rely on *for our survival* in an emergency. This also applies to the rest of this section, and indeed the whole book. My point is that your survival might be at stake. This is why I wrote this book. In Chapters 7 and 8 you'll learn what to do about all this.

## Elevators, Bank Vaults and Buildings

The many systems in our modern buildings that depend on computers and chips and the software within them are at risk. Again, we have no way of telling which ones, and in many cases no way to test in advance. And remember, we can't type-test.

One possible problem relates to the fact that January 1, 2000 is a Saturday, while January 1, 1900 was a Tuesday. This is one of the more obvious problems, but still, expect someone to miss it somewhere. It's just possible some bank vault somewhere may open on that Saturday morning, when it's supposed to be programmed to open only on weekdays.

Fixing bank vaults might be a problem, too. The Yourdons tell of one possibility, a bank vault where the door is built so no one can tamper with the chip without taking the door off. But the vault, as is usual, went in before the building was built around it!

They can't upgrade the chip without demolishing half the building. Perhaps they should abandon the building and move the bank. We could call this an example of more non-productive, but very necessary, "sandbagging" expense, just like the flood scenario we discussed earlier.

Expect to find at least a few buildings in your town with problems, and some that become totally unuseable. Avoid riding in elevators in the last few days of 1999 and the first few of the new Millennium. Air conditioners, security systems, automatic doors, automatic window closers, all are candidates for failure. Ford tested a building, with horrifying results.

These are just a few examples of what might go wrong. Because these chips are everywhere, anything, or perhaps even *everything*, could fail.

Watch that you don't get locked *in* somewhere by a misbehaving security system. It could be very difficult for the security people to get you out. Especially if the service people for the security equipment are busy elsewhere, and the fire department too. The same goes for elevators, and for subway trains.

Start using the stairs in early 1999 if you're not already doing it. A few of these problems are bound to turn up before Millennium Day, so be ready. Every step you take up the stairs, and every two steps down, adds seven seconds to your life. That first step you take toward the stairwell on Millennium Day might add years.

And if the power goes off, we'll be in worse shape yet.

## Vehicles

It's difficult to predict what will happen with chips embedded in vehicles. Some are non-critical, like the digital clock, or the stereo. These may fail, and still leave the vehicle fully useable. Others may render it useable but unsafe, like chip failures in the ABS antiskid brakes, or in power steering systems.

Still others might be in the automatic transmission, or the computer-controlled suspensions of some luxury cars, and so on. These could leave the vehicle still useable, but less convenient, though not actually unsafe. Like the microwave oven, a chip failure in a vehicle *could* even start a fire. Carry an extinguisher, type "A, B, C."

And some failures may be in things that matter only when you need them – airbags, for example. Or an airbag failure might show up right now. What if it your car suddenly filled up with airbags for no reason right at midnight on the Millennium? Or what if this happened to your Toyota right at Japan's midnight? (That'll be 8am MST here in Edmonton.) Very unlikely, perhaps, but by no means impossible.

## Recalls and Getting Your Vehicle Fixed

Getting things fixed may be next to impossible, even if the warranties cover Y2k problems, and there's no guarantee that they will. There might be thousands or millions of vehicles to fix. And what if the parts are not available? If the chip factories are overloaded or shut down, or any link in the supply chain goes out?

Assuming that the crisis does not totally destroy our society, and we're still able to struggle along, we could find that Y2k vehicle failures cause massive recalls, like we've never seen before. This will cost money, which must come out of the auto companies' profits, which comes out of the shareholders' pockets. Does your pension fund or mutual fund hold shares in any auto manufacturers? Basically, they all do.

We just have to hope that the smaller companies who supply parts, and particularly computer chips, are still working and can cope with the demand for Y2k-compliant versions of their products. And can survive the lawsuits from the car companies and others.

All of this will slow down the automobile industry some more. We all know how sensitive the world economy is to the performance of the auto industry. This will be just one more factor driving us into a recession or depression. That is, as well as making it difficult and frustrating to get cars fixed and chips replaced.

The dealers and manufacturers will be having their own Y2k problems. It may be a while before they can address ours.

**Driving on Millennium Day** If you *must* be on the move at the Millennium, try to be sure you're stationary every hour on the hour throughout December 31, 1999. Depending on where the chips in your car were made, midnight in their home town could be any hour of December 31$^{st}$. Police and other emergency response personnel please take note. Given the possible street conditions, it's probably best if as many people as possible can avoid driving altogether that day and the next. Especially right on the hour. *Perhaps all traffic lights should go to red for 30 seconds on each hour.*

People in extreme climates, both hot and cold, will be at risk if they're stranded by a failed vehicle. Think of the story I told in Chapter 3 about the lady from Texas running into the snowditch in Alberta. Those of us who live in arctic and desert climates are aware of the danger of dying if you're stranded, but visitors often are not.

Don't willingly place yourself at risk in the last few days of 1999 or the first few weeks of 2000. Make sure you don't drive beyond the easy reach of help in case of an emergency. Remember the helpers will be busy, and maybe out of touch by phone. Wear your seatbelt.

Many chips in vehicles will fail. No one knows how many. Finding them all beforehand will be impossible. Fixing them afterwards will be difficult and expensive. I'm keeping my 1981 Chevy van because I *know* it'll run on Millennium Day. It has no chips. I'm keeping my 1986 Toyota Camry, with six chips, just to see if it runs. And I'm buying a Dodge truck in 1999, but in the 2000 model year, in the *hope* that it'll be Y2k compliant.

## Medical

Chips are *everywhere* in medical equipment. Practically everything that gets connected to or stuck into a patient these days is computerized. And because of the problems over type-testing, we can't trust any of them until they have been tested. Patients' lives are hanging in the balance here. But there's more to it than just that.

We saw in an earlier chapter how it's impossible to guarantee that software is bug-free. So just because your pacemaker, blood-sugar device, or electronic thermometer is working on January 1, 2000, doesn't mean you can forget about it for the next 1000 years. There could easily be more bugs hidden in the software that won't show up until a few days, weeks or years into the new Millennium.

For many patients, particularly the elderly, their survival *day by day* depends on getting the correct dosage of a number of drugs. This in turn depends on accurate measurements of blood sugar and many other blood chemicals, and blood pressure and other such numbers.

If the measurements and dosages get screwed up, these people will have many kinds of problems. Some will die; others will be permanent damaged. Diabetics may go blind, etc.

And then there are those major diagnostic machines that find so many problems at an early, *curable* stage. CAT scans, MRI scans, even the basic X-ray and ultrasound – they're all totally computerized. CAT, after all, stands for "*Computer*-Aided Tomography."

Someone anonymous gave Peter de Jager a list of about 30 medical devices that *will fail* on Y2k, with a description for each one of exactly how it'll fail.

The British Department of Health has admitted that "The resources do not exist . . . to investigate every item of hardware and software in use . . . let alone put right all those that have not been correctly designed for the year 2000." Based on an estimate of a 10% failure rate of electronic equipment, they expect hospital and medical Y2k problems could cause **between 600 and 1500 deaths in Britain alone.** So a one percent failure rate might give 60 to 150 deaths. Still an intolerable number, especially if it's *you* that dies.

Expect some deaths, and some serious damage. I hope and pray it won't be too many, but I fear the worst. Be prepared to check and double-check every reading taken of yourself or a loved one, and watch for differences from the day before. You'll find more detailed advice in Chapters 7 and 8.

## Canada Has CYNCH

The good news for us in Canada is that we are putting together a central place for hospitals and health workers to share information. It's called *Canadian Year 2000 National Clearinghouse for Health* (CYNCH). It's being run by the Province of British Columbia Ministry of Health, for the benefit of health organizations across Canada, and elsewhere.

A center like this provides a one-stop place for people working on medical Y2k problems to ask for help from others who have had a similar problem. It allows for sharing of information and ideas, problems and solutions, and could be of enormous benefit. There is a definite need for other industries to do this as well.

## Industrial Processes

More and more our factories, chemical plants and everything else are run by computers, embedded and otherwise. As with the patients in the previous section, if things go wrong it could be fatal. In this case, it could be fatal just to the process itself, or possibly to nearby workers and neighbors as well.

What if the readings screwed up in an oil refinery or some such plant? Temperatures and pressures could rapidly exceed safe limits. We could be faced with explosions, releases of toxic substances, and possible loss of life. Don't forget Bhopal. And in Chapter 6 you'll discover the size of the lawsuits that followed the Bhopal incident, huge especially for a non-litiginous country like India.

Power plants, telephones, nuclear facilities, ships, missiles, trains (with and without drivers), train control systems, assembly lines, refineries, chemical plants, breweries, food processing and packaging plants, fertilizer plants, toxic waste disposal, any of them could malfunction on Y2k.

Some might blow up and kill hundreds of workers. Others might release clouds of chemicals and kill thousands of neighbors, as at Bhopal.

## Airplanes

Our modern aircraft have so many places where chips are used. And because stationary aircraft tend to fall out of the sky, some of these chips can be considered critical. Very critical. "Fail-safe" for aircraft has to include getting them safely down when something goes wrong. But we've seen already how often programmers forget, or are too busy, to make software fail-safe.

A modern jet airliner can contain hundreds of microprocessor chips. As with vehicles, some failures will be trivial, some inconvenient, and some could be disastrous. Because all airlines and air traffic agencies are so concerned with passenger safety, we can expect to see a rather extreme effort to fix things.

However, there has already been some significant procrastination. And even airplanes suffer from the inability to type-test, and for them it's more critical yet. Airplanes are so critical, that I have included them in the next section, on "Critical Systems."

# Critical Systems

Most of these I have discussed already, so I mention them briefly here to stress just how important they are.

## Electric power

I've said a lot about this earlier, and that's because it's the utility we depend on the most, worldwide. Here we'll look at some factors that will add to the stress on the electric supply. These factors will not only make failures more likely, they also mean that when the power does fail, the effects will be made worse. They'll increase the domino effect and ripple effect, described at the end of this chapter.

And so many power plants, nuclear and conventional, will be on the **"Max Downtime Approach,"** or **WFITFAFIT**, as you'll see on the next page.

## Weather

July 1996 was the peak of a California heat wave. Eight states and two provinces went out. The Auckland, N.Z. power outage was also at the peak of a heat wave, the hottest summer ever recorded in Auckland. Y2k will not be heat wave time in California, but it will in Auckland, Sydney, Johannesburg and other southerly places.

January 1st is:

* Tornado season in parts of the Southern hemisphere
* Typhoon season in the South Pacific
* Hot, hot, *hot* season along the Tropic of Capricorn, south of the equator. This includes northern Australia, southern Asia, and sub-Saharan Africa.
* Early summer everywhere else in the southern hemisphere.
* Blizzard season in the Frozen North.

The power outage in Auckland New Zealand in January 1998 was caused by the weather. The rather elderly underground lines failed because, in the extreme temperatures, the ground was not conducting the heat away quickly enough.

Mind you, after the experience they've had without power for almost six weeks, Auckland will probably be in better shape than any other city in the world to handle a Y2k power outage. They now have more generators per capita than any city in the world. They'll also most likely be best prepared to *prevent* an outage. That is, as long as they still have a power company, and the lawsuits don't drive it out of business.

At the other end of the globe, Y2k is in blizzard season in Canada, Scandinavia, Siberia and Alaska. And everywhere else in the snow belt. Extreme cold makes huge demands on the electricity supply, as Quebec found last year. Severe damage to buildings can occur if they're not kept heated. If power goes out seriously, livestock and people will die, as in Quebec.

People in severe climates, both hot and cold, will be at risk if they're stranded by power outages. Without air conditioning, a stranded elevator may get extremely hot. The elderly and people with heart problems may suffer serious consequences. There are many other equally distressing scenarios.

## Embedded Chips and Electric Power

Here's another scary one, a story out of New York that I first heard courtesy of Ed Yourdon. The Con. Edison power company in New York reportedly tested one of their coal-burning standby plants for Y2k compliance.

The first failure was a chip in the system that monitored emissions. The plant shut down. They replaced that chip, tried again, and another chip shut the place down. They replaced it, and started up again.

The *third* time the plant shut down,

# It Took 13 Days to Bring it Back Up!

Then in Hawaii, the Hawaiian Electric utility tested their system, with shocking results. According to one of their systems analysts, "basically, it just stopped working." If they had not found this and fixed it, some customers would have been in the dark.

You can probably see a couple of serious problems with these stories. First the more obvious one. In the first days of Y2k, how many power plants might shut down in this way? If some of them take 13 days, or 26 or 39 days to come back up, we just might have our own "Dark Continent" right here.

At that time of year, we couldn't have more than six "Dark Continents" world-wide, but that's how many we just might end up with. (Antarctica is *always* daylight that time of year.)

But there's a more subtle portent to this. Many people and organizations around the world are planning to take this "Wait-for-it-to-fail-and-fix-it-then" (WFITFAFIT) approach. Faced with the prospect of finding and testing (and sometimes fixing) the 25 Billion embedded chips in the world, many are choosing this path of least effort.

## WFITFAFIT: Path of Maximum Downtime

It's also called *Fix-On-Failure*. This approach means that each bad chip will bring the power plant, factory, elevator, medical monitor *or whatever* to a standstill, for somewhere between a few minutes and (current experience) 13 days. And this could happen to any power plant, factory, elevator, medical monitor *or whatever* anywhere in the world.

This really is the *"Max Downtime Approach."* Any plant that does have problems is guaranteed to have some downtime. Managers are choosing to do this because they see it as less hassle than spending time and money *now* to find, test and fix. What they're neglecting to consider is the effect on our larger society when so many plants and factories are out of service being fixed, *all at the same time.*

Besides, it'll be a lot easier to justify spending the money when everyone can see that the plant is down and must be fixed. Right now, shareholders, boards of directors and company presidents are not willing to spend money on Y2k fixes, because they still don't believe it'll happen. As the psychologists would say, they're *"in denial."*

## Nuclear Power

A special case. A very special case. The two big extra fears here are a *melt down* or a *blowup*. Up or down, it's not a nice prospect. While I don't think either of these is certain, as usual I refuse to regard any of it as *impossible*. I'm lucky I live 2000 km (1300 mi) from the nearest nuclear power station. I still worry. Ed Yourdon now lives in New Mexico.

Chernobyl and Three Mile Island are the models we have for how these things were handled in the past. Could we cope with 2 or 3, or half a dozen, or perhaps 50 Chernobyls and Three Mile Islands, *all at the same time?* Based on our record so far, I doubt it. Worldwide, there are a couple of hundred of them. Even the oldest use *some* computers. The modern ones are riddled with them, of course.

Yardeni and de Jager have a few things to say on the nuclear topic. They're not happy at the way the U. S. Nuclear Regulatory Commission (NRC) has so far handled things.

For one thing, the NRC has declared that basically there isn't a safety problem because the safety systems at nuclear plants don't rely on date-related data. Well, we have already seen how one chip manufacturer can produce a compliant chip, while another provides a supposedly identical chip that fails the test. So good luck.

They also claim that 90% of the safety systems are analog, and so not vulnerable to Y2k. Great. But as a skydiver and a programmer, I believe in Murphy's law. It's that other 10% that worries me. And the programmers who have gone and used the occasional date reference in the software when a simple time reference would have done.

But there are dates in the databases they use for running the plant, as opposed to safety systems. So their goal, as far as they have gone toward achieving it, seems to be to keep the plants safe, but they have not spent much time and effort on keeping them *running* through Y2k. For me, this just makes the whole power-outage thing a little more worrisome.

When the NRC talks of a "worst-case scenario," they "believe" that the safety systems will work. They also claim that if the instruments for monitoring the reactor all fail, the plant staff have procedures for a safe shutdown. Can we be sure those backup procedures ***don't use even one embedded computer chip***? If they use even a single one, it becomes a gambling game, which is not a good idea when it's nuclear.

Another problem. This one affects the entire electric power industry in the U. S., but it's scariest in the nuclear part. Since the electricity industry in the U. S. was deregulated, many plants have been "not operating as designed" because they're trying to **cut costs**.

They have been cutting corners to make ends meet. Just to make the point, there are some 37 nuclear sites out of 108 in the U.S. that might shut down soon because their cost to generate electricity is higher than the market price expected over the next few years. Will these companies be able to afford the extra costs of preparing for Y2k? Of course not, if they're already struggling to survive. So what will happen?

Go back to the sandbag example again. If you're bleeding to death in the local hospital, will you send the doctor out to lay sandbags? Not unless the water is running into the emergency room, right? You'll fix the life-threatening problem, or die, before you let him go out there.

Of course, by insisting that the doctor stitch you up first, you've increased the chance that the entire town will be washed away, by keeping the doctor from helping the sandbag crew. It's not much of a choice, is it?

Some of these uneconomic nuclear plants will no doubt shut down before Y2k. Some of the smart operators will do it because of Y2k coming up. That reduces the number to worry about. But any shutdown means layoffs, and that increases the chance of recession. And it increases the chance of overloading the rest of the power grid.

Every nuclear power station that closes before Y2k reduces the backup generating capacity, and steps up the chances of a "Dark Continent." Each one that struggles to keep going may increase the risk of a "nuclear incident." We're damned if they do, and we're damned if they don't!

Some of those that remain will hit Y2k inadequately prepared. *That's* to worry about.

Nuclear plants also have a lot of other safety issues besides those related to a possible meltdown. They use computers for:

- Simulations for training and planning, where the computer simulates the plant.
- Monitoring the radiation dosage each person gets
- Assigning properly-trained personnel to the various jobs
- Tracking the training these people have had to make them suitable for critical jobs.
- Inventory control for radioactive materials
- Maintenance schedules for the plant and its hardware.
- They use off-the-shelf software and hardware, such as programmable logic controllers.

Errors in any of these areas have the potential to be fatal. And some might not be discovered until well into the new Millennium. The big question still to be answered is, will the NRC have the guts to close down any plants that are not *proved* compliant in time? IATA (air travel) and IFAP (pilots) said they would close airports. Will NRC turn out the lights?

At the time of writing the NRC was just beginning to show its teeth, and had stated that non-compliant nuclear plants would be forced to shut down safely before Millennium Day. They're warning that "control room display systems, radiation monitoring and emergency response" are particularly at risk. But really, they're between a rock and a hard place.

If they allow these plants to go into the new Millennium improperly prepared, they risk unplanned shutdowns, accidents major and minor, and possibly a nuclear disaster. If they shut them all down in advance, that could be 5% to 10% of the north American generating capacity. Since the spare capacity is about 15%, just this one problem cuts the emergency power by up to two-thirds!

This puts us in a far riskier position if we have to deal with other problems in the continental power supply. Ed Yourdon's new house in New Mexico has solar panels. Many of his neighbors have windmills.

If this is the sorry situation in the world's most technologically advanced nation, are the rest of us any better? I think not. I don't have facts and figures, except to say that nuclear power generates 17% of the world's electricity in 30 or so countries.

In Canada, Ontario Hydro has recently published an updated Nuclear Emergency Plan (Globe and Mail, August 29, 1998). Before, they assumed that whatever happened, "everyone would be able to go back home, if they got evacuated at all." But that was before Chernobyl.

Now they figure they should plan for a "catastrophic accident," where "a large area might become uninhabitable for an extended period of time." Pregnant women need to wait for a much lower level of radioactivity, because a fetus can easily be deformed by radiation.

They talk about a "devastating atomic incident," with "refugees needing resettlement, huge economic impacts from shuttered commercial enterprises in the radioactive zone, and a long-term blockage of transportation routes because of radiation hazards."

They don't think it's likely ever to occur. But I think Y2k makes it just a little less unlikely. What do you think?

If it ever did happen, most likely it would be a leak of "heavy water." This stuff looks like regular water, but it weighs almost twice as much per liter or gallon. It has two uses. It controls the atomic reaction, and it cools the reactor.

Much like Chernobyl, if it leaked out faster than the technicians could replace it, the reactor would start to overheat. When the heavy water boiled, it would build up steam pressure, and force the radioactive heavy water out into the air.

I've had much the same kind of thing when I boiled my truck and blew a radiator hose. Antifreeze everywhere.

And speaking of Chernobyl, listen to this:

There are 65 Soviet-made nuclear power plants in Eastern Europe. Russia has 29, and *11 are the same model as Chernobyl.* The London Sunday Times says that "Western experts believe many are already unsafe." (April 12,1998. www.sunday-times.co.uk )

The Times quoted an unnamed Moscow source as saying. "Russia's nuclear industry is in dire straits. Throw in Y2k and you could have a giant Chernobyl on your hands."

I'm expecting large numbers of nuclear power plants around the world are going into Y2k inadequately prepared. I fully expect that we'll have at least one nuclear disaster, somewhere in the world. We need to have the (analog) emergency response and rescue teams ready and on alert. Worldwide.

And of course Saddam or someone like him may have their own plans for a nuclear disaster while we're all busy trying to survive. There are still many Soviet warheads unaccounted for.

Hospitals and other users of radioactive materials will have similar safety issues.

## Airplanes

Talk about critical! Get them out of the sky *safely*! But without reservation systems and maintenance scheduling systems, we may not get them up there in the first place.

**Reservation Systems**  With the possibility of millions of stranded travelers, as we discussed in Chapter 3, it's not difficult to imagine all kinds of scenarios where people's lives could be seriously affected, financially and otherwise.

People *will* be stranded by the airport closures and flight cancellations, as IATA (International Air Travel Association) and IFAP (International Federation of Airline Pilots) have promised. You'll remember it was mentioned above that they'll refuse to fly into any airport unless they have *complete confidence* in the entire system. Every link of the chain.

There'll be a certain percentage among the stranded ones who are dependent on drugs or other things to keep them alive. It's a numbers game, really. If we have 'X' millions of stranded travelers, we can expect small percentages to be affected by every possible problem.

We could have 'Y' number of airport heart attacks, with elderly travelers who become over-stressed by the experience. There'll be 'Z' number of babies born in airports, 'P' number of asthmatics, 'Q' diabetics, and others, who run out of their essential medication while stranded, etc., etc., etc. Meanwhile everyone else will get hungry.

And while airports can probably be expected to have first-aiders on hand, other help may or may not be available. 9-1-1 calls for paramedics may be difficult or impossible, depending on the state of the phones. Even if we get an ambulance, there may not be any hospitals available to accept cases. They may be overloaded with all that's going on, and/or having their own Y2k problems.

**Maintenance Schedules**  There'll be a number of software bugs will show up in the early days and weeks of 2000. These will be dealt with and corrected, although not without hassle and difficulty. The real problems will be the few bugs that get through unnoticed, and cause safety and performance problems for aircraft that are not properly maintained.

A few of these will show up when the embedded software in some parts of the aircraft complains about improper maintenance. Because of the date problem, the software may think the maintenance was not done. It might just complain, and tell the pilots to get the job done. Or it could be that the apparent lack of maintenance will not let the airplane start, or perhaps not let it take off.

The worst case would be software that behaved like the 1990 Honda 750 motorcycle, or the Aussie-designed aluminum smelter software. Software that shuts down without considering the safety of its users has no place on an aircraft. But how would we know? Other than waiting for The Day. And being unable to do type-testing makes it worse.

Aircraft software needs to be fail-safe, as does any software where people's lives and property are at stake. But I just don't have that much confidence. I'm a programmer.

**Airport Operations and Administration**   We have to get the people to work, qualified people to do the critical jobs. Also we need all the people who handle the crowds of travelers, and the customs and immigration officers and such who are required by law to be there whenever the airport is operating.

Then we need electricity, vehicles, security systems, security scanners, administrative computers, all the equipment an airport uses that is (a) computerized, and (b) run by electricity. It's that chain concept again. All these things must be in place and functioning for the airport to run. Break a link, and the chain no longer does its job. IATA won't fly there. Nor will IFAP.

**Communications and Air Traffic Control**    As I said, one link missing from the chain, and IATA and IFAP will simply refuse to allow airplanes to fly there. These are the critical chains, totally necessary for survival. And the news is not good.

IBM recently sent a letter to the U.S. Federal Aviation Administration (FAA). In it they stated that there's a problem with the dozen or so mainframe computers that the FAA uses for communications across North America for air traffic control. *They will not run in the year 2000*. At midnight on December 31, 1999, they *will* malfunction.

They didn't say "need to be tested," or "should be upgraded," or "may give problems."

## They *will not* run.

On January 1st, 2000 these computers *will not* function correctly. They *will* have errors.

They can't be fixed, either, because IBM stopped supporting them *eleven years ago*. And I would guess that many, if not most, of the programmers have retired (and/or died.) These are the ones who wrote the operating system software for these machines. The few still around have forgotten how by now. With 620 days to go from the moment I'm writing this, *there isn't time to fix it, even if it could be done*. Nor is there time to replace them. **Don't fly on 2kY.**

**Navigation and GPS**    When the GPS week rollover happens on August 21/22, 1999 we probably won't lose too many ships and planes because they all have other navigation systems as well. It wouldn't be safe for them to rely on any one system, no matter how good, since any piece of equipment *can* fail. Murphy's law says "*Always have backup*."

But land vehicles are different. Used to be that trucks, police cars, off-road vehicles and so on didn't have any kind of navigation device, but now many of them have GPS – and nothing else. So any of these vehicles venturing into dangerous areas may be at risk. But if they do get lost or into trouble that August, we'll have search and rescue organizations and helicopters and stuff to rescue them.

Y2k could well be different. If any trucks get lost, ships run aground (or into each other), or airplanes crash-land or just crash, and we may not have anyone to send after them. Or any aircraft or equipment working. If the emergency services we do have are able to operate, they may well be far too busy already. Don't fly on 2kY.

**Onboard Control Systems**    These are riddled with embedded chips. Need I say more?

There are 3 million parts in a Hercules aircraft. Bigger aircraft have more. A modern jet airliner has hundreds of embedded chips in the control systems, that is, the systems needed to fly the airplane. That includes motors, flight controls, instruments, radar, navigation etc.

Then there are hundreds more in passenger-related roles. The telephone in the back of the seat in front of you. The microwaves the cabin staff use to heat your meals. The heating and air conditioning, the movie/TV screens, the 15-channel stereo feed, and so on. These are not life-and-death, mostly comfort things. But one or two of them could be serious or even fatal if the right set of circumstances happened along.

**A Scenario:**    What if all the navigation systems on board your airplane either fail or disagree with each other? Then the radio doesn't work. The motors, the landing gear (wheels), and the controls may all give problems. Most of the instruments quit, and of course the radar and the landing lights do too.

Once we've (crash)landed, the locator beacon doesn't locate any more. The searchers have no aircraft or equipment working, and they couldn't get to work this morning anyway, so they stayed home.

When those of us who are still alive stumble out of the bush a day or so later, there are no vehicles running to give us a ride. Then we find the hospitals are closed because nothing worked there either, and the staff couldn't get to work.

Because the phones are down, we can't phone home to tell them we survived the crash. The crash which they haven't heard about yet, because the TV and radio stations are out, along with the cable companies. And even when we make it onto the news, no one will notice because there were so many other bigger, deadlier crashes that day.

Get the picture? Don't fly on 2kY.

## Smugglers and Other Undesirables

Even if we manage to avoid wholesale crash-and-burn, we will have problems. And while we're struggling, our transport and communications will in a state of some disarray. Will all the bad guys be sitting around sympathizing? I think not!

Smugglers, drug runners, escapees and just plain undesirables will have a field day, taking advantage of our problems to cross borders and commit other sins. It's automatic. The term "antisocial" applied to these people means, by definition, that they don't care.

These people don't care about you, me, our families, or this complex society we've spent hundreds of years building. They just want their wants, and the rest of us don't matter. Whatever the cause, the point is that this is what criminals *are*.

If there is a serious crisis, they *will* take advantage of it. Some of them *will* try to hurt us. We must first ensure our survival, and that of our families. After the crisis, we'll once more take up the research into rehabilitation, and the treatments that may change people from bad to good. But it can only happen if we survive.

On page 153 you'll see more about weapons, and why they're not always a good idea.

## Weapons Systems

This is *so* scary, but *so* hard to predict. At one extreme it could mean our own weapons going amok and hitting *our* people. At the other extreme it could mean Saddam's weapons going amok and landing on *our* people. If there's war, I'm convinced it'll be ten times as dangerous, because of the unpredictable failures in software, and especially embedded chips.

Here's a couple of actual examples of what could go wrong. During maneuvers, a U.S. submarine fired a torpedo, which turned around and headed back at the ship that fired it. During a simulation of a Gulf war, the mission planners watched their screens blank out. In a real war, this could have made them cancel 2700 air strikes. Both were software problems.

## Military MIS Software

This is the software that manages inventory, people, logistics, and so on. All the things an army must do to get its soldiers to a fight in good condition, properly supplied with food and equipment. This would be in very good shape if all went well with the Y2k conversions. Under normal conditions, remember, the military use far more care and achieve much higher reliability in their software.

But the reports filtering out from the pentagon and in from field officers are not good. Like everyone else in the U.S. federal government, they're behind. So for the military programmers, these are not going to be normal times. As the pressure builds, their error rate will climb like everyone else.

If someone starts a war, we're going to be very unprepared. The only upside to all this is that the aggressor too can expect to run out of things by the time he has marched a little distance from home. And his weapons won't work any better than ours. But tyrants can be expected to sacrifice perhaps millions of their own people to achieve a personal goal. They could take thousands of ours with them.

If we do have a war, I think it'll be bad. I expect we'll be spread very thin, and still trying to cope at home. But I think, at least I hope, that it'll die out before the aggressor can cover much territory.

## Military Communications

All our police and military groups need good communications, especially for Millennium Day and any problems there might be in year 2000.

We need to protect our communication links from penetration by terrorists and spies. We must expect that they'll be penetrated to some extent, and there could be some sabotage this way. This becomes critical if there is any chance of a war.

Terrorist groups or just plain hackers could make it very difficult for the authorities to handle riots or other disturbances. While most hackers are responsible citizens, there are those who like to screw things up just because they can. If someone dies as a result, I firmly believe this should be treated as a terrorist murder, with whatever penalties are appropriate under the laws of the place where it happens.

# Riots and Civil Disturbance

Ed Yourdon's home in New Mexico is in a town of 6000 people. My guess is it's a town that "no gang member has ever heard of." It's 500km (300mi) from the Mexican border, or "more than one tank of gas." If there are disturbances in the cities, or in the poorer parts of the world, this sounds like the right kind of place to be.

Most of us don't have the resources or the portability to up and move like that. We don't have the money, and we need to stay on the job. If there is a job after Y2k. I don't have a new house with solar panels, but you can bet that if I did, I'd be doing the same as Ed..

But isn't this exactly what all the business and government managers have been saying? "We don't have the money to spare to fix the software, so we'll sit tight and hope it all washes by us." If we don't do *something*, we'll be sitting smack in the middle of the road when Y2k comes crashing along.

Edmonton, Aberta, is about a million people when you include the suburbs. It's an oil town, and a cowboy town (but has the only symphony orchestra ever to have a #1 hit!). It's not New York, but it *is* big enough to get ugly if things get out of control. It's also *very* cold in the winter, right around Millennium Day.

About the nearest thing we've had to riots is a bunch of boisterous drunk (ice-)hockey fans after the Oilers won the Stanley Cup. It's generally pretty quiet, but Y2k is like we've never seen before. I think I would rather be somewhere smaller and quieter yet. Like my new home in Victoria, British Columbia.

### The Unhappy Masses

I'm quite convinced there'll be riots. Any little thing can get people going, especially if they're angry or hungry. If the poorer members of our society are without food and electricity for a week or two, and then their welfare, unemployment and social security checks don't come, they'll be angry alright. A confrontation with police here and there could touch off riots even worse than the Los Angeles ones in 1994.

### Urban Problems

Traffic accidents where the lights aren't working, storekeepers chasing or shooting looters, turf wars, road rage, any of these could be a tinder-point that starts the fires going. Literally. Once a riot starts, rioters will beat up and shoot each other and innocent passersby. We all saw it on the tapes of the L.A. riots. Then they start fires.

Police, soldiers, firefighters and paramedics will be spread dangerously thin by all this. And expect that the rioters will block them in any attempt to rescue people or tend to the injured. Communications will be the key to coping with this.

### Emergency Communications

If there are any, that is. With embedded chip failures, possible terrorist or hacker intrusions, and what-all, I'll find it surprising if they can talk to each other at all. And every General knows he can't win a battle if he can't direct his troops.

## Weapons Systems

My comments above apply here too. We may have a lot of trouble with laser sights and infrared snooperscopes and such high-tech equipment. Better our law-enforcement forces stick with simple *mechanical* rifles, shotguns and handguns wherever possible. As long as it has no computer chips, we can trust it.

## Injuries

As with everything to do with Y2k, try not to get hurt. If a riot or disturbance begins or looks likely, you must *leave*. Stay out of it, don't get involved. If you're involved already, behave in a way that will help to end the problem, and leave as soon as you can.

Stay away from angry crowds. If a fight begins, don't crowd in to watch – *leave!* Whether it's a couple of guys or a couple hundred. You can bet that more people will get involved, and the police will intervene. Either way, people will get hurt. **Don't be there.**

No matter how angry you might be about whatever is going on, swallow your anger and leave. It's for the good of your loved ones. Even if there are food riots in your part of the world, hungry and living is better than fed and dead.

If Y2k gets really bad, the police and the military may not have much patience left. Any riot could quickly bring on a serious response, from tear gas to bullets, or perhaps even choppers with rockets. Don't be there to get hurt or killed.

No heroics. *A live coward is way more use than a dead hero,* especially to his own wife and children. Once it starts, a disturbance could progress very quickly. In a matter of minutes it could turn ugly, and guns might be drawn. Figures I have seen would suggest that currently, in a public crowd in the U.S., one person in 7 or 8 is carrying a gun. Other parts of the world are worse. Angry people with guns tend to use them.

If things do get bad after Y2k, expect that the number of people "packing" (i.e., carrying a gun) will increase all over the world. If the guns are present, there's always a chance that they might be used. *Leave when it starts, if not before.*

Better still, live somewhere else. Join Ed Yourdon and me in moving to a small, quiet, protected place.

If a riot starts, and *I'm sure there'll be some,* I think it'll get bad, and quickly. I expect that people will die. Don't be one of them.

## Ambulance & Emergency Services

If you're hurt, will the rescue team be able to get to you? Will their trucks be running? Their medical technology? Will they be able to get to you through the battle? Will you even be able to call them if the phones are down? Will they even be at work? First aid knowledge will be very important. Take a course.

## Hospitals

We have discussed how many systems could fail in a hospital. Their MIS systems at risk range from patient admissions and records, to wages and shift scheduling. They have embedded chips in all kinds of medical technology, including a lot of technology that's supposed to be keeping people alive.

If they're open, of course. Their building systems include security, elevators, fire-protection and so on. We just have to hope it's all still working if we need it. *Try not to need it.* Prevention is always better than cure, especially if our world starts falling apart and cures become uncertain. But if you or a loved one do end up in hospital, you'll find in Chapter 7 some advice that will help.

## Personnel

Throughout this book, I have been making the implicit assumption that the police and the army will be there to restore some semblance of order, and perhaps perform some rescues. But will they? These people have families that they worry about. If things fall apart, why would we expect them to stick around and look after us? Especially when they'll feel a need to go check on the spouses and children at home.

The day before the Quebec ice storm in January 1998, a large contingent of civilian employees from the military base near Montreal arrived at the Edmonton base for a stay of a week or so. When the ice storm hit, they worried. Many were men retired from the active military, older, with older wives who were now alone with no electricity.

The big problem was that the base personnel were so tied up keeping the base from further damage, there was no one to spare to look after abandoned families. They ended up moving many of these older wives, and a bunch of young families, into the gymnasium for a week or two. At least there they were warm and fed.

Both the Canadian Armed Forces (*Operation Abacus*) and the RCMP (Mounties) are specifically addressing the care of families left behind when forces are deployed for Y2k.

My fear is that after Y2k the emergency services may be struggling to stay afloat, or even alive. They'll be busy rescuing their own operation, and worrying about their own families, and coping with enormous demand for their services. How much can you and I reasonably expect from these people in helping us? Whatever happens, I think we'll be much better off to be self-reliant as much as possible.

Hospital workers, paramedics, police, fire fighters, soldiers, doctors, all those people we depend on when we're in trouble. Can we assume they'll be there the way they always have been in the past? Some will, I'm sure. But I'm not even sure we would have the right to demand this of them, given that they have families of their own.

# The Bottom Line on Crime, Looting, Prisons, Riots, War and Disturbances

Generally I'm not one to be identified with the ultra right-wing, law-and-order extreme, but for Y2k many things may change for many people. I fully expect that governments around the world will need to use whatever extraordinary powers are available to them by the laws of their country. If your government doesn't have any, then perhaps you need to start agitating for some specifically for Y2k.

In Canada we have the War Measures Act, which I believe was last used during the FLQ crisis in 1970. Most other countries have something similar. Martial law may be necessary in many places. It may be necessary to read the riot act (literally) over TV before Y2k hits, while we still have TV.

Watch New Zealand and Australia on TV to get advance warning of what's coming. In Europe and North America we're fortunate that midnight hits those countries, along with Japan and all of Asia, before it gets to us. This just might give us the time we need to get things in motion if it becomes clear we have a problem.

### Out of Control

What scares me is that civil disturbances can turn into riots and quickly get out of control at the best of times. And these are going to be the *worst of times* for these things to happen.

In the Times Square scenario at the beginning of this book, you saw depicted a soldier shooting a mugger. The legal term for this is "summary," meaning he was shot because he was guilty, without the benefit of a trial and "due process of law."

I'm not one to advocate summary executions like that. But I'm beginning to think that martial law with all its horrors may turn out to be the least of half-a-dozen evils. If things get bad, I can see it happening in many countries, including the richer ones, and including Canada and the U.S.

Orders to shoot looters on sight, curfews enforced with live bullets, tanks and machine guns responding to stones and Molotov cocktails, any of it is possible. A few prison riots or a mass prison break-out somewhere might make the difference between disturbance and disaster. Manhattan without water pressure could become the biggest torch the world has ever seen.

And how could we justify placing our police officers and soldiers in the line of the worst riots ever seen, without permission to defend themselves? In all fairness, they must be allowed to shoot if attacked.

If they can't stop the riots, the riots won't stop themselves.

## Gaining Control

If things get as bad as we think they might, we may find that any disturbance that's not promptly quelled could quickly become a riot. Not long after that it might become totally unstoppable. I believe that we need our military forces to be prepared, practiced and deployed for Millennium Day. We'll need them to be on patrol *everywhere* for the big day and night.

*Operation Abacus* is one of the most encouraging pieces of news I've seen for a long time. I believe we need them to be on alert for at least the entire year 2000. They must be ready to deploy to any disturbance site in the country on a moment's notice. We need some specialist commanders with experience of riots and mobs. Where will we find those?

If a disturbance becomes a riot, I believe it must be stopped. In normal times, I approve of rubber bullets and riot shields. With our society struggling to cope, and our police, hospitals and emergency services spread thin or maybe out of action altogether, we may have no choice. We may have to simply do what it takes to stop the fighting and disperse the people.

I have a chilling feeling that I just advocated a massacre. I hope it never comes to anything like that. But if some people choose to beat, burn, shoot and kill, whatever valid grievances they feel they have, I'm sorry, it cannot be tolerated. Not if it's going to destroy cities. And people.

If Y2k gets this bad, all of us may have some serious thinking to do about our priorities. This may be more than just a few fights with the cops. This could be as bad as an urban war. Things are different in a war.

## If There *Is* a War

And if there's a regular international war, all the same reasoning applies. If a hostile government (or two three) attacks, naturally they'll push for all they're worth while we're busy, weakened and spread so thin. And it makes little difference whether they attack the U.S., NATO, or a small country like Kuwait or Tibet.

Again, I hate to advocate violence. But it may be that the only effective response is the devastating one. Knowing that this time Saddam or Mladic or whoever will not stop until stopped, and knowing his disregard for the lives of his own soldiers, our generals may be forced to respond with weapons that are *guaranteed* to halt the aggressor.

Given our weakened state, and knowing we can't handle a prolonged battle, the generals may decide that slowing him down is not an option. In the Gulf War, the U.N. countries had the reserves to continue more or less for ever. Stormin' Norman and friends knew that their level of engagement was sustainable.

This time around, we won't have that luxury. We'll have only limited resources and limited time to deal with an aggressor. *He will stop only when stopped,* so he must be stopped. Now. Right now. Before he really does release anthrax. Or use a Soviet nuclear device he got from Kazakhstan.

And even if the levels of violence we have to deal with are nothing like as bad as the picture I just painted for you, our medical system is going to have trouble keeping up.

# Hospitals and Medical Equipment

Besides the radioactive issue (see earlier this chapter), and problems from riots and war, there are some pretty serious things for the medical community to address. For you and me: as I said before, be there for your loved ones, check every instrument reading, and try to avoid surgery, childbirth or medical treatment around The Day.

Avoid unnecessary risk of injury. As a former skydiver and stock car driver, I love to do exciting things. At 54 years of age, I pretty well limit it to motorcycles and wind surfing these days. But I'll park up the dirt bikes until 2001 or so. And the Coast Guard may be too busy to chase after an errant sailboard.

## Drugs: Illegal

I'm sorry, but if you can't survive without these, then you very likely will have difficulty surviving at all. Like every other distribution system, the one for illicit drugs is vulnerable to Y2k. Not only that, but when a vehicle or a cell-phone or something else doesn't work, these guys will be way more ruthless in finding one that does.

Especially in areas where drugs and dealers are already a problem, it could get bad when law and order break down. In the absence of effective policing, existing gangs will be out looking for trouble. New and ad-hoc gangs will form. Short supply of street drugs will push up prices, increasing thefts and violence to pay the new prices. Then there'll be battles over the few drugs that are still out there.

Expect these areas to become worse than any of Brooklyn, Chicago or LA are at present. If you're involved in or on the fringes of any gang, drug or gangster-related activity, you could find yourself drawn into something you weren't really expecting. My advice is to leave before it happens.

Even if you just live in these places, expect bad areas to get far worse. Move, now, *before* it happens.

## Drugs: Legal

Drugstores and hospitals could be closed or out of business, and those that are open may suffer shortages. If you need regular drugs, you must plan and acquire them in advance. If you get hurt in a fight, accident or riot, beware, you may be in trouble.

The blood supply may be equally unreliable.

## Surgery

In the mountain city of Baguio in the Philippines, our host, the owner of our "pension-house," or motel, was an eye-doctor, an ophthalmic surgeon. In the week following the 1990 earthquake, he spent nine hours a day in a U.S. Air Force surgical tent in the parking lot of his own hospital, *amputating*.

He had no anaesthetics, no antibiotics. Just cut them off, stitch them up, and if they could move send them home, because there were no beds. None of the buildings were useable, including hospitals. "Come back in three days time," he told them, "When the Americans have got some antibiotics in here. You're going to need them." Well, I guess so!

Baguio was totally cut off from the outside world, except for U.S. and Philippine Air Force helicopters. We watched streams of choppers flying supplies and equipment in, and injured out. If Y2k is as bad as we think it might be, anyplace in the world will feel just as isolated.

## Post-Traumatic Care

In modern medicine, it's recognized that this is as important as the early treatment to ensure proper recovery. My ophthalmic surgeon friend in the parking lot in the Philippines expected the U.S. Air Force would bring in antibiotics, which of course they did. We might not be able to count on that for Y2k, because the entire world will be in the same state we're in. Don't be one of these. Don't get hurt.

Remember also that when someone has a major injury, there's a "Golden Hour" to get them to hospital. If they get to serious medical treatment within an hour of the injury, the recovery is usually much quicker and better. This may be difficult to manage in a world with many injuries, and few phones, ambulances or functioning hospitals.

# Fire and Emergency Agencies

I've said a lot about these guys above. Here, I want to repeat the warning that your chances of fire, injury, food poisoning and all those misadventures will be much greater if things get bad. At the same time, you will have *less* chance of being rescued and being looked after.

Our emergency services will be spread thinner than ever before, *and* they'll have their own Y2k problems, *and* they'll have their own families at home to worry about. You and I need to plan on looking after ourselves as much as possible.

## Weather Forecasting

This is a highly-computerized function, and one that airplanes in particular have need of. The accuracy of today's forecasts is incredible compared with 20 or 30 years ago. Back then, no one dreamed of trying to predict five days in advance, but now it's routine, even expected.

But it's all done with software and satellites. Don't expect reliable forecasts for the first little while after Millennium Day. How long? As usual, I've no idea! However unstable the rest of our world becomes, that's probably what will happen to weather forecasting as well. Once society stabilizes, however long that takes, the forecasts should begin to recover.

# Conclusion

It would seem that for the first time in history, our entire world will be at risk. Every system in every area of every country in the world is certain to have problems at some level. We must expect that at least some of these problems will be severe. Then two things can happen:

## 1. Synergy

The problems will bump into each other. Problems in one area may affect existing problems in another area, and help to make them worse. The effect could spread through our society. Some of these will spread rapidly; no power means candles and fireplaces, which means more fires. It also means no traffic lights, and more accidents.

Add these two effects together, more fires and more traffic accidents, and they can become a disaster. All this could cause fights and perhaps riots. These and other problems could overwhelm the police, fire, ambulance and hospital services in a matter of perhaps ten minutes to an hour. Not to mention overloaded or dead phone systems for calling for help, and no water to fight fires.

One problem we could maybe handle. Two might make it three times as bad. Three might be six times as bad. Dozens together could mean total disaster. This is synergy, as we defined it on page 33.

Other problems will spread more slowly. As in the sandbag example, if we're all out there saving life and limb, or stuck at home unable to get to work, no work will get done! And if welfare and other checks don't arrive in the mail, and electronic banking doesn't deliver paychecks, many people will have nothing to spend.

As the velocity of money through the economy slows down, stock exchanges fall, factories close, and the downward spiral gathers speed. Over a period of days, weeks and months, we can expect to see the world economy slow down and stumble. And if hospitals close, what effect might that have on the events in the previous paragraph?

## 2. Domino Effect

If we find that fires and traffic accidents do overwhelm our emergency services, what can be done about it at that point? Call in more staff and volunteers? On what phone system? If the phones are working, our calls will just add to the overload. How would they get to the hospitals through gridlocked city streets? Emergency crews are likely to become part of the traffic problem, instead of being the solution. Fly in more equipment, like they did in Auckland? Is the airport open? Fly in from where? If we're having problems this bad, you can bet that everywhere else in the world is too.

The Auckland power outage demonstrated how this can happen. One line went out because of overheating, and so extra load was placed on the other three. It took a week for the next one to break, and then a day later the last two went out.

Then the power was out for 80,000 residents and many businesses, and things started to fall apart. Businesses went bankrupt or lost money. Fax machines and computers were damaged by voltage spikes as the power went on and off unpredictably through this period.

Millions of dollars that no one could afford were spent on generators. Step by step the problem spread from one part of Auckland's economy to another. As each problem happens, it causes more problems. It's just as if we lined up all the parts of our society like dominoes, and then knocked over the first one. We may only be able to watch in horror as each piece of our civilization goes down, and in turn knocks the next one down.

And the people and organizations who we usually turn to for help may be falling apart as well. The military, other countries, all may have their own problems. We rely on backups of many different kinds to keep our society running. But these days, *everything* involves computer technology, and each piece of technology is backed up by more technology, more computer chips.

# Chapter 5: What We Can Learn From Other Disasters

## I Was There

### The Wahine Storm (Wellington, New Zealand) 1968

www.wellington.net.nz/about/past/traged01.htm

In 1968, on April 10 in the southern Autumn, Wellington the capital city of New Zealand was hit by the edge of a typhoon (a.k.a. *hurricane* in the Atlantic, *cyclone* in the Northern Pacific). There were 170 km/h (120 mph) winds downtown in this city of 250,000 people. Children and small adults can literally blow away in these winds.

Power was out for the entire day. Mine was the only floor in the building with coffee that morning, because I had a propane camp stove in my van. Damage, naturally, was extensive, and two people died in the city.

There were stories of heroism all over. One ambulance was blown end over end attempting to reach other vehicles blown off the road. With his seatbelt on, the driver escaped serious injury, and radioed for a replacement. A second ambulance parked around the corner, and the driver crawled 400m (1/4 mi) on his hands and knees pushing a stretcher. The two loaded up their patient, and crawled all the way back.

But more died in the harbor. Wellington has a peaceful landlocked harbor, 8 km (5 mi) across, with a narrow entrance. That morning there were 12m (40ft) waves in the harbor, with a water temperature of 5° C (40° F). *Survival is about 20 minutes* at this temperature.

At 6:00 a.m. the ferry *Wahine* ("*Wa*-hee-nee") with 734 people aboard ran aground on the infamous Barrett's Reef outside the harbor entrance. She lost all power, and the 200m (600ft) ship blew *sideways* through the 270m (800ft)-wide channel into the harbor.

At 11:30 she was 400m (1/4mi) off one of the harbor beaches and began to list. The order was given to abandon ship, but only half the lifeboats could be used. The radio stations in Wellington began calling for pleasure-boat owners to assist, and soon more than a hundred small boats dotted the waves. The N.Z. Railways rail ferry *Aramoana*, in for repairs, went out into the harbor on one engine.

At 2:30 p.m. *Wahine* rolled on her side and sank, leaving the side of her hull and one end of her bridge showing above the water.

Passengers in the powered lifeboats made it quickly to land 400 meters away, *upwind*. Except for the first boat, which was swamped and blown across the harbor. Those in rafts, or floating in life jackets, blew the other way, and had to be picked up out of the water. Several pleasure boats were destroyed on the rocks on the opposite side of the harbor, fortunately without loss of life. Crewmen from the Aramoana hauled many people in through her stern loading door, and several crewmen jumped into the water to assist exhausted survivors.

Approximately 50 people died out of 734 on board. That's about one in 15. There were heart-rending stories in the papers, such as the family who were to board a ship for England the following day. Their raft turned over and trapped the five of them underneath. The father had a jackknife in his pocket, and cut a hole in the canvas floor above them. He got his three children through to safety, but his wife had disappeared.

The big story in the media was when the remaining four were boarding the bigger ship next day for England, the four-year-old was asked, "This one won't turn over will it Daddy?"

I'd like to share with you the lessons I learned that day:

- Be prepared. I had a camp stove that *lived* in my van. That was its official storage place; it had no spot on the shelf in my apartment. Here in Alberta we do that with sleeping bags and such in the winter. Their place is in the vehicle, at least one in each.

  Emergency and survival gear needs to be kept in a place where you can get at it **when you need it**, not just when you're **planning** to have a disaster. I learned as a student skydiver that any time you say "I'll remember to bring it when we need it," Murphy's Law kicks in. For skydivers, Murphy's law is life and death. It might be like that for everyone around Y2k.

- Carry a pocket knife. A Swiss Army Knife or something like it is best, with lots of tools. But not too big – it has to go in your pocket! You may also wish to carry a stronger hunting knife in case you need to do some serious cutting, or perhaps even skinning. That could be kept in a vehicle.

  Be careful about using knives as weapons, even for self-defense. If an assailant manages to get it out of your hand and use it against you, you'll be in worse shape yet.

- **Cold can kill.** Much was written about **hypothermia**, a new word to me at the time, in the N.Z. media in the months and years following. When I moved to Canada in 1970 I found it to be a critical factor in Northern winters too.

- Physical condition and fitness affect your chances of survival. First there are the obvious things, like being able to climb out of things, or jump over things, or run away from things. But the less obvious one came to light in something I noticed in the death statistics from the Wahine.

Of the 50 or so people who died in the frigid waters of Wellington harbor that day, only *five* were in the age range from 5 to 40. Most of those who died were either infants or *older adults*. I put this down to the fact that most younger adults are in better physical shape than their elders.

Their bodies are stronger, and their strength lasts longer when tested to the limit like this. We all will need to be fit and in good shape for Y2k. My wife Nina ran her third marathon this summer. I'll be running my first one next summer (1999).

This should also remind us that our elderly relatives are the ones most at risk.

Your body heals more rapidly when you're in good physical condition. Stirling Moss, a Formula One driver in the 1950s and 1960s renowned for his fitness, once staggered out of a wreck and walked ten paces on two broken legs. He was unconscious at the time. He came to on his hands and knees.

Two weeks later the doctors had Moss walking at a press conference, with no casts on his legs. Six weeks after the crash he won a race, a Le Mans start, where the driver must run across the track and jump into the car.

So work out regularly from now until Y2k. *A good idea even if there's no crisis.* And the bonus is that physical activity from now until old age will extend both your life and your active years. This is now well established in the medical research. Former Canadian Prime Minister Pierre Trudeau was skiing this year at 78 years old!

## The Frozen North

Here in the Canadian North we can almost be regarded as a permanent disaster area. While in the Spring, Summer and Fall our prairie towns, cities and farms look much like you'd find in the plains of Nebraska or Oklahoma, in the winter it's a different story.

Those who live in areas with extreme climates, heat, cold, desert or whatever, learn to adjust. We take certain precautions, and think it quite normal. Visitors from milder climes can sometimes be rather shocked, however.

In the 28 years I've lived in Alberta, I've learned a lot about survival, both in general, and, especially, in extreme cold. Minus 40° is the point where the Celsius and Fahrenheit scales meet. It's the same on both scales. In Edmonton we get temperatures of -40° one or two days a year, usually.

Winnipeg is even colder, at the other end of the Canadian prairies. All across the prairie provinces of Alberta, Saskatchewan and Manitoba, we plug our cars in overnight in the winter. An electric "block heater" keeps the antifreeze (not water!) in the radiator "warm" so the car will start next day. In this case, "warm" means somewhere between -20° and freezing point.

In the 1970s when I first came to Edmonton we had this kind of cold a week or two each year. Earlier, in the winter of 1968-69, there was a period of eight weeks when the temperature didn't go above -30° C (-20° F) at any time of the day or night. Driving on city streets in this climate is an adventure in itself!

In the 70s and 80s Alberta would lose *someone* every winter stranded in a car. Usually they would be on a public road, and die stuck in a snowdrift. Once the gas runs out, the heater doesn't work, so if you don't have a few basic emergency items you can freeze to death in a few hours. Stranded vehicles and downed airplanes can become frozen coffins.

In chapter 8 you'll find a list of things you should have in your vehicle when Y2k comes around. There's a list for warm climates, and an additional list for cold places. Also, rent the movie "*Alive!*" a true story about a South American soccer team stranded in a crashed aircraft in the Andes.

So my education about hypothermia, begun with the Wahine Storm, continued in Alberta. I also learned that you don't need snow and ice to have a problem. A wet hiker or cyclist on a cool rainy day is at risk, especially if there's a wind blowing.

On my first-ever long-distance cycling trip in 1977, 160 km (100 mi) out of Edmonton on the morning of Day 2, I headed off in shorts and a nylon windbreaker shell. There was a light drizzle of rain, and a gentle breeze, with temperature around 15°C (60°F). I was alone, with no friends to monitor my speech and coordination.

Though it was summer, I was at risk because of the chilling effect of the moving air as I rode. The wind evaporated the water off my clothing and skin, cooling me down rapidly.

I discovered there are no restaurants or coffee in the next 120 km (80 mi)! I stumbled into a general store and asked about coffee. They didn't serve it, but the girl behind the counter offered to make me some. Foolishly, I declined, and staggered out. It wasn't until much later that I realized why she had a sort of shocked look on her face. She could see what I looked like, but I couldn't.

A mile or so down the road, a farmer who had been in the store pulled his pickup onto the shoulder ahead of me. He gave me 20m (60ft) to stop a slow bicycle, but I cruised in a daze into his back bumper and stepped off my fallen bike. He threw my bike in his truck, turned the heater up in the cab, and drove me to a restaurant in the town of Edson, where I spent three hours warming up. I think he saved my life.

That night was the only night of the trip that I stayed in a motel. I hung my stuff all around my room to dry, and spent 20 minutes in the sauna. By then my muscles were completely on strike, so I oozed up the stairs to my room and slept the sleep of the dead. Figuratively, that is. Not the real sleep of the dead, luckily.

Here's a summary of what I've learned about hypothermia:

- Hypothermia happens when the core temperature of your body drops below the standard 37° C (98.6°F). Before that happens, your body cuts off blood flow to your hands and feet to conserve heat. Then you shiver. Later you die. Your body can't function at less than its normal temperature. It just stops.

- *Put on a hat.* Did you know that *forty percent* (**40%**) of your body's heat loss is *through your scalp*? This is because it has so many blood vessels near the surface of the skin. If you cover your head, you cut the heat loss, and the body is able to restore some of the blood flow to your hands and feet. The old Canuck saying is literally true, that "If you put on a hat, your fingers and toes warm up!"

- Carry a *space blanket.* You should have some in each vehicle, one in your backpack, and one in your aircraft carry-on and your "go-bag." These are ultra-lightweight aluminized waterproof, windproof plastic blankets that give warmth like a woollen rug. They work by reflecting heat back onto you, developed from the technology of NASA spacesuits.
  You can get one-time emergency space blankets for $3 to$5, or stronger ones for $10 to $12. They need to be looked after carefully, as they're more fragile than fabrics, but they're light, compact and warm.
  Use them as bivouac or groundsheet, sleep under them, sling them behind you around a fire to reflect heat onto your back. Put them over your tent shiny side *in* for warmth, *out* for cool. I've slept beside my motorcycle in a rain shower under one of these, on the back roads of Montana. *They work.*

- When someone begins showing signs of cold, watch each other carefully. Slurred speech, lack of coordination, stumbling, and confusion of mind are sure signs. *Get heat into them.* The first thing is to wrap them in a (space) blanket *right now*, over wet clothing and all. Get them down out of the wind, and then get them dry.

- Mildly hot sweet juices are great (a bit above body temperature but not too much.) Best to avoid coffee, until they're feeling a bit better, and *definitely no alcohol.* Alcohol may give a warm feeling, but it *drastically* reduces the body's ability to survive cold.

- If you can get them indoors, a tub of hot water will help. Not too hot, just a bit above body temperature. Don't let the tub cool down. Dry them off, feed them hot juice, hot chocolate or other sweet drink, and put them in bed or in front of a fire.

- In an isolated place, caught in a storm, lost in the dark, or stranded in a blizzard, heat can be difficult to come by. *Start a fire* with your fire-starter cubes and your waterproof matches, or your roadside flares. Strip the person to their underwear and put them inside two sleeping bags, one inside the other, with a hat on. Lay the person on top of a space blanket and wrap the whole mess in another one.

- A warm person should also strip and climb in with them. Skin to skin contact is often the only way to get heat into the person when you're stranded or lost. Ladies, no bra – the breasts are one of the best sources of heat, since they also have many blood vessels near the surface. It's that or risk losing this person. *Time is precious*, and so is every little bit of heat. Everybody wear a hat.

- Once they can eat, see if they can handle an Access Bar (see page 157).

- **Once the stumbling and slurred speech begin, *Death May Be Only an Hour or Two Away.***

If the core body temperature drops too far, the body is unable to get it back up, and without your prompt assistance, your friend just quietly dies.

## The Edmonton Tornado (Canada) 1987

When The Tornado hit our city on Black Friday, July 31, 1987, it killed 25 people that day, and two more died in hospital. It injured 300, destroyed $300 million in property, and left 750 families homeless, all in just 30 minutes. In the Evergreen Mobile Home Park it killed 15, and smashed 200 out of 600 trailers. 91 trailers disintegrated beyond recognition.

Eighteen-year-old Kelly Pancel was killed with her body protecting her four-week-old daughter Meagan. Her husband Louis says "She gave her life for our child." Mark Ernewein found only a ghetto-blaster and an "I Love Edmonton" sticker where his trailer had been.

No one expected a tornado that day.

- We had a week of temperatures above 30° C (90° F) with 90 – 95% humidity. We all know *now* that this means tornado danger.

- In those days in Alberta, tornado warnings were not broadcast on radio and TV stations until an actual touchdown was sighted. Government policy was that we shouldn't react to funnel clouds for fear of causing a panic. As a result, by the time warnings went out it was too late. Nowadays, we hear tornado alerts several times a summer in Alberta.

  **Right now we have a Y2k alert. Is it also coming too late? I hope not.**

- I had problems calling into Edmonton to check on friends and relatives, and out of Alberta to call my father in Hawaii. This shows what's likely to happen to the phone system in a crisis. So does my friend Ravi's call home after the LA quake. But Y2k will hit not just one city, province or state. It'll hit *everybody*, everywhere, all on the same day. And right on the busiest long-distance night of the century. So if things start falling apart, we'll have the worst load on the phone system *ever*. Even if the computers and chips in the phone system are still working, and we know there's no guarantee of that.

- After the tornado had bulldozed industrial areas and the trailer park, the emergency services began work. Edmonton has a well-developed disaster plan, which got some serious testing and tuning that day. More than 100 fire trucks and 30 ambulances still weren't enough. There were several thousand volunteers, and a thousand or so trained soldiers from the local army base.

  There aren't enough trained firefighters, paramedics and police. Part of the Y2k planning for all governments must be to train more emergency professionals. The military forces in every country should be focusing on first-aid, rescue and disaster training for their soldiers over the next year or so. In addition, they need to make the same training freely available to civilian volunteers.

  I have not read of any such government training programs as yet. Hopefully *Operation Abacus* may identify and partly fill this need for us here in Canada. This kind of training would be a good idea even if there's no disaster on Y2k.

- Emergency communications will be the key to keeping order. Hams, CB clubs and any other such volunteers must be ready. City, state, provincial and federal disaster agencies need to spend time, energy – and, yes, *money* – making sure that both official and volunteer communications are equipped and ready to go. Equipped with gear that will work, of course. Old and low-tech, or brand new and guaranteed.

## The Baguio Earthquake (Philippines) 1990

In the three days following the Richter 7.9 Baguio earthquake in the Philippines, much of the rescue work was done by American soldiers and airmen. The US then had several bases in the Philippines. We saw one ambulance and three fire trucks in the three days we were stranded there. I'm sure there were more. But not like we were used to at home in Canada.

The AM radio stations were calling to some mines 30km (20 mi) away in the mountains. The mines had heavy equipment, rescue equipment, and trained rescue workers. But there was no disaster plan or emergency communication system.

I must stress for this comment that I am an outsider, and I'm not part of the politics and feelings of the Filipino people. Nor am I American. As an outsider, it would seem to me that in the long run, it may not have been a good idea to remove the American bases from the Philippines. The events of the Baguio earthquake, and later the Pinatubo eruption, would suggest that these bases were a definite asset.

I'm quite sure that having a large corps of trained and disciplined personnel available on the spot made a difference to the lives and survival of many Filipinos. I'm sure many are living today who couldn't have survived without the American and other soldiers.

This is not to play down the efforts of the Philippine armed forces, police and volunteers. It just seems a pity they'll have to handle the next one without all those trained helpers, and the expensive equipment they had with them. All available for free.

It'll take more effort, hassle, and time getting large quantities of people and equipment sent back in for the next earthquake or volcano. Some will arrive slower, some not at all.

Nina and I spent an entire day in 40° C (104° F) humidity at the San Juan airport in the province of La Union (Lown-yon. "Lown" like "Brown"). We watched Hercs in, choppers out. Most were American, but many other countries sent aircraft, people and supplies.

This was *Day Four*, and it had taken that long for the rescue effort to get into full swing. Mostly this delay happened because of *communications*. The phones were down, the power was out, the one and only airport runway was broken. All three mountain highways into Baguio were out. An entire kilometer had disappeared into the gorge on one of them.

It took three days for the rest of the country to find out just how bad it was in Baguio! And for us to hitchhike out in a chopper chartered by the Japanese NHK network, in return for letting them use our videotape.

- Lack of adequate emergency communications was one of the biggest problems, and threatens to be a problem for Y2k as well.

- The Third World is woefully lacking in disaster awareness, preparedness, personnel, equipment and plans. All of these things cost money, and only in the First World is there anywhere near enough spare money and resources to do a good job of disaster planning. And even here we still have work to do.

- Since, as I've pointed out earlier, the Third World is almost totally unprepared for Y2k, they're likely to be hit with a triple whammy:

    - No communications
    - No disaster plans and few services
    - For many people, total unawareness of impending Y2k doom.

Now that you've seen my thoughts on a few of the things that I've seen, let's look at some that happened to you. Or at least, to some of you.

# Some of You Were There

Many of my readers have already experienced disasters of various kinds. Many of you have survived, sometimes "sadder now, but wiser." I would invite those people who feel they learned something relevant to Y2k survival to drop me an e-mail. I'm at flykiwi@home.com and be sure to include your name so I can give you credit if I tell your story.

Here are a few of these events, with some lessons that I have drawn from each.

## The Watts Riots, Chicago 1965

This was the first really widespread rioting in the US this century. It shocked many. Especially, it was for many the first time they had ever seen looting taking place. The looting and violence were shown on TV around the world, and Americans saw Americans helping themselves to the contents of the stores.

Nowadays, we automatically associate looting with riots, as we saw in Los Angeles more recently. If there are large numbers of hungry people in your country and mine, and all over, we could see a lot of it after Y2k.

## Earthquakes.

My friend Ravi, as we saw earlier, was able to call his wife in the first few seconds. *Then he couldn't get long distance anywhere for 48 hours.* Phone systems can get overloaded. Any crisis sends the usage level skyrocketing.

## Loma Prieta Earthquake, San Francisco 1989

After the October 17, 1989 San Francisco earthquake, we saw on television all around the world how police, firefighters, paramedics, soldiers and volunteers were working. Thousands of them.

Communications were excellent. Disaster services worked well.

At one stage we saw on TV a large crowd watching firemen at work. One fireman began haranguing the people, telling them to go home and fill a bathtub with water. He told them there was no way of knowing how long power and water would be on, and when they might go off, so they should be seeing to the safety of their families.

He was giving good advice.

Then in the days and weeks following, fire departments in towns and counties around San Francisco patrolled all the acreages and rural houses, checking for damage to buildings, water and propane tanks, and for any banks or bridges that might give way.

You can read a full report on this quake at www.eqe.com/publications/lomaprie put up by the US Geological Survey. I quote: " . . . with the 34 fires and more than 500 responses (in the San Francisco area), the department was taxed to its full capabilities. The Marina fire was difficult to contain because mains supplying water to the district burst during the earthquake. *If more fires had been ignited by the earthquake, it would have been difficult for the fire department to contain them.*" (My italics.)

And: " . . . years of planning and drilling enabled police and fire departments to respond quickly and efficiently to what could have been a safety planner's ultimate nightmare – a major earthquake during (both) rush hour *and* the World Series."

Well, Safety Planners, we have a worse one yet coming up! Take the crowd at the Candlestick Park baseball game that day, and replicate it many times around the world. Put half the population of the world all at the same party. Then let loose the disasters.

Here is another list of learnings, to add to those from the Baguio Earthquake:

- Communications will be the key to handling all the things that might go wrong.

- Planning is essential. Disaster plans, backup plans, contingency plans. You must have your own "*Plan B*" in place in case things get out of hand.

- There might still be time to prepare after it begins, but I wouldn't count on it.

- Any large-scale disaster needs thousands of trained, skilled, disciplined personnel. There aren't enough.

- Because Y2k will hit everywhere, we won't be able to bring in people, equipment or any kind of help from outside. There won't be any "outside." They'll all be fighting their own battles with power and phone outages and so on. Auckland and Quebec will have to rely on generators that they already have in place, this time around.

This time we'll all be on our own. If we're not ready, there'll be no one to call. They'll all be too busy to help you and me.

## The L. A. Riots 1992

The Rodney King riots in L.A. are a chilling reminder of how angry people can get. Footage shown on TV depicted passers-by being pulled from their vehicles and beaten, some to death. Reports said the police made a number of tactical errors that only served to make it worse. (See www.citivu.com/ktla/sc-ch1.html )

Next thing we knew, we had a full-scale riot with fires, looting and everything.

For Y2k, we could have a number of factors that could help to cause riots, and worse:

- Humungous crowds at the biggest party ever, mostly drunk.
- Hungry welfare recipients.
- Hungry prison inmates.
- Inner cities with no food or services.
- Third-World cities with no food or services.
- Policing practically nonexistent in inner cities.
- Ideal conditions for terrorist strikes.

If things get bad, expect these riots in city after city. Some at the stroke of midnight, many over the next few hours, days and weeks. Be prepared, however, in case they start *before* Millennium Day. Riots always mean fires, and Molotov cocktails. If there's no water pressure, be prepared for *"Acres of Fire."*

## The Quebec Ice Storm 1997

The *Canadian Tire* chain of hardware stores learned a severe lesson. They have a "no questions asked" full return and refund policy on everything they sell. They got a whole pile of used generators brought in for refund after the ice storm. Nothing wrong with them. Just not needed any more once the power came back on.

This is an example of a well-intentioned policy meeting an unforeseen circumstance. We could have a lot of that happening around Y2k. If Canadian Tire have any sense, they'll suspend that policy temporarily through Y2k. But they must still give a full Y2k warranty, or we buy elsewhere.

Buying elsewhere means buying early enough, while there's still someplace else to buy! If we wait too late until the rush and the shortages begin, we may not have the luxury of being able to say "No thanks" and walk out.

We need to remember that generators also have chips in their ignition and fuel injection, and even in some of their instruments. They're just as susceptible to Y2k failure as cars are. So if you buy a generator for Y2k, make sure either it's old and sure to run, or very new and guaranteed (in writing) to run after Millennium Day.

Hospitals and other essential services will have backup generators. I hope they all start when needed. And I hope you have all your equipment plugged into power bars in case of surges and spikes when the power keeps going on and off.

## The Union Pacific Railroad 1997

We saw on page ? How this is a classic and scary example of the mess a few software problems can cause. And what if it's not just one railroad? *Y2k problems will hit everybody, all at the same time.* We could have several railroads in this kind of trouble, *all at the same time.* And all the others will have problems too. None will escape completely.

This one took three months or more to clean up, and affected thousands of Union Pacific's customers. And multiply every dollar lost by seven. Not only that, but all the effort that went into fixing this mess has taken resources away from their Y2k project. This event has been a good lesson in how much damage a few software problems can cause.

And then we could have a bunch of airlines with problems this size. And bus lines and trucking companies, factories and warehouses, and power plants, and . . , and . . , and . . . **All at the same time!**

## The Auckland Power Outage 1998

Many businesses saved themselves from going bankrupt by moving to the edge of the city, out of the affected area. This option probably won't be available in a Y2k power outage.

In an article published on www.infotech.co.nz Ross Stewart is quoted as saying that the Auckland "fiasco" (his word) highlighted what could happen if the millennium bug brought down a major utility. Which I'm quite certain it will. *At least* one.

He says the six-week power outage in Auckland demonstrated that while an interruption of a few hours is no big deal, a long-term problem affects "power, hospitals, sewage, telecommunications" and so on, and is nothing less than "catastrophic." It also showed "how poorly most companies are prepared for a disaster." The World Trade Center bombing showed us some of that too.

Ross Stewart is a director of Year2000, a Y2k subsidiary of New Zealand consulting firm Wilson White Ltd. He operates the www.year2000.co.nz site, which has had some very interesting comments and news comparing the Auckland outage to Y2k.

Floods and Hurricanes

Watch out for shortages. Every time a hurricane is forecast to hit the U.S. coast, we see the TV pictures of people trying to buy food and supplies at the last minute. I'm always struck by the emptiness of the shelves. Not a good sign if you're still shopping.

No one expected the World Trade Center to blow up when it did, or the 1989 Loma Prieta earthquake in San Francisco to hit in the middle of a World Series baseball game at rush hour. No one was ready. Be ready this time. We know *when* this one will come. We just don't know *how big*.

Get your preparations done *early*. This advice comes to you from the worst procrastinator my wife has ever known. This time I'm acting completely out of character, and getting it done. *"Just do it!"* While hurricanes last only a day or two or three, it can take months to clean up afterwards. So it will with Y2k.

Prepare in advance for a crisis in utilities and supplies, and prepare for the worst. Prepare for the longest duration you think could happen, even though you expect it'll be shorter than that. And plan for a long cleanup. For me, I'm *expecting a month* of isolation, and I'm *preparing for a year*. Your motto must be "Hope for the best, Prepare for the worst."

## Bhopal, India

December 3, 1984, someone let water into a chemical tank at the Union Carbide plant in Bhopal, India. The resulting chemical reaction caused a cloud of toxic chemicals to be released. It drifted over the town, killing 3,800 people and injuring 2720 more.

I think the big lesson from Bhopal is just how drastic a chemical leak can be. And how easily it can happen. Almost four thousand people lost their lives, because of a single leak. It's a credit to the Union Carbide company, and others like them, that such a thing had never happened before, or since. It took an act of employee sabotage, along with the deliberate cover-up by many other employees, for such a horrendous thing to happen.

On Y2k we could be faced with thousands of minor spills and leaks around the world. And at least a few major ones. Check on the companies in your area, especially those located upwind from you. Find out who they are, and what they do, and see if they'll tell you what chemicals they use and which ones they store near your house.

But there's a second and perhaps more ominous lesson to be learned. Bhopal has been described as "the greatest ambulance chase in history." Within days of the tragedy, American lawyers were *flying to India* to sign up claimants. Expect similar things in the U.S. and around the world, as everybody sues everybody else over Y2k problems.

There were 145 million dollars made available voluntarily by Union Carbide for the victims. It's grown to double that, because it's still sitting in an account somewhere. The victims haven't seen a penny of it! Indian government officials seriously impeded all the investigations, and they're still arguing over how to get this money into their own pockets.

Practically no money got to the victims. There's even a report that the Indian government bulldozed a partly-built rehab center when they discovered it was funded by the company! You can check the web sites listed in the Appendix, "To Find Out More."

### Could it happen here?

Peter de Jager reports that one chemical plant manager told him about an embedded chip that *will* fail if it isn't fixed, and would likely cause explosions involving chlorine gas. It's the tip of an iceberg. However many we hear about, there's several times more still hidden.

Downwind of a chemical plant or oil refinery is probably not a good place to live, in the months following Y2k.

# We all saw it on TV

Here are the classic disasters that are now famous. Their names are recognized anywhere. They can all teach us something about being prepared.

### Chernobyl

This is what happens when a reactor comes close to "melt down." It took a lot of assistance from other countries to get the reactor (unsatisfactorily) buried. Right at this moment, the Ukraine is seeking help from the developed nations to re-seal the leaking cement that has encased the Chernobyl reactor for 10 years now.

Tens of thousands died, a hundred thousand lives were ruined by radiation sickness and birth deformities.

For any reactor in trouble over a Y2k problem, there may not be any help from other countries. The U.S. is as worried about its own nuclear power stations as it is about those in the former Soviet Union. Rescue and repair crews may be fully tied up at home, and simply not available the way they were for Chernobyl. And there's 11 more of that model.

*We can't count on outside help* if we have a chemical or nuclear "incident" in Y2k.

### Three Mile Island

This one teaches us not to trust the people to use common sense. When the instruments say there is something wrong, *they must believe the instruments!* Three Mile Island happened in spite of alarms and warning messages. The alarms sounded, and the crew on duty didn't bother checking!

So what if they'd had a zillion false alarms in the past? Even though the boy cries "Wolf!" every night, you risk losing sheep if you ignore him. This is a *nuclear plant*, for God's sake! **Every** *alarm must be checked* **Right Now!**

Crews on duty at nuclear plants, or anywhere else that might give severe problems, need special coaching about *reacting* to alarms and not just ignoring them. A good idea even if there's no Y2k disaster.

## Everest / IMAX/Into Thin Air

Recently we watched a TV documentary entitled "*Into Thin Air*." Nina has since bought the book by Jon Krakauer, which she finished long before I did. The story is about the weekend in May of 1996 when nine people died in bad weather while climbing Mount Everest. One of the many heroes that weekend was a Sherpa called Tenzing, the son of Tenzing Norgay (see below).

The weekend also included setting a world record for the highest-ever helicopter rescue. A daring colonel in the Nepalese Air Force flew a stripped-down chopper way above its operational ceiling, alone, with no crew to assist him. He was able to rescue two severely frostbitten climbers, *one at a time*. Both suffered later amputations, and lived.

I've never done any climbing beyond a one-week beginners' course in the Canadian Rockies, but I've always had a special interest in Everest since Sir Edmund Hilary was a boyhood hero of mine. You'll no doubt remember that he and Tenzing Norgay were the first people ever to reach the summit of Everest. I plan to discuss Hilary in some detail in an upcoming book about the psychology of why people should have heroes.

Another version of the story is depicted in stunning color and sweeping panoramas in the IMAX film "*Everest*." The IMAX team made it to the top a week later, with their huge camera. All they could carry was five minutes' worth of 72-mm film! In fact, on the bad weekend, before they did their own climb, the IMAX crew were instrumental in saving the lives of a number of the injured survivors.

The story of that terrible weekend is at once as inspiring as it is horrifying. There are tales of heroism, of heroes risking their lives, and some dying, to save strangers and friends. There is the story of the New Zealand professional guide Rob Hall, who lay immobilized in the severe cold and thin air, totally unable to save himself, and far beyond the reach of his exhausted friends. He was able to talk by radio and phone patch to his wife in New Zealand, for several hours until he died.

Inspiring tales, to be sure. But do we want to be part of adventures like these during Y2k? I don't think so! For your own sake and that of people who depend on you, do not expose yourself deliberately and unnecessarily to physical danger. There might be plenty of unwanted danger around, so don't go seeking it out.

For Y2k, refrain from climbing, skiing, motorcycling, skydiving, car rallies and races, stunt flying, airplane racing, drag racing, power boat racing, snowmobiling, and anything else with a risk of getting hurt. No polar, mountain or other exploring expeditions over Y2k.

At least until the party is over, and we know how things will be.

If you get hurt after Y2k, there's no knowing what hospitals and other services may or may not be available. And if you get hurt prior to Y2k, you may still be disabled (temporarily, I hope) when things get bad. You and your family may need for you to be able-bodied and healthy if things get really bad at Y2k.

As an experienced skydiver, stockcar driver, motorcyclist, etc., I'm here to tell you don't deliberately put yourself in a position of risk at the Millennium, or early in 2000. Take *special* care if you *must* have surgery or go on expeditions in the first few years after Y2k.

## Piper Alpha Oil Rig Fire (British North Sea)

The Piper Alpha oil rig disaster (www.bbc.co.uk/education/disaster/piper.shtml) in the North Sea was caused by people error. It became a disaster because of lax safety precautions and poor emergency training. This is typical of most oil rigs, petrochemical plants, and other critical industrial sites.

Now, that one wasn't a software failure, but *we're* going to have a *lot* of embedded microchips failing around Y2k. Do you think it likely we might lose an oil rig or two? An airplane or two? Or a nuclear power plant or two?

## Murphy's Law Hits Y2k Project

I saw this story in ComputerWorld magazine in the (northern) fall of 1997. This one company had done their software corrections for Y2k, and set a weekend for a system test.

All the programmers came in Saturday morning, they rolled the clock on the mainframe computer ahead into 2000, and did the tests. Everything went fine, just few details to fix. Sunday night they rolled the clock back, and went home.

Monday morning, they discovered that they had no backups of anything. All their backups had disappeared! Their backup system had an automatic test that deleted anything more than two years old. They quickly ran a new set of backups, and all was OK.

But for a period of 15 hours or so, they were exposed. A building fire or a lightning strike during that time could have lost *the only copy they had* of all their databases. They could have lost *all* their business information. That could easily be bad enough to drive a company out of business.

*Always make extra backups of* everything *before trying* anything*!* This should be outside your regular backup procedures, and not subject to any automatic deletions, etc. ·Do this also before you start playing around with dates on your PC. Don't trust anything or anybody, especially when they give glib assurances like "Sure, no need to back up. It'll work just fine!" Famous last words.

Be careful when putting fake dates into a computer. Something else that can happen is that you might trigger a "*software license bomb.*" This is a piece added into the software, to make it "bomb" and stop working after a certain date.

You'll often find these in "free trial" software that can be downloaded from the Internet, and is not supposed to be a permanent copy. You're supposed to *buy* it sometime, though many people just use it until it bombs, and then download it again.

These are also found in software that you buy with a time-limited license, and you have to buy a renewal by a certain date. If rolling the clock forward detonates the bomb in this case, you'll have some explaining to do to the vendor. Either way it's a hassle.

There are a lot of details to watch for, and it helps to learn from other people's mistakes. We can also learn a lot from the minds of fiction writers. There have been a number of movies in recent years that can have something to teach us.

## Lessons From the Movies

The movies have given us some fairly realistic and quite convincing scenarios about what happens when the computers don't work.

### Jurassic Park

This movie is such a beautiful example of how *not* to do things that the Computer Security course in my college uses it as a case study! While the story line is perhaps a little far-fetched for the real world, it does illustrate the chaos that could happen when the computers go down.

This is a story about computerized *security systems*. Now extend this from a little island to an entire continent, even with no dinosaurs. We do, by the way, have computer-controlled security systems in our prisons. Hopefully they're fail-safe. Prisoners, tyrannosaurs, raptors – I imagine they're all equally friendly.

And what about the MIS software that prison systems and parole boards use to track when prisoners should be released? Will we end up keeping some in too long? Or, worse still, releasing some who shouldn't be out?

### The Net

In this movie, Sandra Bullock's character finds her identity has been removed from all the databases. Her credit cards are all canceled, she has no passport to get back into the U.S., and somebody else is selling her house! This time the problem is in a series of government and business *MIS systems.* The story tells how she, a programmer herself, copes with all this, and finally destroys the villains who caused it.

Her experience is a scary one. It illustrates just how dependent we are on the multitude of government and other computers for everything, even just to prove who we are. But imagine if something like this happened not just to one unfortunate but very capable woman, but to hundreds of thousands of people *all at the same time.*

## Speed 2

As in The Net, it's again a villain who screws up the programs in this one. But this time, it's *control and navigation systems* that malfunction. While I doubt that we're likely to end up with a cruise ship in the main street of a Caribbean town this time around, we could certainly have collisions or groundings. Keep in mind that even the radar is computerized.

## Alive!

"*Alive!*" is a true story about a South American soccer team stranded in a crashed aircraft in the Andes for two months in the winter. They're rescued only after two of them hike out of the mountains in the spring. It's an inspiring story of heroism, leadership, loss, death, and eventually joy at being rescued. The film also deals with one or two deeper social issues, in particular the legitimacy of cannibalism under desperate survival conditions.

## Post-Nuclear Holocaust Movies

While I don't for one moment suggest we cavort around the post-Apocalyptic Australian outback with the likes of Mad Max and Tina Turner, or even swim along in Waterworld, there are some more serious movies that have treated this topic. Here is a sampling of some that I think can help to raise our awareness.

They show what our world could be like if we lost all the trappings of modern (computerized) civilization. You will note that they were all made in the "Soviet Era," back when there was a Soviet Union. Because of this, the nuclear exchange is always shown as being between the USA and the USSR.

## The Morning After

A made-for-TV movie about the aftermath of a nuclear exchange. Numerous other apocalyptic movies have suggested what might happen when our civilization collapses totally, but I think "*The Morning After*" was one of the most realistic.

## Threads

This is a British movie set in the 1980s. It has very little story, but I think it's devastatingly accurate about the conditions that would follow a sizable nuclear war. In particular, it shows how frightening and dangerous pregnancy and childbirth could be in a world gone awry. And how easily they could happen in such a world.

*Threads* briefly addresses one very difficult moral and ethical issue. It shows looters some months after the holocaust. Caught by soldiers, they're executed on the spot, even though what they were actually doing was foraging for food to stay alive. You be the judge, and hope it never comes to this.

## On the Beach

This is based on the novel by Australian writer, engineer and test-pilot Neville Shute. It tells how World War Three devastates the Northern Hemisphere, leaving Australia, Brazil, New Zealand and South Africa as the only habitable countries. Eventually, however, the fallout spreads there too, and the story is about what people do with the remainder of their lives, knowing they have only a year or so to live.

## IMAX Movies

### Fires of Kuwait

Shows how devastated a landscape can be when it's on fire. It shows how the ingenuity and courage of modern engineers and workers can deal rapidly with a major threat to the world environment. And it shows just how ruthless, self-centered, uncaring, and just plain *evil* men like Saddam Hussein and his ilk can be. Beware these people. They will take advantage of our weaknesses.

### Everest

Also TV documentary *"Into Thin Air,"* (book by Jon Krakauer.) At once a demonstration of human folly, and a celebration of human courage and endurance. Shows graphically what can happen in extreme cold, *when the comforts and facilities of our civilization are not available*. (More on page 102.)

## Software Failures

Just to review, here is the list of software failures we've seen already:

Airline Reservation Systems: The 89/90 Decade Rollover
The 1990 Honda 750 EFI.
The New Zealand Aluminum Smelter
Apollo VII Lands in the Wrong Ocean
Home and Desktop Computers Fail Software Tests
Murphy's Law Hits Y2k Project

### What These Software Failures Teach Us

Now the summary of what we have learned from these:

- Software is complex and unreliable.
- It *always* has bugs.
- Expensive military-style methods can reduce the number of bugs, but not eliminate them
- Programmers sometimes do weird things.
- Most software is *not* fail-safe.
- An error message is *not* an appropriate way for software to fail if it involves human lives or the safety of property.

Beware. Be careful. Be prepared. We have no way of knowing when and where the problems will happen. Some will occur in the months leading up to Y2k, and many will crop up in the months and years following. In the next chapter we'll take a look at some of the possibilities.

# Chapter 6: How, When and Where It Will Happen

We've been looking so far mostly at *what* will happen, and now I'd like for us to think about *when* and *where* these things will take place. We've seen already that Y2k will hit Tonga first and then New Zealand. But how different will its effects be in the different countries around the globe? How much difference will it make if you're rich or poor?

## Problems Begin 1998 and 1999

First, lets talk about *When*. Already Y2k bugs have been showing up, as with the lady who tried to enrol in one of my courses. Her experience shows us that if a software program for any reason looks ahead in time will become vulnerable as soon as it starts looking ahead into the new millennium. We say its "look-ahead horizon" or "event horizon" extends into the year 2000.

As we journey through 1998 and 1999, we'll see more of these incidents. More and bigger. By the time we reach 01/01/2000 they may well have grown from a trickle into a deluge. Each will have to be hunted down by the programmers and fixed.

Except, that is, for the ones where the software is abandoned. Perhaps it's going to be too expensive to fix, so this software becomes a victim of the triage process. Perhaps there isn't time to fix it before Y2k. Or there's no programmers available. Or (d) All of the above!

As we approach the millennium, we can expect there'll be an increasing number of companies going out of business because of Y2k bugs. Some will hit a major bug and will declare bankruptcy because there isn't enough time, money or programmers to fix it, and the business can't run without it.

Other companies will die because a Y2k bug does too much damage to their databases, and the data can't be recovered, or there's not enough time, money or programmers. Still others will lose their databases entirely, and go under because nobody pays them what's owed to them.

And a few others will literally give away (or throw away) their stock or their assets or their money because of a Y2k bug, and never be able to get it back.

More and more of these incidents will be reported as we approach Y2k.

## Levels of Damage

It's difficult to estimate how much damage there'll be, since no one knows exactly what will and will not go wrong. Any physical damage will likely be more limited than a hurricane or tornado, but will be spread over a much wider area. Like the entire planet. Y2k will happen to everybody, everywhere, *all at the same time.*

But business damage is another thing entirely. I believe that most of the pundits are being too conservative, with the possible exception of Gary North (www.garynorth.com ). I can see just too many things that *could* go wrong, and I can't see how we can escape without having a whole bunch of them go wrong. A small percent of a small percent is still a large number.

I believe we'll have a serious recession as a minimum, and a full-blown depression is most likely. Much like the 1930s. Maybe worse, maybe not as bad. But *bad.*

### No Outside Help!

As we said before,

# Who Ya Gonna Call?

This is one of the worst and most terrifying features of Y2k.

Y2k will hit us all at the same time. The rest of the world will be far too busy to help you and me. There'll be nowhere to fly in generators from, like they did in Auckland. There'll be no one to send UN troops. Canada will have all its peacekeepers fully employed keeping the peace in Canada.

In the Loma Prieta earthquake in San Francisco, the fire department was just able to handle all the fires. If it had been any worse, they'd have needed help from the military and from surrounding municipalities. If the fires get out of hand on Y2k, or anything else does for that matter, *there won't be any outside help available.*

And don't forget the emergency crews will also be called upon to get people out of stranded elevators. Broken security systems could trap people inside buildings, or even bank vaults. And some of this could be happening in burning buildings.

Stay out of elevators, and don't trust any kind of automatic door you can't climb over, for the first few days of Y2k. The firefighters, police and paramedics will be stretched too thin. They'll be totally overloaded, none of their equipment will work, and they'll all want to stay home to protect their families. We could have *"Acres of Fire."*

*There'll be* **no one** *to call, that's who!*

We must all plan on being totally self-sufficient through whatever crisis that may occur.

## Culture, Economics and Geography

In the different nations of the world, we can expect the effects of Y2k to vary somewhat. This will depend on the culture, the climate, and the wealth. Let's take a look at how these differences will affect four groups.

We'll look at these four groups in Third World nations, and the same four groups again in the developed nations:

- Urban Rich and Poor.
- Rural Rich and Poor.

### The Third World

Although these countries are much less dependent on computers than the rich nations, they have two major problems to face:

- The computers they're using are older, and in many cases the vendors are no longer supporting them. The IBM SAFE product used by so many Asian banks is a good example of this. IBM years ago stopped supporting both the SAFE software and the computers it runs on.

  The same is true of computers and embedded microchips in Third-World electric power and telephone industries. Much of the equipment used by these industries is very old, and uses very few chips, if any. Most of that equipment will be safe from Y2k. But they have a lot of stuff that was acquired second-hand from First-World countries, with a lot of computer chips in it. This equipment is very much at risk!

- Governments and businesses in Third-World countries are seriously, and perhaps tragically, unaware of Y2k. With a few notable exceptions, the vast majority of all their software *will not* be converted. MIS software, air traffic control, banking, electricity and telecommunications, to name but a few, are terribly at risk in South America and all of Asia. And Eastern Europe is not doing any better, either.

### Rural and Urban

Third-World cities will not be fun places if things go bad on Y2k. When utilities and food distribution chains fail, hordes of hungry people will be competing for very limited quantities of food. Since many of them are already living on the edge of starvation, *many will starve*. Large numbers of dead in crowded conditions will mean epidemics, and these are people who don't have access to basic medical care even in good times.

Cities like Cairo, Manila, New Delhi and Buenos Aires concentrate millions of people in a small area. Each of these cities is 16 to 18 million, and around the world there are a dozen more the same size. And in cities like these, more than 70% of the population lives below the poverty line. *Their own* poverty line, that is. Not what we in the wealthy nations think of as poverty.

Life in the poorer parts of such cities can be a violent business, as it can be in parts of some First-World cities too. When Y2k disrupts the small amount of policing we do have, we can expect serious crime and violence. More bodies, more orphans, more epidemics.

The rural areas of the Third World are different. They tend to be subsistence farming (i.e., peasant farmers). They grow food mostly for their own needs. These farmers sell for cash only a portion of what they produce.

They don't have power and phones anything like we do. Even their urban cousins in third-world cities use more technology than these people. They're much less dependent on technology than we are, and so they're less vulnerable to Y2k.

They could still be affected by a worldwide depression, however. But *how much* it will affect them depends on their use of cash markets, and how much they export, and so on. If they get most of what they need from trade with local people and businesses, and they can feed themselves, a world depression will have very little effect.

When Nina and I were in the Cook Islands, we were talking to the locals about standard of living, unemployment, and so on. "Unemployment!" they laughed. "Breakfast is on a tree, and lunch is in the lagoon! A little cash from the tourists, and that's all we need."

These people should be in great shape to weather a depression, or any other Y2k problems. Even if there's no tourists for a while. It also helps being so far away from the inner cities of the First, Second and Third Worlds. But if large numbers of Y2k tourists from the First World are stranded on these islands, they could become a severe drain on their resources.

The more they depend on exporting products to places outside their own town or province, the more they stand to be hurt by world economic upheaval. And there's no one to call for help. The wealthy nations will be busy at home, perhaps just trying to stay alive, perhaps trying to get their money out of the bank.

It would seem that people in the Third World will be better able to weather the Y2k storm in rural areas, growing most of their own food. They'll still need to stock up ahead on things that can only be had for money, even though that will be more of a struggle than in rich nations. Even for us it's difficult enough!

## Rich and Poor

In the poorer nations of the world, the rich few do lead a soft life. My wife Nina has at times expressed that she feels some discomfort when she visits rich friends in the Philippines. In Canada, we are certainly well off, but we in the middle class are not used to having uniformed maids serving every meal, or uniformed nannies and driver-bodyguards taking kids to school.

It's difficult to say what effect a serious Y2k crisis might have on the lifestyle of these people. In rural areas, no doubt some of these people will turn their farms and haciendas into safe refuge for employees and neighbors. Such people will be leaders in the survival effort, directing preparations for the feeding and safety of a large number of people.

Even though it's unlikely that they will have prepared in advance, many will manage since much of the food will come from their own land. Those among them who are capable of caring and effective leadership could save a lot of lives this way.

In the cities, however, the rich are more likely to find themselves struggling amongst the masses for nonexistent food supplies. Their riches may be of little help when a crisis hits the overcrowded cities. We saw in the movie *Titanic* how useless cash can be at a time when only survival counts.

And the poor in the cities will fare just as badly, or in many cases worse. If the food-supply chains to Third-World cities fail, *everyone* will starve, rich and poor alike. Watch for mass exodus of hungry people to nearby farmland.

Both rich and poor will fare better in the countryside. Whatever level of crisis we end up with, whether it's a brief interruption to food supplies or a long one, the people on the farms will have more to eat than their city cousins.

Mind you, if it gets really bad, they'll need to be prepared for a mass migration out of the cities. Those nearer the major cities could have a real problem with this. And remember that hungry people do a lot of unusual and sometimes violent things. Like locusts, they may devour everything in their path.

## Developed Nations

In the richer countries we depend much more on the complex systems and chains that make our society function. Utilities, delivery supply chains, food supply chains, any or all could fail and leave us stranded.

Mail, banking and finance, government operations, government funding and revenue collection, all these systems are needed if our society is to continue to function the way we're used to. And they're all heavily computerized.

## Rural and Urban

As in the poor countries, the countryside will probably be a better place to survive Y2k than the cities. There's more chance to grow food, and less chance of violence. If things get bad, we too may see a mass exodus from the cities, so those in the suburbs or on acreages near major cities need to be careful, alert and prepared.

Also, those in high-class residential neighborhoods will need to watch out in case mobs or riots overflow from poorer areas. You need to think about defense, or about how and where to hide or take refuge. *Now* is the time to do a little thinking about these things, not when the mob is approaching your door.

## Rich and Poor

Wealthy people have the resources to spare, so they can afford to buy extra food, and make various other preparations. But only 1% of them will bother doing anything to prepare.

Unlike Third-World countries, the rich in the First World have relatively few domestic help. They're more used to doing at least some things for themselves. Hopefully, this might tend to make them a little more self-reliant in an extreme crisis. But in a fight for food, they're just people like the rest of us. Like us, they too can starve, or be trampled in a riot.

Poor people in the rich nations will be hit almost as hard by Y2k as their cousins in Cairo, Manila and New Delhi. Food chains and supply chains may be a little more reliable, but where they do break down there could be trouble. What's different with the poor in the rich nations is that many live on welfare, unemployment or other government money.

People who are used to having the government supply them with food and money are going to feel hard-hit and angry when food and other services cease. They'll be both hungry *and* angry. A double-edged sword.

Some of these troubles will occur in the days and weeks and months following 01/01/2000. Others will happen right on the dot of midnight. But midnight will be on the move, marching relentlessly around the planet over a 24-hour period.

# Time Zones

Twelve midnight, and the first second of the first day of year 2000, will happen initially in Tonga, (pronounced with a soft 'ng' – the 'ng' is like 'bringing.') They have about 100,000 people, on 700 sq. km (270 sq. mi) of land area. The capital is Nukualofa. They are, somewhat artificially, 13 hours ahead of GMT, the "zero" of time zones.

At about the same time, in the Chatham Islands (*chat*-im) of New Zealand, a similar size population will see the year 2000. Then it's New Zealand with about 3 million people, and a highly-developed, computer-dependent society. Watch them closely!

After that, midnight will progress to Australia, to New Guinea and Japan, Korea, Indonesia, the Philippines, Hong Kong and the rest of Asia. Russia and Europe will be next. Then the Americas will see it, and finally the Galapagos, Easter Island and the other islands of the Eastern Pacific. If there *is* to be a disaster, it'll show up in this sequence.

I suggest you videotape Y2k midnight as it rolls around the planet from Tonga and New Zealand to the rest of us. But do it on your older, non-digital TV, hooked up to a battery. You'll see celebrations (hopefully), or maybe disasters, all over the world.

### See It Up Close (*Not!*)

There seems to be a growing number of "Y2k Tourists" making plans to head for New Zealand and the South Sea islands for Millennium Day. They want to be among the first to enter the new millennium, but of course I'm not so sure that's a good idea.

If you're a tourist on tour, you probably won't be carrying a year's worth of food and batteries with you. If the crisis hits hard, you'll not only be in a difficult position yourself, but you're likely to become a burden on the local support systems, especially if you can't fly home.

Australia, Hawaii and New Zealand are wealthy First-World nations, but the smaller island countries are most likely not well prepared for a crisis. And they don't have the resources to feed and shelter hundreds or thousands of stranded tourists. Such people might end up putting their hosts' survival in jeopardy as well as their own.

There'll be a great view from orbit for any astronaut brave enough to let the computers put her/him up there for the Millennium. Who knows, he or she might get to stay up for the *entire* millennium! But for you and me, there'll be some preparation required.

# Chapter 7: What Should I Do?

## Start Now!!!

Whatever you decide to do about Y2k, there's only one time to get started on it.

## That time is now

However much *you decide* you should prepare, do it *now*. Not just now, but *Right Now*. You and I face the same major problem that programmers face, and government, and businesses big and small:

### The Immovable Deadline!

Y2k, like time and tide, waits for no man. Or woman. It *will* happen at midnight on December 31, 1999, whether we're ready or not. Procrastinate at your peril – perhaps literally. If it gets bad, early preparation might make the difference between survival and possible death.

I'm convinced that there'll be people die because of Y2k. I want it to be as few as possible. The purpose of this book is to make sure *you* survive. And those you love.

### How to Use This Chapter

It's very important that you should use this chapter and the next one carefully. For everything that I recommend here, you must make up your own mind how bad it might be, and how much to prepare. Then you can choose whether to do everything I say, or something less, or maybe more. The decision has to be yours.

And make sure that, as far as possible,

> *Everything you do is something that would be* **a good idea anyway**, *even if there's no big Y2k crisis.*

### Avoid Lineups, Shortages and High Prices

Lineups are mostly just an inconvenience. But of course, if you're running around trying to prepare for Y2k *after* the lineups form, then you're doing it too late anyway. "Better late than never" still applies, but *earlier* is best of all.

You should do all or most of your shopping in the first half of 1999 (or sooner.) For things you need to buy, or to get from government departments or other bureaucracies, get them done before the masses wake up and start panicking. Get things like passports and ID, immigration and citizenship records, school transcripts. Get pension records and such from your employer's HR (Human Remains) department.

Mind you, if you waste major time in lineups, and it means you end up not properly ready, then they're more than just an inconvenience. Like so much of this Y2k stuff, if things get really bad, even lineups might turn out to be fatal for a few.

## High Prices

High prices just push up the monetary price of survival, or at least the price of comfortable survival. As we approach Y2k, you can expect an increasing number of software errors in the news. Each news story will push a few more people to begin taking all this stuff seriously. As more people hit the stores looking for food and supplies, *up will go the prices*.

And at the same time, down will go the selection.

## Shortages

These could get serious. Get what you need *while it's still available*. Doing without could be very uncomfortable.

We've all seen the news shots on our (computerized) worldwide TV networks, showing people in the path of a hurricane. With those marvelous (computerized) modern weather forecasts, we know very precisely when and where a storm will hit. And we see shots of people shopping, and stores running out of food staples, coal-oil lanterns, batteries, and so on. Expect to see all this and more as Y2k looms near. All over the world. *Everywhere*.

But don't go hog wild. Get only the kind of stuff that would be a good idea anyway.

# Do What Would Be a Good Idea Anyway

Kind of a strange thing to say, isn't it? It works this way. We don't know just how bad this all might turn out to be. I sincerely hope that I'm way off base here, and I hope Y2k ends up being no big deal. I don't think so, but I hope so.

So everything you do to prepare for Y2k should be something that's a good idea anyway. Even if there's no disaster, and no panic. Everyone should have a fire extinguisher in the kitchen and another in the garage, anyway. A stash of food in storage is a good idea anytime, especially if it gets you buying at bulk prices.

Even things like a large stash of food, or a huge pile of firewood, can be used up over time if Y2k doesn't need them. Extra supplies of life-preserving drugs are always handy, but watch expiry dates, and make sure you use them up in order. Watch food expiry dates.

A course in first-aid or bicycle maintenance, bush survival or disaster preparedness, is never wasted, especially if it was something you had always thought of doing but never got around to. These are the key points. If you have a bunch of "that-would-be-a-nice-idea-someday" activities that you dream of doing, now is the time to turn them into reality.

Right now, with a year (or hopefully a little more) still to go, you should be getting all these "nice idea" plans under way. Call up and book yourself and a friend for a course in something, and *"Just Do It!"*

Been thinking about extra insulation in your house? Now would be an excellent time for that, in case the power goes off. And if the power never goes off, you'll have the extra comfort and reduced heating bill that you were planning on.

It's important that you apply this principle to *everything* you do for Y2k. Everything you do should be a good idea *even if there's no crisis*. And if you do a few things that are *solely* because of Y2k, then that's OK too. Just make sure they're not too expensive, whatever they are. And be prepared to take responsibility for that decision, if in your own estimation you think those things were absolutely necessary.

And now my "ulterior" motive! I'll be quite honest with you. If all this blows over without much hassle, I'd like to think that maybe I helped improve your life a little by prodding you into buying a fire extinguisher or two, and taking a couple of courses you had never got around to.

If Y2k is nothing much, and I become "the boy who cried 'wolf!'" I'll be embarrassed, but happy. If on the other hand it's as serious as I'm predicting, I'll be greatly saddened. But I'll feel better if my efforts have caused you and a few others to be better prepared, and able to make it through with a little less hassle.

Now let's talk about more specific things you need to do, beginning with whether you'll need to work on Millennium Day.

## Your Job

If your line of work is one of those often called "essential," then you can expect to be needed on, before, after and around Millennium Day. Doctors, nurses and hospital staff are used to this. Police, firefighters and paramedics do it routinely also. We'll need all those.

The military are quite used to being given odd orders at odd times. We need them too.

Then we'll need people who keep things running when we're asleep. Bus drivers, train drivers, cabbies and all those who work in some kind of transportation. City workers, tow truck drivers, snowplow drivers too.

And we'll need the people who keep all our systems going. We'll need engineers and maintenance crews from the water department, power company, gas company, phone company and cable TV company. Even if Y2k is "not too serious," these guys will have a lot of work to do that night.

If your job is in this list, or you think maybe it should be, please make all the arrangements well in advance. Start now talking to your employer about the personpower needed for that weekend and the period following.

Prod them into making contingency plans for getting people to work, especially if extras might be needed and transportation systems might be out. Make sure rosters are drawn up and people told what's expected. And make sure your employer has read this book and understands the seriousness of the problem.

## Fix Your Own Computer

You'll need to run a check on your own PC or Mac, if you have one. If not, skip to the bit about "Get A Job."

First thing is: Backups, Backups, Backups! You absolutely **must back up** *everything* that matters before you start. It's best if you can do your entire hard disk, but you must at least do all your documents, spreadsheets, and databases. And don't forget your e-mail. Netscape keeps it in its own directory, so you'll need to find it and add it to the backup list.

Don't trust anything or anybody. *Back it up.* Believe me.

### Business Data

Backups, Backups, Backups. Business data should always be backed up in three, or better five, generations, and one of them stored "off-site" in another building. Check that your system administrator has this properly set up.

Then you can try the tests.

### Test Everything:

August 21 and 22, 1999 (Especially for GPS-related software.)

Before the Millennium
After the Millennium
February 29 and March 1ˢᵗ, 2000
January 1ˢᵗ, 2001

If you have any GPS equipment, contact the maker and get assurance of Y2k compliance.

Set the clock on your PC to 11:59pm on December 31, 1999. Wait 2 minutes. Check the time again. Even if the date and time are correct at 12:01 a.m. January 1, 2000, there's more to check. Shut down your Windows 95 or 98, and choose "Restart the computer." When it reboots, check the date and time.

Some machines work just fine. But most 486 PCs and many Pentiums reboot to the date of January 1, 1980, the birthdate of DOS. You can reset it each time you reboot, and it'll work OK. But it'll always go back to that date every time you reboot. However, there are software products out there now that can be used to work around this problem. Or you may just have to reset the date every time.

You can find more about testing and fixing your PC in any good book from your local computer bookstore. Don't hesitate to ask a knowledgeable friend for help in either doing it, or finding the right person to do it.

For a small business computer where time is money, do the research and find someone trustworthy and experienced at Y2k to do the testing and fixing. Pay a little more now, and save a bundle later.

And don't forget to back up *everything* before *anyone* does *anything*!

## Get A Job

If you've been thinking of a career change, or you're entering or re-entering the job market, here's a suggestion. If being a programmer appeals, now is the time to go for it. The market for programmers is heating up drastically already, and there's more coming. For all kinds of computer professionals, the demand will skyrocket in 1999.

There may not be time for a full degree in computers before Y2k, but there are short-term training programs out there. Talk to your community college or technical school. Plan on getting some short, intensive training, and *continue with part-time schooling* for a full degree or diploma once you're employed.

Remember that after Millennium Day, programmers will be going flat out fixing all the problems that were missed, and all the software that was put aside until later in the triage process. And then there'll be all the projects that were postponed in favor of the Y2k project! By 2001 or so, those ones will really be getting urgent.

Programmers will be in extreme demand for at least a couple of years into the new millennium. I expect there'll be plenty of work for a decade or so, long enough for you to become experienced and valuable. The Yourdons advise that you print numerous copies of your resume *before* things go haywire on The Day.

## Accumulate Some Cash

It may be difficult or impossible to use banks and ATMs during the crisis. You'll need enough cash to live on for the duration of the crisis. That's easy to say, but for most of us it won't be easy to do. In March of 1933, the U.S. government closed all banks in the country for 10 days. Any government in the world could conceivably pull this or a similar stunt if they wished. Be prepared.

What if your job or pension disappears for a month or three? Or for a year? Could you survive? Even if your job is still OK, there's always a chance they may not be able to produce paychecks. Especially if they try to pay you by electronic bank transfer.

Since most families live more or less from paycheck to paycheck, this could be extremely difficult. Even in the developed nations about one quarter of the population have no savings, and no liquid assets. In the poorer nations, this is like 95% with no liquid assets.

If you think the crisis will last just a few days, well OK, anyone with a steady job can manage enough cash to see them through that. If we don't have the cash on hand, we just run up the credit cards and the overdraft a bit. But if like me you think it'll last a month or more, possibly a year, that's a different story altogether. Even if it becomes impossible to put aside enough, you must still do what you can.

Short-term borrowing on lines of credit or credit cards very likely won't work. Don't count on them. Bank machines (ATMs) might be down, banks closed, and all those high-tech money sources could dry up for a while. Or perhaps for good.

Cash is the only thing you can rely on through the crisis. Later, under "Investments" we'll discuss using gold and silver bullion coins as an investment hedge. If needed, these coins can be used for spending as cash also. At their investment value, not their face value!

The big thing is, *start now!* This means setting some money aside each month, every month, from now until Y2k. *Do it!* Decide what you can put aside, and deposit that amount to a special savings account every month without fail. *Just do it!*

I realize this means that you're putting aside money at the same time you're spending extra each month on food and supplies to stack in the basement. I won't pretend this is easy. But if it gets bad, every little bit of preparation will make a difference. And if it doesn't get bad, you'll have a nice little nest-egg to spend on a family treat, or put in a retirement fund..

Sometime late in 1999, but not too late, you'll need to take that money out of the bank and keep it in a safe place. Or you might choose not to put it in the bank at all, if you don't feel you can trust the bank to stay open long enough. We should all have at least one month's living expenses in cold, hard cash, kept in a safe place in the house. Three months worth would be even better, of course, but more difficult to arrange.

If you can pull some or all of your cash reserve out of the bank, and put it away in a *safe* place, that will protect you against possible early runs on the banks. Count the small amount of lost interest as an insurance premium. If there's no crisis, put it all back in the bank in February 2000, and you haven't lost much.

Be careful, though. A run on your bank could happen sometime in 1999 if enough people around the world take notice, and start to panic. Or it could happen as late as 2001.

But make sure that safe place really *is* safe. It would be heartbreaking to lose it all just before you need it. A month or three in cash and a year or so in savings accounts spread over several banks might be a good compromise.

## Investments

Probably the best advice I can give you is *see your financial adviser*. But find one that cares about Y2k! If you already have one you trust, feel free to buy her a copy of this book.

I'm not qualified to advise on investments. You'll find here a few ideas and suggestions. They have come from a variety of inspired and trustworthy sources, but don't do anything without advice from a trusted, qualified adviser. Take these ideas to your financial adviser, and the two of you make the decisions, after reviewing what I have to say.

First thing I have to say is to quote Baron Meyer Rothschild, who knew about Napoleon's defeat at the Battle of Waterloo hours before anybody else. He went on to the floor of the London stock exchange, and *sold* everything. Everybody panicked, and they all sold everything too, thinking Napoleon had won! The market *crashed*.

Two hours later, he quietly bought it all back again, plus a whole lot more, for "pennies on the pound." Then the official news arrived, of Napoleon's defeat, that the British Duke of Wellington had won, *and they all bought*. The market went way back up, and Rothschild became the wealthiest man in England.

Obviously, this happened last century, before computerized satellite communications networks. He didn't get to watch the war in real time as we all watched Baghdad.

His words of advice have been adopted by John Davidson and Lord William Rees-Mogg as the title of their first book. He says you should buy when "blood is running in the streets!" (See "*Blood in the Streets,*" in the Appendix, "To Find Out More.")

There could be much blood in the streets of the world around Y2k, financially, and perhaps literally. As with any crisis, misfortune, war or disaster, there'll be a lot of people lose a lot of money. And there'll be opportunities for some to make money, perhaps a little, perhaps a lot. Which group do you want to be in?

Be careful! Be guided by your *financial adviser.*

The first piece of advice, then, is to *see your financial adviser*. Trusted and trustworthy; choose carefully.

The second piece of advice is to get Tony Keyes' book "*The Year 2000 Computer Crisis, An Investor's Survival Guide.*" He has a more in-depth approach, suitable for the layman and casual investor as well as for the seasoned professional. Those who wish to protect their retirement investments will do well to read it, then consult their own adviser.

Here are my comments, some drawn from Keyes' ideas, some of my own, and some from Davidson and Rees-Mogg in their other book "*The Great Reckoning.*" They have an investment newsletter called "*Strategic Investment,*" which I think is well worth reading for its commentary on the world economy. Even if your only investments are in your retirement plan and your pension.

## Stock Market and Mutual Funds

If you have much of your money in the stock market, even indirectly through pensions or mutual funds, there are a number of questions you may want to ask. These are questions you should ask at shareholders meetings, or by mail. Ask directly of the managers of the companies you hold stock in, and ask the investment managers of your mutual funds or pension fund.

You need to know specifically what they're doing, and how much they have done, and *how much is still to be done.* How many programmers (and what percentage of the total programming staff) are working on the Y2k problem?

How many lines of program code do they have to scan and convert? How many have been done? How many will be victims of triage, and scrapped instead of converted? How many will be triaged into 2000 and 2001, to be repaired after the crisis instead of before?

Do they have contingency plans so they can operate without the delayed software fixes?

The answers to these questions are important in planning your investments. Try to stay away from companies you think might be heading for Y2k troubles.

## Protecting Your Retirement Savings

First of all, don't go overboard moving money around! Check whether your plan allows you to move it from fund to fund for free, otherwise you must factor that cost into your decisions.

There are two main areas you should put a fairly large proportion of your money into, and they are *Precious Metals* (gold and silver bullion coins, *not* mining stocks, and **take delivery of the coins**), and *Cash Equivalents* (T-bills and Money-Market funds). Government T-bill bonds and money-market bond funds will go up as the stock market falls, but you *don't* want corporate or municipal bonds. Companies and cities may go broke.

You want *Federal* T-bill funds, and hope that the U.S. and Canada don't go broke. If that happened, nothing would be safe anyway. State and provincial bonds are not as safe as federal, but should be OK.

Gold and silver have always been the twin hedges against crises. It's not easy to work them into a retirement plan, so you may have to buy coins with your savings money.

I've moved a small amount of retirement money into precious metals funds, because those haven't been star performers in recent years, but I'm expecting them to react a little to Y2k.

The plan is that once the stock markets have fallen, they'll always come back up in the long term. That might be months, or it might be a year or a decade. Whenever it is, my investment adviser and I will be watching. We'll move my money back into equity (stock market) funds, and leave it there for 5 or 10 years as the markets recover.

These moves will be within a family of funds, and most such families allow you to do this with no penalties. In fact, the fund managers will welcome it, because we'll be putting money back into equity funds just about the time they're ready to snap up bargain stocks.

## Other Investments

If you have any other money to invest, I believe the best place for it is precious metals. The actual metals themselves, not stocks or mutual funds. Gold and silver bullion coin are the best for the small investor. Silver can give a larger rise than gold, but gold tends to be more reliable. So get some of each.

Also you should have some money in "cash-equivalents." These are highly liquid invest-ments, such as T-bills. But since a T-bill costs a minimum of $25,000 (or so, depending on the country), we will have to use T-bill mutual funds, as we did for our retirement money. An equal amount should also go into money-market funds.

And then you will need that cache of hard cash. As to the amounts for all these, I suggest that you and your financial adviser decide first how much you will pull out of your stocks and other investments. Then take that amount, and start by considering 25% of it in each category:

- Cash
- T-bill funds
- Money-market funds
- Gold and silver bullion coins (in your possession.)

The coins should probably be about half gold and half silver.

Use this breakdown as a starting-point, and then you and your adviser should ad-just these proportions whatever way you decide is appropriate.

Both Keyes' book, and *"The Great Reckoning"*, discuss exactly which coins to buy, and give names and addresses of dealers they recommend.

## Take Possession of the Coins

Don't let the dealer or your adviser talk you out of this one. *Take possession of the coins*. They're no good locked in some bank vault, and the only record that they're yours is *in a computer*! Possession, in this case, is all *ten* points of the law. Even the legendary Swiss and Liechtenstein banks will have Y2k problems, just like the rest of us.

## Nationalized Gold

Can you believe that, in the 1930s, the U.S. Government, bastion of freedom and capi-talism, *nationalized* gold? For about 15 years or so, it became *illegal* for U.S. citizens to own gold. Can you believe that? And what's to stop them or any other government doing it again?

*Don't leave it where they can find it!* Keep your bullion coins well hidden from the tax man, and make sure there's no paper trail to tell the government that you have them. Davidson and Rees-Mogg have quite a bit to say about this in *"The Great Reckoning."*

You may need to make an arrangement with the coin vendor that he will keep no record of your name or identity, so the tax man has no way of knowing you have the coins. You may wish to check with your lawyer (verbally, not on paper), but I think you'll find in most countries this is perfectly legal. You can sell candies and groceries for cash with no record of who the buyer is, so why not coins?

But be careful about finding a safe place. Under the mattress won't do. Nor will safety deposit boxes. Most banks if they close down on Y2k will reopen after a "short" while. Some won't. Don't trust them to be there when you need to get to your safety-deposit box.

Be sure and have some of the gold and silver in small-denomination coins. In a bad crisis you may have to actually spend them. Of course, you'll do this at the going rate for the weight of metal, not the face value of the coins. Silver coins are generally better for this because they're smaller in value.

Don't buy Bre-X, or anything like it. I would advise leaving the mines and stuff to your investment-fund managers, in the precious metal funds. That is, unless you enjoy speculating in the market, and you can afford to lose that part of your fortune. In that case, for you Y2k is going to be *fun!*

Even cash will be an investment. *If* things get really bad, people will be selling every-thing at fire-sale prices (perhaps literally). Those with cash in hand will be able to pick up bargains. Maybe cars and trucks, houses, businesses, furniture, books. Certainly stocks.

Davidson and Rees-Mogg predict, and for very good reason, that if we have a de-pression it will be deflationary. This is unlike Argentina and Brazil,who had runaway inflation at about 500% a few years ago. In a deflationary economy, cash will be king, and debts will kill you. (See *"The Great Reckoning."*)

However long it takes for the stock markets to reopen and stabilize, there'll be solid stocks available at rock-bottom prices, at least for a while. Diversify, since some of them won't make it. But some will, dramatically.

Fortunes were made after the 1929 crash. Look at the Kennedys. Joseph Kennedy put his son Jack in the White House on money made by selling out just before, and buying again after, the 1929 crash. There was a now-famous schoolteacher in the 1930s, who each month spent her salary on General Motors shares, and later became a million-aire (back when a million was still worth something.)

## Beware Too-Good-To-Be-True Schemes

Above all, watch out for the people who offer a fabulous way to cash in on Y2k, whether it be stocks, or any other scheme. Remember the most basic adage of investing: *If it looks too good to be true, then for sure it* **is.**

Get to know a reliable stockbroker and an investment adviser before Y2k. When the crunch comes, listen to their advice. You'll buy some good stocks, and expect to buy a few bad ones. That's normal. But stay away from Get Rich Quick schemes.

In the panic before Y2k, and the mess after, there'll be opportunists out to separate the unwary from their hard-earned cash. You must be as diligent about the quality of investments as you ever were. Don't get caught up in fire-sale fever. Always ask your qualified financial adviser, the one with the proven track record, and who allowed you to talk to all her satisfied clients for references when you began with her.

There could be a lot of such worthless schemes arising *before* Y2k, claiming to protect your money against the Y2k disaster. Read what I have to say in Chapter 8, and the books I recommend there and in the Appendix. Don't trust someone who promises "total safety" for your money, without consulting your financial adviser first. There's no such thing.

But many people will fall prey to these schemes. It's a fact of life and human na-ture. Enough suckers will fall for them to make it well worth while for these predators to do it. Just make sure it's not you or yours. Much money will be lost by a large number of unfortunate investors, adding a little more fuel to the recession.

Perhaps the most repellent side to this issue is that they'll go after the old folk. The elderly are one of the groups most at risk for these schemes, in good times or bad. If you have seniors among your family and friends, brief them about the dangers, either before or after Millennium Day, as you see fit. Warn them not to do anything unusual with their money without checking first with you, or their children, or someone trustworthy.

Also, be cautious about any bank or financial institution that starts advertising loudly in 1999 that they're "totally compliant," and you should be moving all your money and banking to them. They might be "totally compliant," but that may not mean "totally safe."

They're also at risk from the massive ripple effects that could go through the banking systems of the entire world. All the banks in the world are tied together by enormous computerized networks. Any bank that gets into trouble could affect other banks it deals with. No bank anywhere can guarantee to be totally protected.

Third-World banks are less dependent on computers than banks in the richer nations, but are no safer. As we saw earlier, the computers and software they do use are older, not Y2k-compliant, and in many cases not supported by the manufacturer. Much of it cannot or will not be converted. All banks are at risk, *everywhere*.

And remember that anywhere you have assets or debts, you're really no more than just a record in a computer. You'll need to protect yourself there too, by filing your documents.

# File Your Documents

Bank statements, credit card bills, utility bills, mortgage statements, pay stubs, canceled checks, you may need any of these to prove you paid, on time. If some companies you deal with lose or corrupt their computer files, this may be the only way to avoid some expensive problems. And when it comes to paying parking tickets and speeding fines, it could even keep you out of jail.

Insist on paper receipts when paying by credit or debit card. *File them*. Have a special, designated place to put all this paper. It must be somewhere convenient, so you'll remember to drop this stuff in each day. Then you must work to make it a habit *doing* it each day.

A filing cabinet is perfect, but a drawer or a shoebox will do the job. Just make sure it's kept in a place where it'll be easy to get to, and then make sure it's used. A filing system is pretty well useless if there's nothing filed in it! Organizing them is important, but it's less important than *making sure they're collected*.

File at least six months to a year's worth of **everything**.

Keep all your canceled checks. If you don't use a checking account, open one now, right away, and use it for *all* your bills. And keep your canceled checks, bundled by month.

For stocks and certain bonds, you can demand the paper certificates from your broker. He will resist, but you *must* insist. You're entitled to the physical paper certificate, even though most people never bother.

But you're not "most people." You're reading this book, and that's not "most people." And these are not "most times." If your broker says you don't need the physical certificate, you tell her/him that you insist on having it anyway.

This is another "Good Idea Anyway." You should be filing all your bills anyway in case you need to check for an error. I think it would be a great idea to get a file cabinet. If you're an organized sort of person you probably have one already. I'm not, but I do.

You must also check all your bills each month to see that there are no errors. Get in touch with the company promptly to sort out anything that appears wrong. Especially in the last part of December 1999. Any errors you may find this late need to be cleared up promptly *before* Millennium Day.

Here's a less-than-complete list of some of the documents you should have on file. Some, like drivers' licenses, will need to be photocopies:

| | | |
|---|---|---|
| Bills | College transcripts | Insurance policies: vehicles, houses, life |
| Wills | Pension statement | Welfare check stubs or photocopies |
| Passports | School report cards | Divorce Decree and Agreement |
| Contracts | Firearms licences | Vehicle and drivers licenses |
| Citizenship | Canceled checks | Unemployment check stubs |
| Utility bills | Birth certificates | Guarantees and Warranties |
| Scholarships | Marriage licence | Stock and bond certificates |
| Immigration | Adoption papers | Mutual fund statements |
| Naturalization | Bank statements | Certificate of Marriage |
| Paycheck slips | Rent receipts | Financial statements |
| | | Custody agreements |

## Demand Warranties – For Y2k As Well

You'll need to ask for receipts and warranties for all your purchases between now and Y2k. Get warranties that say the product will still work properly in the year 2000, and will not suffer any date-related failures. Do this for all but the most trivial of purchases. Insist on this, it's your legal right. Then make sure you file them all.

When things start failing after Y2k, you're going to need these warranties! Vendors may lose all their computerized records, and the only way you're going to get service is by having the piece of paper right there in your hot little hand. The onus will be on you and me to prove that we bought and paid for it.

Anything you buy between now and the Millennium *must be warrantied to work after Millennium Day.* Really, when you stop and think about it, Y2k is just another software bug. We expect cars to start, and microwave ovens to stop on time. If they don't, it's a problem, and any warranty *should* cover it. But they'll try to get out of it, believe me.

Under any other circumstances, we would expect these things to be fixed regardless of the date. Why should Y2k be any different? (*WhY2k?*) No reason, other than it's the worst problem ever, worse than anything that ever happened before. But it's still just another problem, and warranties must say specifically that they'll fix it for Y2k problems.

## Stick to Your Guns

Expect a lot of argument from some sales people over this one. Many may have been told specifically not to agree to cover Y2k-related problems. Insurance companies are writing clauses into their policies to exclude Y2k. Manufacturers may well do the same with warranty contracts. This won't do.

Insist that it be there. Don't take "No" for an answer. Write it onto the agreement, contract, bill of sale or other document and sign beside it. Then insist that they also sign it *before you pay.* After you pay the money you'll be arguing from a position of weakness. Remember the old saying, "Possession is nine points of the law."

And if the sales person pleads (as they will) that "I don't have the authority to do that," get someone who does. Even if they have to phone at all hours and wake the manager. If they won't, buy elsewhere. It's far too dangerous to buy from a company that won't warranty its product through Y2k.

Once they have your money it's going to be much more difficult to get it back. You must get this all settled *before you hand them the cash,* or let them get hold of your credit card. By all means wave the card or the cash around in front of them, but don't let go of it until they sign.

Be prepared to walk out on them. They'll throw everything at you, fire with both barrels, so to speak. Mr Slick the Salesman, along with Slicker the manager, will have all kinds of reasons why it can't or shouldn't be done. They're good at what they do, these guys. And what they do well is *sell.* They don't have to care *what* they sell, or whether it's any good, they care only that they sell it. Get the warranty.

But right up until the moment you part with your credit card, you have the one good reason why they *should* care. You still have the money. Get the agreement sorted out to *your* satisfaction **before you let them have a penny.** Or leave.

Every salesman knows that if you walk out the door, there's a *90% chance that you won't be back*. And that's in good times. They know they have to sell you *now*. They want to make the sale, *now*. You're in the driver's seat *until you pay*. Demand what *you* want, and don't sign unless you get it. There's always another store just around the corner.

## Insurance

Basically, don't count on your insurance for anything related to Y2k. Many home, auto and life policies are now specifically excluding any claims to do with Y2k. Others figure they already have enough disclaimers and things in their policies to be able to deny Y2k claims.

Besides, if you did have a claim, they could be too busy with their own Y2k problems, or they could be closed down. Insurance companies are among the heaviest computer users.

Read your insurance policies, or have a friend read them. Check just what you might or might not be covered for out of all the calamities I'm predicting in this book.

Keep all your documents, and your canceled premium check.

## Stick with Low-Tech

From here on, try to avoid anything digital. If you can. That's the whole trouble; it's practically impossible to do that! Everything these days is computerized. But the lower the tech, the fewer computer chips involved, and the less the risk of a Y2k failure. But it *could* still happen to anything *digital*.

Analog watches and car dashboards are a good idea. But beware. If the dash on your new car is electronic, it uses computer chips, even if the gauges are displayed as analog.

For emergency radio receivers, get the ones with a sliding pointer for the tuning dial, *not* the digital readout. Sliding scanners are mechanical and therefore reliable. I have a couple of old 2-channel CB radios from the 1970s. I have a collection of batteries for them, and I'm quite certain they have no digital chips.

Kids 2-way radios are usually on CB Channel 14, so they can be used for emergency communication. Older ones definitely have no digital chips, newer ones *probably* not. **Any stereo with a CD is digital**, and could go wrong. CDs are a digital recording medium, so they can *only* run with computer chips.

Cars, trucks, microwaves, TVs, VCRs, clocks, radios, all-terrain vehicles, snowmobiles, cameras, video cameras, cassette recorders, all used to be made without microprocessor chips. If you have an old one that still works, keep it. Don't dispose of it until after Y2k, even if you do get a new one before then.

## Take Pictures

All of those things mentioned above are things that could be useful in the days following Y2k. Cameras may not be needed for survival, but they give an excellent record to show to an insurance company, or in court if you need to. Make sure you have an older camera in addition to any modern ones. Remember all those cute little point-and-shoot cameras on the market today are *totally computer-driven*.

So, of course, are digital cameras. But hopefully any camera you buy in 1999 should be Y2k-compliant. Get that y2k warranty!

Take lots of pictures of everything that goes on, for two reasons. One is for protection later, insurance or in court if needed. The other is that, whether we want it or need it or not, this will be *memorable*, if nothing else. It'll be an adventure, although not likely an enjoyable one. *Memories are best preserved as pictures.* Videotapes only have a life of 20 years or so, but photos last forever. And most video cameras contain microchips.

You'll need something to show your grandchildren.

In the days following the 1990 Baguio earthquake, my wife Nina and I took a lot of video. But there was no power to recharge the batteries. Once my two batteries were dead, that was it. We were traveling in a van, which still ran. But I didn't have a charger that would work off the van! Now I have one to plug into the cigar lighter. Make sure everything you need to recharge can be done from a vehicle.

You can buy an inverter to plug into the vehicle cigar lighter and give 110 or 220 volts. These are a cheaper and more compact alternative to a gas-powered generator. They usually come in 100, 250 and 600-watt sizes. Bigger is better, of course, but also more expensive. In Canada an inverter costs about 50 cents per watt. I have a $135, 250-watt unit that runs my computer nicely, or a karaoke, or electric drill, but not a hair dryer.

# Travel Plans

If possible, don't travel at all around Millennium Day.

## Don't fly
## On 2kY

At Maligaya Travel, we'll be advising clients not to travel in the last week of December 1999 or the month of January 2000. Better still, avoid travel all of December, January and February. IATA and IFAP may close a whole bunch of airports, at least for a while.

If you can't avoid traveling, be prepared in case you get stranded. Make sure your carry-on has a change of clothing, plus all your bathroom stuff. You'll need some kind of food, Granola bars and things that you can munch on if you're stranded and the restaurants are not open, or maybe open but overcrowded. Or running out of everything. In an emergency a can of food may be eaten cold.

Don't expect airports to function the way they usually do. Instead, be prepared that you may have to look after yourself for perhaps several days.

Nina and I have an Egyptian friend who was living in Kuwait at the time of the Iraqi invasion. He told us how he and his family escaped by driving from Kuwait across Iraq to Jordan and home to Egypt. This took almost two weeks, and much of it was spent in lineups anywhere from eight hours to three days long. They had very little food, a few pieces of cheese each day for a week.

They had a little money, but there was no food to spend it on. All they could think of was getting home. Make sure you have plenty of money with you. Wear a money belt, and carry half in travelers' checks (assuming the banks are OK) and half in cash.

If there are crowds stranded in airports, and you have to sleep there, it's likely there'll be thieves. So buy a money belt, now, *before the rush* in the last few months. Traveler's checks are the safest way, but in a crunch you may not be able to cash them, so you'll need plenty of cash along as well.

Carry your cash safely in your money belt, with more in a number of other *safe* places just in case. Ladies, it's a good idea to carry some in your bra. If things get so bad that it's not safe there, it's not going to be safe anywhere.

### Don't Travel At All

Air travel will not be the only problem. The movie *"Speed II"* suggests what might happen when the computers fail on a cruise ship. Railways are heavily computerized too. And we've spent some time already discussing what could happen to cars, buses and trucks. Bridges, tunnels and toll highways with computerized administration and control systems will be having troubles.

The best advice I can give you is *don't travel at all* in the last week of December and the entire month of January. Better yet, avoid all travel in December, January and February.

## Prescription Medicines

Make sure you carry at least *3 times* enough to last the trip, stored in three different places. One can be in your carry-on, another in your jacket or your checked baggage, and perhaps another in your money belt. This way, if something is lost or stolen, you'll still be OK. If the trip takes twice as long as it's supposed to, you'll be OK. More below, under "Medical."

## Commuting

The only thing you can do about getting to work is to arrange backup, just in case. Arrange for car-pooling in case someone's vehicle doesn't start. If you commute by train, be sure you know how to use the bus, and vice-versa. Maybe you should buy a ticket in advance.

In warmer climates, consider walking or going by bicycle. Those don't involve computers. But wear a helmet and perhaps a dayglo vest on your bike, avoid heavy traffic, and beware in case the traffic starts going nuts. Y2k could cause gridlock, maybe 24-hour traffic jams, who knows what?

Even road rage. Watch out for angry drivers. Some may be carrying weapons. But then, every driver is behind the wheel of a weapon! Especially when *you're* on a bike. Just be extra careful, OK?

# Where Should I Spend the Millennium?

Your best bet is to be at home for the Millennium, or at least somewhere close by. Driving home may not be a good idea that night. If you do end up celebrating somewhere other than your home, I'd suggest you arrange to stay overnight.

Gather with a large group of family and friends. It's best if they're all well prepared, of course. (Feel free to send them a copy of this book along with the invitation!) Arrange for cable or satellite TV (or both just in case) to watch the celebrations around the world. Check in advance which channels will be showing New Zealand and other early-bird countries.

This way you'll get advance notice of whatever is happening, be it good or bad.

Physical location should be a house with full stocks of everything we talk about in these two chapters. Be prepared that your guests may well spend the night, and maybe a whole lot of nights after that.

A well-equipped cabin at the lakeside or in the mountains could be a good way to avoid possible urban problems. Make sure it's *totally* self-contained, and get to know your neighbors if you haven't already. In the countryside, coping with any disaster has always been, and must be, a community affair.

Avoid big cities, and especially avoid rough neighborhoods. Gangs and other ne'er-do-wells will be out in force, partying, drunk, stoned and otherwise uncontrolled by what you and I would call "normal" inhibitions. And once they see that the police are overextended, or worse, have lost control, rest assured they'll take advantage of it. Don't be there.

## Should I Move?

Ed Yourdon did. If you can find a suitable place, you may want to consider either moving there, or at least planning to spend the Millennium Days there. If you do spend these critical days away from home, then you'll need to prepare both locations. The cabin will need preparation for being used through Y2k, and the your home for being empty.

If you've been thinking of moving to a quiet little town, *now* is a good time. But move early, or it'll be difficult and expensive. There's no knowing what might happen to real estate prices if a selling panic happens in the cities, at the same time as a buying panic in the small towns.

But I would suggest that you only move if it's something you've been thinking about doing anyway. Or if you're really convinced it's going to get bad in the cities.

Always remember that I could be totally wrong, and we may not have a serious crisis at all. I don't think it would be a good idea to go through an expensive move, and end up in a difficult job search, and so on.

If it all comes together for you, and it's something you want to do, then here's my advice. These ideas are what I think would be best. I present them for you to use as guidelines in making decisions to fit your own needs and circumstances.

- Choose a small town, as far as possible from main centers. But choose one with an active town administration that works well and looks after the place properly. You may want to check Jack Lessinger's book, "*Penturbia*," about the move to small towns.

- Pick a moderate climate. The ideal is moderate levels of heat in summer, not too cold in winter, and modest rainfall all year. This will make it easier to live without utilities.

- One man, Russ Voorhees, has built a Y2k community in Arizona. He calls it "Heritage Farms 2000," and it looks like a well-thought-out approach to the problem. 1-800-383-2489 or www.heritagefarms2000.com (See Appendix "To Find Out more.")

- This is not a survivalist camp. Those are often right-wing extremist groups, or anti-government, anti-everything groups. If you go looking for "Voorhees Village" or one like it, beware the survivalists, and all extremist groups.

  Because such groups are often totally convinced that their view is the only correct one, they can often turn to violence. Their camps are sometimes bristling with weapons. You and your family need to stay well clear of extremists around Y2k. Especially if, as in our family, most of the people you love are non-white.

- If you've been thinking of moving to a bigger city, with more night life and whatever, *forget it!* At least until about 2001 or 2003. Wait until after the Millennium, and see what things are like.

- If I lived anywhere within Scud range of Saddam or Moammar or one of those, I'd consider moving.

- If you're already living in a big city, and moving is not really an option, consider leaving for a vacation around Millennium Day.

## Should I Take a Vacation?

If you have friends or relatives who live in the countryside, a month's vacation might be a good idea. Be careful that you leave your home or apartment in such a way that it won't be damaged if things go wrong. You don't want to come home a month later to frozen pipes and flooded bathrooms. Or fire damage. Remember your neighbors may be gone too, and if things get bad there could be looting and break-ins, even in "nice" neighborhoods.

Also keep in mind that there's always a chance you may get stranded in the countryside, and not be able to get back home to the city at all. Make sure your employer and your friends know where you're going and how to get in touch with you – once the phones and the mails are working again.

So in this case your preparations will have to be made with this trip in mind. You'll need to take all your emergency food and supplies, or arrange in advance for them to be at your vacation place. You'll also need to have some serious advance talks with your hosts about their preparations for Y2k.

## Don't Party

I really would advise against going out to join the celebrations. Even if there is no disaster, large public parties have a habit of sometimes getting out of control. The drinking doesn't help. And this will be the largest party the world has ever seen. If there *is* a disaster, I believe the opening scenario of this book is not beyond the realms of possibility.

## Stay Out of the Third World

Those of us lucky enough to live in the First World sometimes don't realize just *how* lucky we are. Emergency services are a luxury, that we take for granted in countries rich enough to afford them. Safety is expensive, and there isn't the money to spare for such things in countries where 60% or more live below the poverty line.

After the Edmonton tornado in 1987, with 27 dead and homes and factories flattened, the emergency services swung into action. Edmonton's more than 100 fire trucks and 30 ambulances weren't enough, nor were the thousands of volunteers, and a thousand soldiers.

After the 1989 San Francisco earthquake, the TV showed all the police, firefighters, paramedics, soldiers and volunteers. Thousands of them. In the rich nations we're used to having these skilled specialists and volunteers to call on when we need help.

In the three days following the 7.9 Baguio earthquake in the Philippines, we saw one ambulance and three fire trucks. Not like we were used to seeing at home in Canada.

There are more guns, and fewer protections, in the Third World. This is just a fact of life. In good times travelers are not affected too much, but on Y2k all the rules may change. There and elsewhere. I really think most of us will be better off to stay home for Y2k.

# Preparing Your Home

Your home needs to be prepared in case utilities go off, especially if it's going to be empty. In cold climates, you'll need to prevent the pipes from freezing and bursting. Shut off the water at the *outside* tap. Open a tap inside, and drain the pipes. *Then close it.* Be sure you *find* the outside tap in mid 1999 or earlier, and figure out how to use it. Practice again after the snow comes.

## Legionnaires' Disease

A serious caution here. In Auckland during the power outage, the water pipes were stagnant for three weeks. There were news announcements warning people to *flush the pipes well* when the pressure came back on. Stale water in the pipes for any more than two weeks is an excellent breeding ground for Legionnaires' Disease.

## Burglar Alarms

If you have a fancy alarm system, check it out and test it beforehand (in about July 1999), and then continue to use it on into the year 2000. Test it again as soon as possible after Millennium Day. If the phones are OK part of the time, and the alarm still works, your house will be protected at least part of the time. But a large number of false alarms around Millennium Day may make it less helpful. Don't rely on the alarm company to respond.

I *don't* recommend spending large sums of money on (computerized) alarm systems, unless it was something you were thinking of doing anyway. If you do, demand that it be Y2k-compliant. Make them sign the warranty, *before you pay.*

If you've been thinking of getting a dog, that may be a good idea. But don't buy a cute little 4-month-old puppy in October of 1999! Get your puppy early, like *now*, and take the time and trouble to train her properly. Or get an older, *already-trained* dog. But remember, dogs need food. Lay in supplies. (How about a doorbell that barks?)

## Fire and Smoke Alarms

*Smoke detectors are a definite must!* If the power goes out, and we're relying on candles and fireplaces, our risk of fire increases. There **will** be more fires. At the same time, it may be very difficult to get help when we need it. So it's very important to have that early warning if things go wrong. Get several different types and brands, in the hope that at least one will be Y2k compliant.

Also get some **A-B-C** fire extinguishers.

And don't play the hero. If there's a fire in a house, it takes only *minutes* to go wild. What happens is that once a curtain or some such catches fire, in about *three minutes* the air throughout the entire room becomes superheated. The air gets hotter than the temperature that wood catches fire. So all the walls catch fire at the same moment, in what's called a "flashover."

The room becomes an instant furnace, and you don't live through it.

This is one of the reasons that everything you read about house fires, including your life-insurance policy, says not to go back into a burning building once you've left it. Never go back for pets, papers, money or anything else, except maybe a trapped child. A flashover or a collapse can catch you in seconds.

Once the smoke detectors are sounding, you may have only three or four minutes to get everyone out of the house. Unless you're trained in firefighting, don't play the hero. A live Daddy is more use to kids and spouse than a dead hero.

### Fortification

One of the books available from the Survival Center at www.survivalcenter.com explains how to fortify a closet as a hiding place. I think this may be going a little too far, but some of you may feel that you are living near a danger zone. People just outside a major city may feel the need to do something like this.

If you do, make sure you hide where the invaders will have no idea that you're there. Make sure it's fireproof, and survivable in a fire, as well as bulletproof. Underground is good. So are oxygen or compressed-air cylinders to make sure your little fort doesn't turn into a fiery coffin.

# Medical

The first thing to say about medical issues is that you must avoid them if at all possible. Look after yourself carefully in the months and weeks before Y2k. Avoid nonessential surgery in the last half of 1999. Avoid dangerous pursuits. I love to do exciting things, but we must all avoid injuring ourselves around Millennium Day.

Hospitals and paramedics may be stretched thin. And you don't want to be a hospital patient on Millennium Day. It could be the most dangerous thing you ever did.

Don't get drunk, just in case. You'll need your wits about you if things go wrong. Just reread the opening scenario at the front of this book to see what you might have to deal with.

### Babies and Childbirth

After the Eastern seaboard of the U.S. was darkened for 24 hours in 1977, 9 months and one week later there was a 3-day surge in births throughout that area. Many babies were conceived that night because the TV wasn't working.

Be warned – pregnancies and births, planned or otherwise, may not be a good idea in the early days and weeks of 2000, especially if the medical community remains in a state of disarray for a year or so. Unprotected sex at such a time would be placing both mother and baby at risk.

If things are really bad, delay having your children until the world settles down again. Use contraception, and *stock up*. As a minimum, avoid pregnancy throughout 1999, and probably all of 2000.

### Prescription Medicines

Make sure you have at least *three times* enough to last through the crisis, however long you think the crisis will last. And if the crisis takes twice as long as you expected it would, you'll still be OK. Watch expiry dates, and make sure you use them up in order.

The problem with prescription medicines is that many of us depend on them for our very life. A lot of young and middle-aged people don't realize just how serious this is. Most of the elderly, and a number of younger adults, literally cannot live without their drugs.

My mother-in-law must have her pills four times a day. If she misses a morning, say, she suffers a few hours later. If she misses a day or two, it takes weeks for her to recover fully. After an accidental overdose one time, it took her three months to regain her strength and get back to normal. This is typical of people around that age.

At 54, I must take four drugs daily for my blood pressure. If I stop, my BP skyrockets in a day or so. A couple of days like that won't kill me, but a few weeks or months will seriously increase the likelihood of a stroke or heart attack.

What if a diabetic in your family ran out of insulin? He or she could survive a few days, perhaps. But for a diabetic to be totally without insulin for an extended period is to risk blindness and even death. Asthmatics must have their inhalers available at a moment's notice. For some of us, running out of certain items is simply not an option.

## Non-Prescription Drugs and Medicines

You will need:

- First-aid kit
- Oxygen
- Allergy drugs

And your usual family medicines:
- Painkillers (Watch for allergies and intolerance. Use a variety.)
- Cough syrup
- Antihistamines
- Laxatives
- High-fiber laxatives (e.g., Metamucil)
  (Note: Oatmeal and/or prunes can reduce the need for laxatives. If your lifestyle changes for a prolonged period after Y2k, regularity could suffer. You will need plenty of fiber in your diet, and some laxatives for backup.)
- Anti-diarrheal Medicines
- Pepto-Bismol (Pink Stuff)
- Kaopeptate
- Corn Starch
- Imodium (or cheaper generics such as Novo-Loperamide)

## First Aid

You need a serious first-aid kit, and some training. This is one of those things that we should all have in place anyway, and most of us have a few Band Aids or a small kit around the house. But the kind of kits that most of us have will be inadequate if someone gets seriously injured. 9-1-1 and the Paramedics may *not* be there when we need them.

Go out and buy a big, serious first-aid kit. Check what it has in it first, and get advice from a friend in the business. You must know someone who is a nurse, paramedic, or doctor, who you can ask for help. Dentists, hygienists, vets, St John members, ski patrollers, industrial safety specialists, anyone like that has knowledge and experience that you can use

Chapter 8 has a list of what I recommend should be in a first-aid kit suitable for a serious disaster. One important thing to watch for is the size of the gauze pads, for putting on a wound under a bandage. You need at least a bunch of "4x4s" ("four-by-fours"), that is 10cm or 4 inches square. Bigger is always better. Buy a few very large ones to add.

Make sure your kit has all the specialized things that your family members may need. Diabetics need insulin. People with allergies need antihistamines and some need adrenalin.

If you have to leave your home during the Y2k problems, make sure the kit goes too.

Take a course or two, or more. You need skills in bandaging and basic first aid, and also CPR, especially if you have someone at risk in the family. This might be an elderly grandparent, or anyone with a heart condition, or emphysema or any lung problem.

I recommend a bottle of oxygen. You can buy a small one for emergency use, not too expensive, with a breathing nozzle. I don't consider this as critical as bandages and so on, unless you have someone at risk, perhaps elderly. But it could be a lifesaver in some cases. Severe stress from the crisis could cause a stroke or heart attack in someone at risk.

You'll need to include something for dysentery. If we're all camping out in basements, community halls or wherever, food poisoning is bound to be a problem from time to time. And don't just rely on the Pink Stuff or the White Stuff or any of those. By all means have some of those, Pepto-Bismol, or kaopeptate, or whatever.

But you must also have a package of corn starch (*corn starch* in American, *cornflour* in English). A teaspoon of this with some sugar in a half glass of water or milk will stop the runs. Get some Imodium or Novo-Loperamide or equivalent for more serious control. Be sure to read directions on everything.

## Get Your Shots

Go to your doctor or public health office, or the nurses or safety people where you work. They're probably used to giving shots to travelers, especially those headed for third-world countries. Ask for *all* the shots you would need to go to *all* the worst places in the world.

But be guided by your public-health nurse, or doctor or other health professional. I'm not an expert in these areas, just a concerned citizen. It's up to each of us to check with the experts, and then make our decisions about how to protect ourselves and our families.

One or two of those precautions may not be appropriate, such as malaria. That is, unless you live in a country where malaria is common in some regions. In that case, stock up on malaria pills beforehand. If there *is* a crisis, diseases like malaria may move out of the regions that they're usually confined to, so be prepared.

Vaccinations are a minor inconvenience, but one of them could save your life. Or that of someone you love. As with so much of this stuff, it's really just a matter of making it happen. *In time.*

Typhoid, typhus, cholera, bubonic plague and such things are all possible if our cities stop functioning for a few days or weeks. Flu shots and all the things we sometimes get, this time be sure to get. Make sure your kids are not only up-to-date with their shots, but get them as far ahead as your doctor will permit with any upcoming shots.

Make sure all your boosters are up to date, and will last at least two or three years into the new millennium. Don't forget to give your pets their shots as well, *before* Y2k.

If garbage pickup doesn't happen for a while, or sewage treatment plants don't treat sewage, it won't take too long before pollution and bacteria find their way into whatever water there is around. After the Baguio earthquake, Nina and I saw many residents gathering water from streams. We lived for three days on bottled Pepsi.

It's amazing how things happen. Or maybe it's Murphy's Law. Before that trip, I had decided I would get a typhoid vaccination. Nina, and the nurse, and the travel agent, all said I wouldn't need it, and so did the official brochures. As it happened, I left it too late, and I had only the first shot of the two that are required. I planned on getting the second one when I arrived in the Philippines.

Of course, I was far too busy when we got there, and I never went for that second shot. Then, not long before we were due to come home to Canada, the earthquake hit! We were stranded for three days in a city where 400 people died, and none of the buildings were useable. Was I ready for this? Not on your life!

Here is a list of diseases you should consider when deciding which shots to get. This is a partial list, and there may be others, perhaps some that specially affect your region.

## Dengue Fever

("*deng*-ghee," "*deng*gi," sometimes "*deng*-ga")

This is a mosquito-borne illness for which there is no vaccine as yet. I understand that there is one currently being developed in Thailand, and I hope it will be deployed before y2k. The disease exists in two forms, the worse being the hemorrhagic kind, where the patient dies from internal bleeding.

| | |
|---|---|
| Cholera | This and typhoid, along with a number of other diseases, can become a real risk after a disaster if garbage and sewage are not being taken away |
| Dengue fever | |
| Diphtheria | |
| Hib (haemophilus influenzae B) | May cause meningitis, an infection of the brain and spinal cord. Generally only very young kids are given this vaccine. |
| Hepatitis A and B | |
| Japanese encephalitis | |
| Malaria | If you live in a country where malaria occurs, you may need to think about whether your exposure would be increased in a disaster. If so, you may wish to get malaria pills in advance, or just take extra precautions against mosquitoes |
| Influenza | |
| Pertussis | |
| Rubella. | |
| Measles, Mumps, | Even if you're not planning to be pregnant. (Pregnancy is not a good idea around Y2k anyway.) |
| Meningococcal disease | This is a bacteria that causes meningitis, an infection of the brain and spinal cord. It "can strike with frightening quickness," but luckily it's confined to just a few areas in Africa and Asia. But who knows what diseases may spread to where if our society and all its usual precautions are not working? |
| Pneumococcal disease | This bacteria can cause one kind of pneumonia, and "blood poisoning." |
| Tetanus. | Get your booster. Always wear shoes, since dirt that carries tetanus can get into scratches and cuts on your feet. |
| Polio | Get a booster. |
| Typhoid | See cholera, above. |
| Rabies | If you're in an area where rabies is common, you can get immunized. It's expensive, though, about $300 Can. |
| Whooping cough | |
| Yellow fever | Important for some parts of Africa and South America. |

(Courtesy of BC Capital Regional District Public Health, Victoria, Canada)

Treatment consists of keeping the patient alive, often with expensive blood transfusions, until the body's immune system can dispose of the virus, which can take a couple of weeks.

As I write this, there is a widespread outbreak in the Philippines and other tropical countries. Nina is there right now, and her 11-year-old great-nephew Earl is in hospital in Manila with dengue. After several transfusions, Earl is now on the way to recovering.

Nina saw hundreds of kids in the hospital, a horrifying sight. And these are the rich ones, whose parents can afford hospital care to save their kids. There's no Medicare in the Third World. If you don't have the money, your kid dies.

If we have a serious crisis after Millennium Day, diseases like this could become rampant in some parts of the world. Some with no vaccine or even treatment available. And if our hospitals are overloaded, and drug companies paralyzed by WFITFAFIT, there may not be much care available even in the First World.

Here are some comments on some of the diseases around:

Get any shots you missed as a child. Get vaccinated for all those things *most* of us had, or had the shots, as children, but maybe you missed out or you're not sure. Even "innocent" childhood diseases can be a problem or even fatal if we don't have full medical facilities.

Your health care professional can advise you about which ones are present in which parts of the world. I strongly recommend you get shots for any that are endemic (common) in your region. And remember that vaccinations don't usually give 100% protection. You must still observe good health and protection practices. Wash your hands regularly, and take all the precautions your mother taught you years ago.

All of these diseases have potential for epidemics if the world got really bad. *Each one of these diseases has been an epidemic at some point in history.* Who knows, there just might even be a pocket of Smallpox waiting its chance somewhere. Get *all* your shots.

Typhoid, cholera, hepatitis A, influenza, measles, rubella and polio are all spread in food and/or on your hands. You can reduce the chance of catching all these by washing hands regularly. Make sure children and other group members wash their hands when handling food, and after handling garbage or human or animal waste. Always wash before eating, and after handling animals.

Hepatitis B is spread like AIDS, by body fluid contact, and particularly by sexual contact. Guard against these and other STDs, and pregnancy, by avoiding unprotected sexual contact. Also wear latex gloves if you come in contact with a stranger's blood, such as when assisting at an accident.

Avoid getting hurt yourself, because even if blood is available for transfusions, the blood supply might be suspect after a major disaster. Drive carefully, if at all. Wear seat belts, wear helmets and leather on motorcycles, helmets and long clothes on bicycles. Stay well away from fights and riots.

## Mosquitoes

Malaria, Japanese encephalitis, Yellow fever, Dengue and a number of other nasty diseases are carried by mosquitoes. In addition to vaccinations, you should take a number of precautions against mosquitoes if you live in any of these areas.

Cover up when out of doors, as much as the heat will allow it. Wear insect repellant. Use one with DEET in it – the more DEET the better. Amway d-15 is one of the best, and Deep-Woods OFF and others also have DEET. Use screens on doors and windows, and/or sleep under nets when in the tropics. (I've become quite used to mosquito nets over the beds when visiting Nina's hometown in the Philippines.)

Stay away from crowded areas to avoid TB and a host of other diseases. Crowds, demonstrations, riots, looting, mass meetings, stay away from all of them if the world gets bad after Y2k. Staying clear will help you avoid both illness and injury.

## Third-World Vaccinations

One of my deepest personal concerns here is the people of the Third World. I believe that the United Nations, with the help of the richer nations, should be *stepping up vaccination programs in the poorer countries over the next year and a half.* A good idea even if there's no disaster.

It's important that as many people as possible be vaccinated against a whole slew of diseases *before* any Y2k troubles hit. All over the world, rich and poor. There's not much time to make it happen. If you agree, please write your elected representatives and tell them of your views.

And one of the biggest problems in First, Second and Third-World nations is TB.

## The New TB Epidemic

This is one epidemic we're having already. The August 1998 Saturday Evening Post carried an article on how the AIDS epidemic is helping to spread TB, and how TB has become resistant to so many of the older drugs that used to work against it.

TB was supposed to disappear off the face of the Earth by 2000, but since 1984 it's been growing instead of declining. In 1995, 3 million people died of TB, more than any year ever recorded. A few nurses have died after catching TB from patients, so now it's getting dangerous for them to work around these cases.

New York City has one of the highest AIDS rates in the US. According to Cary Savitch, M.D., in the Post article, *one in every six people in New York City has TB!* He says: "Most of these cases are actively infected, not on treatment, and highly contagious." The subway trains don't sound so good any more.

Does this city sound like a good place to be if things go bad in the new Millennium? Ed Yourdon has already moved out to New Mexico. It's a big continent. There's lots of nice, safe, distant small towns to choose from.

AIDS victims can catch just about anything, because their immune system is weakened. TB is one that they often catch. Or sometimes, an old dormant TB infection flares up full-blown as their immune system declines.

AIDS sufferers never die from AIDS itself. It's always from something else, that they caught because they had AIDS. In Third World countries these days, most AIDS patients die from TB. And nearly half of all the refugees in the world right now have TB.

People with AIDS who get TB as well are almost never cured. Many are homeless in the rich nations, or refugees, or they're poor in the Third World. But they're infectious for the whole time until they finally die! Often they're in crowded shelters, or refugee camps, where the disease spreads rapidly.

*Unlike AIDS*, you can get TB just from being close to someone who has it. It's carried by tiny water droplets in the air that a TB victim breathes out, and another person can catch it by breathing in those droplets. Airplanes are a problem because they cram many people into a small space for hours at a time, and then recycle the air.

The World Health organization of the United nations predicts 90 million new TB cases in the decade of the 1990s. That's about nine million a year. And they predict 500 million new TB cases in the next 50 years, or 10 million a year.

But I don't believe they factored Y2k into their predictions! If the systems in our society break down badly, we're likely to have a lot of people crowded into shelters, and crowding into overloaded hospitals. Perhaps hospitals won't be as clean as in better times.

We could have millions of hungry refugees leaving the cities, especially in the Third World. If their fate is at all like our current world crop of refugees, most of them will end up with TB.

## What can we do about TB?

The only vaccine around for TB is called "BCG." It's a live vaccine, and so it can sometimes have side effects. AIDS victims should *not* get BCG, because their weakened immune systems can allow them to get very sick from it.

BCG is mostly used only for people who are going into an area where TB is common, or for health care workers. It only gives partial protection, but it's the best we have.

Go to your doctor or public health unit, and have a TB skin test. If you've had BCG before, you'll need two skin tests. The protection given by BCG lasts for about 10 years, and then slowly fades. After about 20 years it's only giving a very small amount of protection.

The first skin test will wake up your old immunization and get it working again. The second one will give a rough idea of how well your old BCG is working for you. The bonus is that the skin tests have now reactivated your BCG. While it's still not as good as new, it's giving somewhat more protection than before.

If you've never had a BCG, then you should go for a skin test. There are three possible outcomes:

- **You test negative**. You've never been exposed to TB. Discuss with your health care professional whether you should have a BCG. I would think it's a good idea, but then I'm not an expert. Even a recent BCG doesn't give 100% protection, but some is better than none. And we do have an epidemic already.

- **You test positive**, and you discover you have active TB. Start treatment immediately. These days it's not a difficult treatment, just daily pills to take for six months to a year. Be guided by your doctors and nurses.

- **You test positive**, but you *don't* have active TB. What's happened is that years ago you were exposed to TB, and caught it. You may have actually had the active disease for a while, and then it "went to sleep." Treatment is voluntary, not automatic, but I believe you must get it. One pill a day for a year.

If the TB germs are having a tough time in your body, they wall themselves up in tiny hard-shelled "tubercles." There they wait, hoping that one day your immune system will be weakened, and then they can become active again. This happens to many AIDS victims.

*About* one-third of the population of the world *has active TB or this dormant form of TB.* And about one in six people in New York City. When you're around these people, you have no way of telling who has become active again, until weeks later when they start coughing up blood. Meantime, you and others have been exposed.

The treatment for dormant TB is one pill a day for a year. For both active and dormant TB, the most important thing of all is that *you* must *take* all *the pills, right to the end.* If you don't, you will *not* be cured. Many people stop taking them once they start to feel better, but that's not enough. The TB is still there, and it can get active again years later.

People who do not finish the medicine are helping to develop the drug-resistant strains of the disease. These kinds of TB are resistant to many drugs, and this makes them very dangerous. Most people who catch one of these drug-resistant variants finally die from it.

If things are bad after Millennium Day, you can cut your chance of getting TB by avoiding crowded places. There you can be exposed to droplets breathed out by other people, as well as personal contact with strangers.

Staying away from crowds will also help you to avoid influenza, measles, mumps, rubella, meningococcal disease, pneumococcal disease and diphtheria. These and other diseases are all spread by breathing airborne droplets, or by personal touch.

Discuss with your local TB clinic whether you should get BCG, and what you can do to protect against TB. It's a good idea even if there's no crisis on Y2k.

## Dialysis and Other Medical Equipment

If you or a family member need regular visits to a hospital or clinic or other such place, you'll need to arrange backup. What if you can't get there? What if they're not open, and the staff are at home looking after their own families? What if they're open, but the equipment you need doesn't work? Or they're completely overloaded?

You may want to see about buying the equipment for home use. Dialysis and other equipment can be purchased for about the price of a luxury car, but make sure they give you that warranty for Y2k. Also, the patient and family members need to be trained to use it. And make sure you're able to get them to a hospital as backup in case it doesn't work in Y2k, or there are any complications.

You may want to share with two or three other families in your city or neighborhood. But do it now, while there's still time and you can still get one. *"Just Do It!"*

All this applies equally to glucometers for diabetics, and blood pressure cuffs for those with high blood pressure, and other special equipment. Get one and learn how to use it.

A cylinder or two of oxygen is a good idea if someone in your family has a history of heart disease, stroke, emphysema or some such. Oxygen always a good idea if you have an elderly parent in the group. Make sure it comes with a breathing nozzle, or get one. If you can't practice using it without breaking the seal, ask the vendor to train you.

If one of your group uses oxygen routinely, stock up with plenty. You may wish to check out the rental on a huge cylinder of welding oxygen as a backup, if you feel this person might not survive when the oxygen runs out. Welding oxygen is not medically pure, but it's distilled from regular clean air. So it'll do just fine if the world (and the medical supply chain) falls apart on us.

## If You Have Someone in Hospital

If it gets bad, this will be a very difficult time for the sick and the infirm, the disabled and the elderly. In many cases, these people are unaware of what's coming. Not only that, if you tried to explain, to many older people it would make no sense at all.

You and I have a responsibility to these people. We may have very limited influence for getting hospitals and old folks homes to prepare for Y2k, but we should still try. We *can* do it for the ones who are a part of our own lives.

Through marrying Nina, I have learned many things from the Filipino culture. Theirs is so different from the New Zealand culture that I grew up in, and the Canadian culture we now live in. Both these are heavily British in their origins. One such difference is the practice of always having a family member present with a patient in hospital.

When Nina's mother has been in hospital in Canada, the nurses have struggled valiantly to accommodate this cultural divergence. They expect to do this for an elderly immigrant, and it reduces their load; they're overworked already. It helps that so many of the nurses in any hospital are Filipino! The family member takes over many of the routine care and feeding chores, freeing up the nurses for more serious work.

A year or so back when I had surgery, since I'm a white Caucasian, the nursing staff were a little more surprised at Nina's insistence that she sleep in a recliner beside me. But they coped. I sure appreciated it, since I was totally immobile and dependent for the first time in my life since infancy.

*Plan on doing this yourself through Millennium Day.* Prepare the nursing staff *ahead of time*, if possible. Move in on December 30th or earlier. Arrange a roster of people to take turns, but plan for the contingency that they might not be able to get to the hospital in the first few days of the new year.

Bring all your own supplies, including food and your own medications, if any. Bring clothes, a sleeping bag, an air mattress, books, flashlight, battery radio, spare batteries. Everything you might need if you're stuck in the hospital for a while.

And what will you do once all this is in place? If things are near enough to normal, you'll keep the patient company, help them to the bathroom, and all that helpful, non-medical stuff.

But if there *is* an emergency on Millennium Day, the staff will be far too busy. Perhaps many won't make it to work for their shift. Or some may be sent to the Emergency department because of an overload there. If the power goes off, that's another set of problems. And Y2k problems in the equipment could throw everyone into a panic.

In the midst of all this, your family member could be the only one on the ward getting proper attention – from you! If there's a fire or other evacuation you'll be one more pair of able-bodied hands. *You* could be the only guarantee your patient will be rescued.

With or without a general alarm or panic, you'll need to be there to check and double-check every machine hooked up to your patient. Track all the readings for a few days before Y2k. Learn to read the patient's chart. Write everything down, and draw some graphs as well. Graphs help you to notice sudden changes.

Make sure your patient has no sudden changes in readings or vital signs at Y2k. If your patient is getting medication automatically from a machine, watch out for sudden changes in the dosages at Y2k! If there are, they may be due to a Y2k error in the equipment. Suspect everything. Try to get the readings checked on a non-computerized instrument, or with one from a different manufacturer.

### Ambulance & Emergency Services

If you're spending Millennium Day away from home, check the way to the hospital, doctor, fire station and police station, and any other important services. Walk, jog or cycle the routes for practice. You never know, you may have to walk them in the middle of the night.

# What Should Governments Do?

There are a number of places where our governments should be preparing, aside from the obvious one of fixing all the software. Here is a list of my thoughts on the matter. You may well be able to come up with more. I urge you to write, attend meetings, and do anything else that will agitate and get governments moving. All levels of government – city, state, provincial and federal – should be planning and *doing something* about these things:

- Fix their own software.

- Prepare contingency plans for what to do when (not if!) they don't get it all fixed. Many essential government services will need backup plans for what to do to keep going when the computers fail.

- Passing whatever laws will be needed to cope with Y2k and protect citizens from all kinds of disasters, in case one or two of them do happen.

- In particular, have emergency powers for the police and military in place *before* Y2k comes around. Here in Canada, it seems our Prime Minister is planning to be at the party, so we might have a little trouble finding him at 12:03 a.m. to sign a proclamation of martial law.

- Governments need to publicize the whole Y2k thing. In particular, get businesses of all sizes working on the problem.

- Get businesses preparing contingency plans for what to do when (not if!) they don't get all their software fixed.

- Train riot squads. Train *all* police for riot duty. Expand riot squads and SWAT teams. Arm everybody (police and military) with BOTH rubber bullets *and* real ones.

- Train the military for riot duty. Give them basic police training. Arm them with rubber *and* real bullets. Swear in thousands of soldiers as special police (Special

Deputies in US, Special Constables in Canada, N.Z., Britain and Commonwealth countries. Or whatever the term is in your country.) Your government is going to need all the law-and-order personpower they can get. Canada's *Operation Abacus* is a good model.

- Train lots of dogs to sniff drugs, *and explosives.* I don't know if it's practical, but it would be great idea if we could train dogs to sniff out excessive quantities of gasoline. What we need is some way to detect either bottles of gasoline in a car (in other words Molotov cocktails), or barrels hidden in a van or truck.

- Train other military personnel as firefighters and paramedics. Before Y2k, let them go on calls with civilian firefighters for practice.

- Equip military vehicles and choppers with what they need to help with riots and fires.

- Develop firefighting plans and strategies for widespread urban fires. Have trained personnel and supplies ready in case burning buildings have to be imploded.

- Increase the size of military and civilian rescue units. Expand the 9-1-1 service, and the staff, vehicles and equipment behind the number.

- Install fire sprinkler systems in important buildings that don't already have them. Of course, this assumes there'll be water pressure. I expect there will be, but not everywhere and not all the time.

- Provide generators and water tanks to hospitals and other emergency facilities, in advance of Y2k. In an emergency, a 1000-bed hospital will need about 2000 gals per day for drinking, plus several times as much again for washing.

- Install fire sprinkler systems in any prisons that don't have them, and put prisons at the top of the priority list for this.

- Quietly install sleeping-gas nozzles beside the prison sprinklers. I've always felt that this was the answer to prison riots, fires and hostage-takings. I say we should get the equipment in place, and worry about the prisoners' rights only if it becomes necessary to use it. After the prison has been saved, and the lives of its guards. I must stress that this one is my own personal opinion. What's yours?

Everything in this list is something that would be a good idea for your government to do anyway, even if there's no Y2k disaster.

## Write to Your Government Representatives

We must all begin *now* to prod our governments into Y2k awareness. Write to your elected representatives and to bureaucrats at all levels. Demand that they state publicly how many lines of code must be converted in each government agency, how much has been completed, how many people are on the project, and things like that.

Demand to know how much money has been budgeted, and this will show how serious they are about it. From time to time, ask, how much of that has been spent. That will tell you how hard they're working on it, and whether they budgeted enough.

Ask for firm completion dates, and testing schedules. Ask for details of their triage exercises, and what systems they have decided to delay or abandon. All such questions are good because they bring things out into the light of public scrutiny.

Find out what contingency plans they have for power outages, transportation and communication shutdowns, government shutdowns, and so on. Ask what plans they have to deal with riots, terrorists or wars.

Demand that they deploy police, paramedics, helicopters, and soldiers near any potential trouble spots for the duration of Millennium Day. That includes international trouble spots, of course.

## Project Damocles

Peter de Jager had a "Project Damocles" running on his www.year2000.com web site. If you had first-hand knowledge of something that failed, an embedded chip, a software product or application, or a computer hardware platform, you were invited to visit the web site and make an anonymous report. All information that came in was to be sent registered mail to the legal departments of the companies concerned.

The name, by the way, refers to the fable *"The Sword of Damocles,"* about the peasant who sat for a day on the throne of King Damocles. He didn't enjoy all the power and glory of being king for a day, because he saw a sword hanging over his head by a single thread. At the end of the day, King Damocles explained that it was there to remind him that he ruled only by the will of the people, and his rule, like his life, could end any time.

"The goal" said de Jager "is to fix issues before they become problems."

# Late-breaking News: Demise of Project Damocles!

# Damocles *GONE!!*

It is surely one of the most unfortunate and short-sighted things this world has ever done. Pressure has been brought to bear on Mr de Jager, and because of the threat of lawsuits, Project Damocles is no more.

De Jager is to be commended for trying. His was the only attempt on a large scale to give direct feedback where it's needed. His idea had built-in protection both for the companies involved, and for the employees, customers or others who blew the whistle.

It was a very fair system. But fair doesn't count. Might is always right in a lawsuit. They just made it too dangerous for him to risk sticking his neck out in that direction. God knows, he's had a lot of courage in sticking it out in other directions already!

Killing Project Damocles has destroyed an opportunity to save countless businesses and jobs, and likely some lives as well, in the light of the recent disclosures to Mr de Jager. Because it's no longer there, many more Y2k bugs will get through, just making the whole thing worse.

We have absolutely no way of telling just how many corrections would have happened if the project had continued. It could have been many, or it might have been just a few. Either way it would have helped. And its demise will slow the world economy a little more, and add a little more to the Y2k depression. But there is a way that you and I can help fill the gap left by the death of Damocles.

## Volunteer for Something

Whether it's something directly related to Y2k software fixes, or to keeping our society running after Y2k, your help will be needed. If you've been thinking about volunteering for something sometime, *now* would be an excellent time.

For one thing, whatever agency you volunteer with will need more help than ever during a Y2k crisis. If there's a disaster, rehabilitation hospitals, women's shelters, old folks homes, institutions for the disabled and so on will need as much help as hospitals will. Even police stations will need volunteers, especially special deputies/constables.

You could get involved with your local civil defense, rescue, or disaster preparedness organization. They're probably OK with their general disaster planning, but they might need your input to their Y2k plans. Do you have specialized skills or knowledge that could help in a disaster?

Volunteering for ski patrol, fire fighting, ambulance work, militia, rescue or police assistance all could lead to useful training. And to a chance to contribute in an important and much-needed role if there is a crisis.

This is closely related to the idea of taking courses.

## Take Courses

First there's the obvious ones, like First Aid, and various survival courses. Everyone should take first aid and CPR anyway, regardless of whether you're expecting anything to go wrong. Even in perfectly normal times there are chances to save a life.

Any survival course relevant to your climate is a good idea, especially if you like to go camping, hiking, off-roading, etc. For Y2k purposes, you won't need "*Arctic Survival*" if you live in New Mexico, or "*Deserts for Dummies*" if you live in Alberta or Alaska. If you were planning to do these things someday anyway, then now might be a good time. But if time and resources are limited, choose courses more relevant to *your* exact situation.

Many courses can be found by scanning the yellow pages, or doing a search on the Web. One of the best search engines on the Web is at www.metacrawler.com because it also searches all the other search engines.

Government agencies, especially those specifically dealing with disasters, offer many courses and can help by telling you where else to look. Many governments have "Safety Councils" or similar agencies. Many volunteer or sport-related groups offer courses, such as the Canadian Ski Patrol System, whose members take a superb first-aid course.

If you belong to any club or group that does things in out-of-the-way or risky places, they may well be interested organizing (or having *you* organize) some of these courses. Hikers, mountaineers, canoers, cross-country skiers, mountain-bikers (without motors), dirt-bikers (with motors), off-road or four-wheel-drive clubs, sailing and other boating clubs, scuba divers. All of these groups you might find use some of these courses as part of their normal preparation. A good idea even if there's no Y2k crisis.

Many of these courses can be claimed as a tax deduction in most countries. Check with your tax adviser, and with the people presenting the courses. Check with your employer to see if they'll fund some of your courses. It's always handy for an employer to have an extra first-aider on staff, or a disaster-preparedness expert.

There was a need for people with these skills in the Baguio earthquake. Nina and I saw buildings where perhaps a hundred people died in a single building. And that's with not one building in the entire city more than six floors high. In a third-world country only the rich few have the time and money to take courses like this.

One (untrained) heroine in Baguio led 30 of her co-workers to safety for about 60m (a couple of hundred feet). They crawled and wriggled through a terrifying maze of collapsed beams, live wires and burning rubbish that used to be walls. Their ordeal then ended with a 15m (40-foot) climb down the outside of the burning heap of rubble that had been their building. No one was expecting an earthquake that day.

Here's a partial list. These are courses I can think of that might be useful, and I'm sure you can add to the list. In particular, you'll be aware of courses relevant to your geographic location, your sports and interests, your business or occupation. And don't forget the businesses and industries nearby in your community.

First Aid and CPR
Rescue Courses
Swimming and Life guarding
Disaster Preparedness
Winter Survival
Desert or Mountain Survival
Orienteering and Bush Survival

Outdoor Cooking, Survival Cooking, Camp Cooking, Rice Cooking
Driving or Motorcycling
Vehicle and Bicycle Maintenance
Handyman, Construction, Electrical; Any kind of repair or maintenance courses.

Here are a few comments about each of these categories:

### First Aid and CPR

First Aid is always important, especially if you have elderly family members. Having a doctor, nurse, paramedic or other medically-trained professional in the group is a great advantage. But even then, it can make a big difference if others in the group have had some training and can assist in an emergency.

The serious courses are generally more than 100 hours. St John Advanced is 100, Canadian Ski Patrol is around 160 hours. There are even a few places where you can do full Emergency Medical Technician (EMT) training part-time.

Search the Web or the Yellow Pages, or contact these organizations to find courses:

| | |
|---|---|
| Red Cross / Red Crescent | Safety equipment vendors |
| St John Ambulance Society | Ski Patrol and other sports clubs |
| Local hospitals | Ski stores and other sports stores. |
| Local police, fire or ambulance services | Community colleges |

CPR, Cardio-Pulmonary Resuscitation, or "Rescue Breathing," is another important one. Even in "good" times, many heart-attack victims, especially the elderly, can be saved if someone can start CPR right away. The *delay* is the big problem.

### Swimming and Life Guarding

Along with first aid, swimming is something *everyone* should be able to do. I must confess that, coming from a water-bound island country like New Zealand, when I arrived in Canada I was horrified at the number of Canadians and Americans who can't swim.

If you've been thinking about learning to swim, or taking an advanced course, or joining a club, or just swimming to get into shape, *now* is a great time to start. If you already swim well, Life Guarding skills are always a good idea.

Remember that any fitness activities will help you to survive if things get bad.

### Rescue Courses

I think our emergency services will cope, but they might be stretched a little thinner than we're used to. But I could easily be wrong. They might not be able to cope at all. Any assistance you can give is going to help. Remember all the volunteers who helped in San Francisco after the Loma Prieta quake. We might need all those and more, and not just in San Francisco this time.

On the other hand, if things get bad, and some of my more dire predictions come true, you may end up being the most qualified person around to lead a rescue. You could be dealing with people trapped in elevators, or stuck inside a locked building, or trapped in a crashed airplane, train or vehicle.

Fire rescues are extremely dangerous without proper training. Riots, robberies and other crimes can present their own set of rescue problems. Remember, a live Daddy is more use to your kids than a dead hero.

Contact:    • Government disaster and emergency preparedness agencies
            (e.g., FEMA in the US. See below.)
          • Fire, police and ambulance services
          • Mountain-climbing, hiking or other outdoor clubs and stores
          • Safety companies and equipment vendors
          • Safety councils
          • TEERS (www.teers.org) and ARTI (www.amerrescue.org) Rescue teams.

And once you have the rescue training, you may need to learn more abo[ut]... ...in... for whatever might happen.

## Disaster Preparedness

There are many varieties of disasters, and different training is available for them. If your employer holds training courses within your company, get yourself onto as many as possible.

Many occupations and professions have special needs in planning for disasters and emergencies. As a Systems Analyst, I'm concerned about such things as data backups, off-site storage of one backup copy, and how to quickly replace damaged computers, and people too for that matter. Your work may have its own special needs, and training may be available.

Get yourself onto as many courses in this area as you can, especially if your employer is paying for them. If your company does any of this in-house, be there. Right now, as Y2k approaches, is a good time to become a disaster expert in your own field of work. The time and money spent will be good insurance, both for you and your employer. A good idea even if there's no crisis.

### FEMA Website.

The U.S. Federal Emergency Management Agency (FEMA) has a website where you can take courses on-line. These are free for U.S. citizens, and modestly priced for us foreigners. They're well worth checking out.

### Government Disaster Agencies.

Most governments have a department or agency concerned with all types of disasters. Canada, BC and Alberta each have one. These people not only run courses, but they help companies, towns and sometimes individuals to plan and prepare. Some may have access to funds for equipment, special clothing, etc. Many countries, states and provinces have safety councils or commissions, some run by governments and some quasi-government. These offices will be able to point you in the direction of a great many useful courses.

### Winter Survival
### Desert or Mountain Survival
### Orienteering and Bush Survival

It stands to reason, "Bush Survival" won't be a very useful course if you live in Brooklyn, unless either (a) you're planning to move to a cabin in Montana, or (b) you always wanted to take it anyway, just for interest.

On the other hand, for those who live in mountain, desert or arctic environments, such courses could be very relevant. I've taken winter survival courses and read up, because until recently I lived in Alberta, and -40° is normal at least once every winter.

### Outdoor Cooking, Survival Cooking, Camp Cooking, Rice Cooking

If it happens that we're stuck in our houses in the dark, living off our stored supplies for a period, then any of these skills would be helpful. Check out community colleges, camping goods stores and outdoor equipment suppliers.

### Vehicle and Bicycle Maintenance
### Handyman, Construction, Electrical
### Any kind of repair or maintenance courses.

If things get difficult, we may need to improvise a lot of things around our homes, or find a way to fix things without the help of the local repairman. These are handy skills to have anyway, so if you were thinking of doing some of these courses, now is a good time.

### Driving or Motorcycling

The same applies here. If you've been wanting to do some courses, now is good. It's conceivable, though, I must confess, not likely, that we might need to drive in some exceptional and difficult conditions. Depending on your geographic location, winter driv-

_, desert driving, off-road driving courses could be useful. Any advanced driving course .s a good idea anytime.

As an experienced motorcyclist and instructor, I always recommend new motorcyclists take a good course. Old ones can also find it helpful. I was amazed at how much I learned from the motorcycle instructors' course, even after 20 years of riding.

# If Utilities Fail

If the power, gas and/or water should fail, make sure there'll be no disaster in your house when they come back on! This is especially important if your house is going to be empty for a while around Millennium Day.

## Electricity

Make sure things are turned off. *Unplug* all electrical appliances. There are three reasons.

One is the danger of fire or other malfunctions when the power comes back on.

The second is that microprocessor chips in your appliances may be damaged by spikes and surges in the power supply. Whether or not the lights go out across the continent or around the world, there *will* be all kinds of outages. Whether at the national, regional, or just purely local level, there'll be blackouts and brownouts all over.

As we found in the Auckland outage, there'll be spikes and surges as the power goes on and off. Make certain that anything you absolutely must leave plugged in is connected through quality power bars. Check that everything you don't actually *need* to have plugged in isn't plugged in. Everything.

You may be unpleasantly surprised if you leave a few things plugged in. Many appliances have chips that you would never have suspected. Anything with a digital display, or any kind of LED or liquid crystal display has a chip.

The third reason is that Y2k malfunctions, when they do occur, will be completely unpredictable. Any appliance with a chip in it is susceptible. Some percentage *will* malfunction. Some small proportion of those will be potential fire risks, or other risks.

A small percent of a small percent of *25 billion* embedded chips is still a large number. Be there in person for the post-Y2k test run, just in case. With a fire extinguisher.

## Water

One of the most important things here is to find your outside water (and gas) shutoff valves, and make sure they work and you know how to use them.

If the power and heat go off and you live in the snow belt, you may need to shut off the water to prevent your pipes from freezing and bursting. My house has a valve in the basement, but that doesn't protect the 1.5 meters (4 feet) of pipe sticking up out of the basement floor to reach this valve. The outside valve on the front lawn is the one for that.

Once the water is turned off, open some taps and let the pressure run out. *Then close them again!* You don't want a flood when the water comes back on! I'll say it once more:

## Then close them again!

But when the water does come back again, *flush the pipes thoroughly!* Remember the concern expressed by the health authorities in Auckland, that once the pipes are stagnant for a couple of weeks there's a danger of Legionnaires' Disease developing.

## Gas Supply

Be very, *very* careful what you do with gas. If you do anything out of the ordinary, get advice from a qualified professional. If your haywired gas pipes break, and cause a fire, remember there may not be a fire department, or a hospital, or insurance.

*Don't* mix different kinds of gas, or use the wrong kind of equipment. Propane camp stoves use a higher pressure than the propane stoves in trailers (caravans) and campers. You can't mix the two kinds of equipment. Get advice from a qualified expert, *before* Y2k.

Natural gas can **not** be used in propane burners, and vice versa. The two kinds of gas need different jets, and it's dangerous to use either kind of gas in jets designed for the other one. Gas is not just gas. Get advice from a qualified expert, **before** Y2k.

## Telephones

It's a good idea to have one or two old, old phones, as well as at least one totally brand new one. It's the ones made in about 1980 to 1996 or 1997 that are most in danger of not working. I have some old, old touch-tone phones, and I even have a rotary dial phone!

If your phone company doesn't work, there's not much you can do but wait. Expect them to go up and down a few times, too.

If the landlines go down, the air phones may still work. Nina and I have cell phones from different companies, so if one doesn't work, we'll just hope the other does. Among the extended family, we've got all four local cell phone companies in Edmonton covered.

# Food and Water

This is a fairly obvious problem, and one of the first that people think of. But you have the chance to be one of the few people who *act* on those thoughts.

You must be careful about good eating and balanced diet, and watch for group members with special needs. A serious Y2k crisis will not be the time for fad diets or any other restrictive diet. The longer a crisis lasts, the more important it is to have proper nutrition.

Issues such as dieting and losing weight must be put on hold. Cosmetic weight loss must be delayed until the world returns to normal. Survival is an important prerequisite for weight loss. If things get really bad, the survival of your group members may have to be placed ahead of everything else, at least for a while.

If you have in your family someone who is fanatical about dieting and losing weight, or perhaps even anorexic, you and the other group members must plan beforehand how you'll handle the inevitable conflicts. Bulemia would be an unacceptable waste of sorely-needed food. These people may need constant watching.

Those whose religion or other beliefs don't allow them to eat certain foods may need to think about that *before* it happens. If you don't eat meat, or certain kinds of meat, for example, you may need to ask yourself some questions. What would you do if you and others were in danger of actual starvation? Do you have the right to deny your children the nutrients when they're in a forbidden food? Or perhaps you feel OK making exceptions if it gets bad.

### The Toughest Food Question of All

And just in case you're sitting there reading this and thinking smugly that *you* don't have religious problems with food, let me throw this at you. What about cannibalism? In a desperate emergency, would you, or even could you, eat human flesh?

I bring in this idea simply to make people think about it. I can't say what's right and wrong for you, only for myself. You'll find here a few questions that I believe we all need to ask ourselves. Some you may be unable to answer to your own satisfaction. That's OK. The important thing is that you think about these questions a little, so they're not a total shock if they ever hit you in a harsh reality. Y2k or anything else.

Killing people is of course not acceptable. But if I were to die in a survival emergency, I would want to know that my body was going to be used to help others survive. Right now, that means I carry an organ donor card, signed by my wife. In a crisis, I won't know or care what you do with my body afer I'm dead. I want it used to save those I love.

There was a much-publicized case in the Canadian North, where a downed pilot and his (live) passenger ate parts of a dead passenger. I recommend the movie "*Alive!*," which tells the true story of a Peruvian soccer team who spent two winter months in the Andes in a crashed airplane (See Chapter 5). It's a story of heroism and sacrifice, pain and loss. It tells of real courage that showed in many and unexpected ways.

Most countries have laws against cannibalism, but in a true survival emergency no one has ever been prosecuted. I have not yet seen in the scriptures of any major religion a passage specifically prohibiting the eating of human flesh. I am not an expert on religion, so I stand to be corrected on that one. All religions condemn killing, but not all eating.

For me, my criterion for most things is "What's the *loving* thing to do in this situation?" If it comes to a food crisis, you will have to ask yourself if you have the right to starve your child to death because of religious beliefs, or perhaps just squeamishness. Do you and I have the right to choose to starve and die, thus denying our children the protection of a parent? How will you react if it comes to the crunch?

Some people believe they have that right. Religious groups who prefer their kids to die rather than accept blood transfusions have obviously come to a firm decision already. Where do *you* stand?

Whatever way we look at it, food could easily become an issue. Here are some ideas on what you should have:

## Stock Up

You could load up the fridge and freezer, especially if you're expecting only a short crisis. But do remember that the stuff in the freezer will only last about three days without power, and only if you don't open the lid too often. As long as there are ice crystals in the center of the food, it's safe. Always cook it well, anyway. Food poisoning could be critical if hospitals are closed or overloaded, even for a short time.

A gasoline generator, or an inverter off a car battery, will run the freezer. Check the wattage carefully to make sure the inverter has enough power to run the freezer. Get help from an expert if you're not sure, because this could be a life-and-death matter. But still be prepared that if something goes wrong, you might have to unload the freezer and eat everything in a few days.

Freeze-dried foods are great, but expensive. A few of these could be a good idea. You could use them in the early days of a problem, before moving to the less appetizing long-term stores. Or you could save some for a later treat in case the problems persist. Get them at camping and hiking stores, or from the Survival Center web site (see Appendix).

Prepackaged noodle soups are a great base to add dried beans, peas and lentils for protein. Or you can add skim milk powder or powdered egg for protein. You can add these things to soups or stews, also.

There are some highly-concentrated products that add taste to soups and stews and all kinds of foods, but are not widely used in North America. I recommend you try to find some Marmite, Vegemite (yeast extracts) or Bovril (beef extract). All three, used in minute amounts, add flavor the way soya sauce does.

Buy a few sauces to add zip to basic meals. HP Sauce, Lee & Perrin's "What's-dishere?" sauce. (For some reason, Canadians and Americans seem to have a lot of trouble pronouncing "Worcestershire." As any Englishman, Kiwi or Aussie can tell you, it's pronounced "Wooster Sauce." The 'oo' as in "wood.")

Also get the basics of mustard, ketchup (tomato sauce outside North America), hamburger relish, and so on. Get the ones that don't need to be kept in the fridge.

Fat has become an issue in modern nutrition, so there are a couple of things to think about. One is that you can be careful to buy low-fat foods to be eaten in the first part of a disaster. If the power outages and such last a couple of weeks, low-fat is fine.

But if the problems in the food-supply chain go on for weeks and months, you must remember that the body needs a certain amount of fat. If your meat consumption goes down as you begin eating your long-term supplies, then it's OK to use other foods that are high in fat. Peanut butter is a good one, and any kind of nuts.

Nuts are high in protein as well, making them a good food for a long crisis, but not a cheap one. Sunflower seeds have 17 vitamins and minerals, in addition to fat and protein. High-fat commercial cereals like Harvest Crunch have fat, protein, carbohydrates, and fibre, and would be ideal for a nutritious dessert in these later days.

If it ever got bad enough that we were getting near starvation, then the crucial factor becomes getting enough calories per day. While carbohydrates are still the best, when you're near starvation any calories will save your life. And those of your kids.

When we see starving kids from famine-ravaged countries on TV, this is what we're seeing. Kids whose lives could be saved by a handful of calories. Then, when survival is assured, we need to worry about other nutrients, and not just calories.

Concentrate on starches, protein and fibre. Because a well-balanced diet will be more difficult to achieve, *multivitamin pills* are important, even for people who don't normally use them. Megavitamins and alternative medicines are strictly a personal decision.

## Junk Food

It's OK to stock up with a few days' worth of candies and junk food, as long as you can afford it. But only *in addition* to a carefully-planned food stock in case of a longer outage. After the first couple of days you may need to ration the goodies a bit. Make sure the kids know that when it's used up there is no more. After that they eat healthy food only, and *only at official mealtimes.*

## Starches

Potatoes are a staple in most western nations, but they don't store very well. You should have a few bags, but don't overstock. Keep just enough to use comfortably before they grow shoots everywhere. And don't waste the shoots. They have all the goodness from the potato, so chop them up and drop them in a soup or stew. Get some powdered mashed potato for use after the real thing runs out.

Rice and other grains store better, but keep them dry and sealed. I recommend 20 kg (40 lb) bags. With the number of Asian immigrants to Canada in recent decades, we can buy these in our supermarkets these days. If you can't get them there, try an Asian food store.

Rice is cheap, and easy to prepare. It's also a good idea to get some brown (whole, or unpolished) rice, for the fibre. Fibre could be a difficulty in the kind of crisis we're preparing for. Brown rice does need to cook twice as long, and it works well mixed with white rice. *Try it out in advance.*

Other grains need to be ground or crushed before you can use them, so make sure you have something to do that with. *And try it out before Millennium Day!* If you've never before ground grain for cooking, an emergency is not the time to learn that you can't do it with the tools you have.

Flour is way more convenient, but also more prone to insect infestation. Still, in a crisis, well-cooked weevils are good protein – *ugh!* (I've heard stories of the Navy doing this at sea. Any bacteria dies if cooked at boiling point or above for 20 or 30 minutes.) Seal your flour in the original package in plastic tubs. Make sure some or all of it is whole-grain flour for the fibre. White flour and other white starches don't have any vitamins or fibre.

Oatmeal and cream of wheat are excellent sources of starch and fiber. Get a few bulk boxes of the instant stuff in single-serving packs, and a big bag or two of the old-fashioned kind for backup.

Packaged pasta is also great, and easy to prepare. Put a few frozen pizzas in the freezer. And some multigrain bread.

## Protein

Buy large bags of dried peas, beans and lentils and so on. Get many kinds of beans to give variety. Store them in the original packing, sealed into plastic tubs. Sealed packs of nuts are great, high on protein though expensive. Good for occasional treats.

For long-term storage of meat, fish or eggs, you must use freeze-dried, canned or salted products. Buy lots of skim milk powder, and canned milk. Canned meat is high on fat, but get some for backup.

Dried fruit can be an important source of protein. Raisins and figs are cheap. Prunes can be important as a natural laxative. Dried apples, apricots and other fruits can be boiled for dessert, or munched on for snacks. You also need a stock of canned fruit and vegetables.

## Grow Your Own

In case this becomes necessary, you'll need a supply of seeds. They're not very expensive, so don't scrimp. But watch out for hybrids. Some hybrid varieties grow really well, but won't reproduce. That means you can't collect seeds from your own plants to grow the next year. You want basic vegetable varieties, natural seed not hybrid.

If you have a little garden plot out the back of your city lot, great! Otherwise, 1999 might be a good idea to build one and try it out. For apartment dwellers, if you don't already have them, a few planter boxes to hang on the balcony or window sill would be nice. Just in case the following year you might need to grow vegetables in them.

# Controlled Access to Food and Supplies

Watch out for kids or others who are in the habit of visiting the refrigerator whenever they feel like it. Quantities may not need to be sparse, but because the supply is finite, they will need to be limited. But then again, since we may have no idea how long the problems will last, you may need to set those limits a bit on the low side.

If we have an extended crisis, food quantities may need to be severely limited. In most families it's the teenagers who eat us out of house and home, so they may need some serious briefing. The old saying about "Waste not, want not" will be specially true.

But in general it's the children and younger people who may not understand the seriousness of what's going on. They may perhaps need careful monitoring, after the ground rules are spelled out on food, batteries and other such limited supplies. Everyone must understand that each person gets their own fair share, and that's it. Under survival conditions, all must do their bit, and pull their weight. And waste not.

What children and younger people may not fully realize, and some adults as well, is this: If things get bad, then if one person overeats, or plays with a flashlight too much, or whatever, *they could endanger the lives of the entire group*. Running out of food, water or other essential supplies could become a serious problem if things get bad enough.

## A Sensitive Issue

There is one problem here that might be very sensitive for some people, and that's if you have a compulsive eater in the group. This person may be somewhat obese, or perhaps very obese. *That* makes it a ticklish issue.

But it's an issue that must be considered carefully, because if this person continues their old eating habits, this too could compromise the survival of the entire group. If you find this is what's happening, someone must challenge this person and state the ground rules.

This must be done in the most sensitive way you can manage, of course. But it has to happen, even if the rest of the group get along well enough that no one needed to actually spell it out before.

When the Y2k problems first begin, it may be difficult for many people to realize how serious it is or it might get. Especially for those who weren't expecting any real Y2k problems in the first place. They may not have enough.

A 1-year food supply could be stretched out to last three years if it had to. But not if we started out eating as if this were a one-month party. And since we won't know at the start how bad it's going to get, we need to plan and act for the worst-case scenario.

# Prepare Just In Case . . .

# Chapter 8: Just In Case It Happens . . .

Here's an interesting commentary from a senior businessman. I consider this to be an example of classic British understatement:

> One anonymous senior executive at Barclay's bank in England was reported as saying "The average man or woman does not appreciate what is going to happen. I'm going to plan for the absolute worst – I am talking about buying candles, tinned food and bottled water from mid-1999 onwards. People think that I am mad, but a company director I met last week is intending to set up a commune and buy a shotgun because the potential for looting is also quite high."

The major decision that we have to make is, *how long do we expect problems?* Is it likely to be days, weeks, months or years? Whatever *you* think is likely, you must:

## Hope for the best — and prepare for the worst.

If you think the problems will last a month or two, be ready in case you were a little under. Prepare for six months to a year, just in case. If you think it'll be a year, be ready for it to last two or three years, just in case. Prepare for the duration you think is most likely, and also for *one level worse*.

If you prepare a bit too much, the worst that can happen is that you have a bunch of food and stuff to use up. If there isn't any serious crisis on Y2k, then your grocery bills will be reduced for a while after the non-crisis.

## Watch it happening

As Y2k rolls around the planet from Tonga and New Zealand to the rest of us, watch it with your kids on your older, non-digital TV. The one that you've set up so it'll work even if the power goes off. Do this for good or bad. The TV will be showing live celebrations (hopefully), or maybe live disasters. Either way it'll be an historic occasion to share with your kids. Tape it.

Have an atlas and a time-zone map handy, so you can find everything to show them. A rotating earth globe would be great too. This will be a real learning experience for kids.

And the TV is not the only thing you'll need backup power for.

## Backups for Everything

The only antidote to Murphy's Law is backups. You must always have a Plan 'B'. You need backups for computer data, and you also need backups for everything else in your life!

- To get to work
- Power and utilities
- If your car doesn't start
- If your computer doesn't start
- Heating and cooling your home
- In case the phones are out
- If your bank is closed
- If everything else is closed
- If your life or well-being depends on any kind of medical machine
- In case you need fire, police or ambulance
- Etc., etc., etc

### Backup Your Business Data

Please, please, *please*, make sure everything on any computer you have anything at all to do with is *fully backed up.* Several times over. You'll need to back up your own computer data *in addition* to the official backups done by your Network Administrator.

Make your own extra backups, beginning around October 1999 at the latest. For really critical stuff, that you can't do your job without, take an extra backup using the Windows copy function (drag & drop). Do this one without using anyone's backup software. Even backup software could have residual Y2k bugs in it. Even Windows might.

## Backups for people

Make sure your team are all backed up too. Especially if you're in an "essential" job, one that the rest of us need you to do even when the world is falling apart. You need to be prepared in case people can't get to work. Or in case they can't get home again.

Arrange that people can fill in for each other, that they're able to do each other's job. Rent "*Jurassic Park*" and watch it for how not to treat staff (programmers in particular.) In that movie, only one person knew the computer system, a sure recipe for disaster. At your office or place of work they should all be training and practicing now, to make sure they can back each other up, or function with a bunch of people missing.

# Backups for Utilities and Everything Around Home

## Electricity

If a gasoline-powered generator is something you can make use of then it's a good idea. If you figure you can use it for camping, or at your cabin, or because you live in a rural area with occasional power problems, then get one. Get it *early,* before the shortages start. But it's an expensive item, so I don't recommend it for everybody.

A generator is a good idea if you have somewhere you could make use of it either after Y2k, or if there is no Y2k problem. For farmers, or people with businesses, campers or cabins, a generator is often handy, even in normal times. If you already have one, get it tuned up. If you buy one, insist on the usual Y2k warranty.

Much the same applies to an inverter. This gadget generates 110- or 220-volt AC from a car battery. These are way cheaper, but you do need the car battery to be available. Inverters have less power capacity than generators, so choose one big enough to run the things you'll need. Make sure the inverter has enough power capacity for everything you want to plug into it. With small inverters, you may have to plug things in one at a time. Insist on Y2k warranty.

With jumper cables (the kind for jump-starting a car from someone else's battery) and some *suitably heavy* wire you can connect the battery to a vehicle if you run out of power but still have gasoline. Try it out well ahead of time. If the power in your area keeps going on and off, a plug-in charger will store battery power for use whenever the power goes off.

You may want to get a spare car battery or two, or better, RV batteries. RV and golf-cart batteries are designed so they can safely be drained all the way before recharging, over and over. Car batteries like to stay fully charged, and dislike being fully dead too often.

The Survival Center sells solar panels (See Appendix for web site.) At $1400 US for an average house. An excellent idea if you're an eco-buff, and you'd rather be using a renewable resource anyway. Windmills and water generation are also an option, for a suitable site.

## Electrical and Electronic Equipment

Uninterruptible Power Supplies (UPSs) are a good idea where appropriate. These units sense when the power goes off, and switch to battery power through an inverter. This can be done for an entire house, but that might be overkill. It's usually for an important computer or other electronic gear, or medical equipment.

For your stereos, computers, TVs and other expensive electronics, use power bars with surge and spike protection. For a computer, use one that also has protection for the phone line. It's a good idea to plug it so it protects all your other phones, as well as your modem.

Spend at least $30 on a power bar. There are cheaper ones that claim to protect your equipment, but I'm not so sure. Just remember what you paid for the computer or home theater stereo that you're trying to protect! You can buy cheaper ones to daisy-chain into the good one, however. Just make sure that the one plugged into the wall is the expensive type.

I have read that power bars should be replaced once a year. It seems they do lose their protective power over a period. However, I think they'll last a bit more than that. You don't need to replace all of them, only the ones that plug into the wall. The old ones can then be used to daisy-chain into the new ones.

And if the power does go off, don't forget you'll have to arrange supplies of water.

## Natural Gas and Propane

If you plan to use a tank of compressed natural gas (CNG) connected to a barbecue or fireplace outlet, be sure you have all the necessary hardware pieces. Check it out with an expert, and *try it out* beforehand. It may keep the furnace going for a few days. Make sure you know how to relight the pilot lights on everything in the house.

Get some spare propane tanks for your barbecue and camp stove. Fill them. Early. Store all propane and gas safely in *approved* containers, outdoors.

## Backup for Transportation

Have several vehicles of a variety of makes and models available among your family, friends, car-pool, fellow workers, etc. If you normally drive, scout the *various* public transit routes *in advance*. Get a map of your city and your routes. Plot on the map, and then check out, alternative routes to work, to school, and anywhere else you need to go.

Don't forget escape routes, especially the one for leaving the city if it gets bad. And alternative routes.

# Physical Safety

## Fire Protection, Smoke Alarms

Get some extra smoke alarms. These things are cheap these days, and can easily make a life-or-death difference. Especially if the fire department and ambulances are not doing too well when you decide to have your fire.

Get several different makes and models in the hope that at least a few will be Y2k-compliant. Pay a few bucks extra for the ones with the escape light. Don't be afraid to spend extra on smoke alarms, as the better ones are more sensitive, but give fewer false alarms.

Three or four is the minimum for an average two or three bedroom house or apartment. One for every room is fine. Don't forget the garage, basement, and storage closet.

## Fire Extinguishers  *You gotta have them!*

Here is what I recommend every family should have. You may certainly have more, but you shouldn't have less than this. You should have one in the master bedroom of your house, and some of you may decide to put them in the other bedrooms. Each vehicle should have one. Regard these sizes as minimum; you can always go bigger.

| | |
|---|---|
| Kitchen | 2 Kg / 5 lb |
| Garage | 4 Kg / 10 lb |
| Bedroom | 1 Kg / 2 1/4 lb |
| Vehicle | 1 Kg / 2 1/4 lb |
| Camper | 1 Kg / 2 1/4 lb |
| Backpack or | Kg / 1 lb |
|     Carry-on bag | or smaller |

Be sure they're type **A-B-C** so they'll work on all kinds of fires, as in this Amway story:

Amway love to tell about a youth camp high in the mountains, far from water supplies, but equipped with more than 100 Amway 10lb extinguishers. When one of the wooden buildings caught fire, they saved it by emptying almost every one. You can deal with any fire if you have enough extinguishers. Get type A-B-C to handle all kinds of fires.

If you have quantities of magnesium around where you work, you'll need a type **D** as well. If the "mag wheels" on your car are true "mags" made with magnesium alloy, *they can burn*, and you need a type **D** extinguisher. Aluminum "mags" are not a problem.

If you have other chemicals at work, there should already be suitable extinguishers around. But check it out, *this year*, in case the safety people in your company are a little behind when it comes to knowing what materials are in use where. This is all a good idea even if there's no Y2k crisis.

Courses or some kind of training in using extinguishers can be important, but not always easy to arrange. With all emergency planning, it's crucial to practice. Unless people have been through the motions, under the stress of a real (or simulated) emergency they'll do the wrong thing.

Here's an example of how that works. Ever notice how William Shatner on *"Rescue 9-1-1"* always pronounces it "Rescue, *Nine-One-One.*" If in an emergency you shout "Go call Nine-eleven," under the stress people have been known to freeze looking for the "eleven" button. So even in normal conversation, you must always say *"Nine-One-One."* Practice it the *right* way every time, so it becomes automatic.

This is why simulations are so important in first aid and any kind of emergency training. In an emergency, you must:

* *Know* what to do,
* Be *able* to do it, and
* Do it.

At the very least, if you can't get training, *read the directions*, and find all the controls.

### Regular Fire Drills

This is another place where family, workers, etc. must know what to do, be able to, and then actually do it. And it's all stuff you should be doing anyway. *Even if you don't believe a word I say about Y2k, you still need to do fire drills at work and at home.*

And while you're at it, in earthquake zones you should throw in some earthquake drills too. Everyone dive **beside** a piece of furniture in the *"Triangle of Life"* (see TEERS in Appendix), or if you're in a vehicle stop and stay put until it's over. Remember to put the parking brake on! We had that problem in Baguio. During an earthquake, a vehicle makes an excellent cocoon to keep bricks and stuff from falling on your head.

Get pamphlets, videos and other help from your local fire department. Take your kids to see the "Safe House" and any other displays.

**Exits** Make sure everybody, especially kids and elderly, can find *and open* all the exits. Practice blindfolded, *carefully*, with a sighted person *always* beside the blindfolded one. Check that the exits are clear and safe. No junk, clutter, shoes, furniture, etc blocking the way. Especially no flammables like paint or cleaning fluids. Have practice evacuations through each different exit.

### Family Rendezvous Point

Make sure everyone knows where to meet when they get out. Otherwise, like my sister-in-law Diane when the train attacked my brother, you'll be frantic when someone is missing. Make every practice evacuation end at this place.

### Stop, Drop and Roll!

Be sure everyone, especially the kids and elderly, knows to

# "Stop*!* Drop*!* And Roll*!* "

if their clothing catches on fire. And how to use an extinguisher, or a blanket or jacket, in case the next guy catches fire. Be sure and *practice*.

There's a game you can play with the kids for this. You play "Tag" with a soft foam ball, with a red streamer of some kind attached. You call this thing the "Flame." One kid throws it at another, and if you get hit you must stop, drop and roll, while the others chant

"Flame, flame, flame,
What's your name?
Johnny's in the hole.
Stop, Drop and Roll!"

Of course, you substitute the kid's name where I have "Johnny." Then that kid is "It" for the next round.

## Special Protection from Local Problems and Natural Disasters

If you live in an area where anything in the list below might be a potential problem, you'll need to take extra precautions. Get all the information you can, look for courses, buy the appropriate equipment. Or move, if you're really, seriously worried.

- Snow and blizzards
- Dust and sand storms
- Tornados and storms
- Prisons
- Earthquake zones, volcanoes
- River or ocean flood plains
- Industrial problems, chemical, biological or nuclear
- Typhoons, cyclones and hurricanes

Our new home on Vancouver Island off the West coast of Canada is in an earthquake zone. Since both Nina and I grew up in earthquake zones, we're used to the idea. Our experience in Baguio in 1990 has both scared us, and given us confidence that we can handle things.

We were pleased to discover that in this region, many neighborhoods are organized into groups to plan and prepare for disasters, such as flood, storm, earthquake, forest fire and so on. Check with your local city, state or province disaster planning agency to find similar groups in your area. Educate them about Y2k (and have them read this book.)

## Don't Fly, Don't Drive

Essential workers, drive carefully. We need you to arrive safely at work and be part of the solution, not part of the problem. Others don't fly or drive until things settle down.

As I said above under "Medical," avoid injury (along with surgery and pregnancy.)

### Stay Home for New Year's Eve

That's my advice. *Stay home and watch it all around the world on TV*, surrounded by your children and your emergency supplies. Remember my story in Chapter 1 about my sister-in-law Melda, and the tourists heading for Tonga, N.Z. and the South Pacific. Invite people to your house instead.

### Vehicle Preparation

On page 159 you'll see a list of what you should carry in a vehicle. Start now accumulating all this, so as to spread the effort and expense over a longer time period. As much as possible, everything should have two or more uses. And it should all be stuff that would be a good idea even if we don't have a crisis.

## Some Group Survival Pointers

If things get really bad, and you have to leave your house, some of the basic rules of bush survival become important even in urban areas. If, heaven forbid, your house burns, or some other mishap occurs, you may find your group wandering, hopefully for just a short time.

Or perhaps you might be unable to avoid getting into a large crowd, during or after the Millennium celebrations, even though you tried not to. If any of these things happen, the following hints could save time, trouble, pain, and perhaps even lives.

These ideas are the kind of thing taught to people who must travel or work off the beaten path. Soldiers also learn some of these things for combat situations. A downed military pilot must travel difficult and sometimes hostile territory.

Any good book on hiking or bush survival will have lots of advice and help.

One of the first rules for groups is not to split up.

## Don't split up

Hikers and bush people know not to separate. Looking for lost people can cost a lot of time, and could become dangerous in itself. Of course, it's even worse if they think they're not even lost! Brief people at the start, especially children.

## If You must Split Up:

If there is no other way, then you must recognize the seriousness of the problem of getting back together. I think most people don't realize at the time how difficult this might be, or how dangerous it can be if someone's lost. The first thing is to arrange how to get back together.

## Rendezvous

You must decide on a rendezvous place and time, and make sure everybody is quite clear about it. Not just one person per group. They must all understand clearly when and where to meet, in case the smaller groups get split up too.

They also need to understand that they must avoid splitting up any further, and have backup plans in case there's no one at the rendezvous point..

## Stay Put

If one person or a small group does get lost or separated, they should stay in one place as much as possible. They might need to move to avoid danger, but they mustn't go running around looking all over. If you're all looking for each other, you can easily get everyone lost!

## Communicating

If you go into a crowded area, or you must travel in strange places, take along any equipment you may have that will help you stay in touch with each other. Cell phones are great, if they still work. CB radios or any other two-way radios might be more likely to work after Y2k.

The celebrations on Millennium Day will be the biggest party the world has ever seen. I would guess that about half the population of the world will be partying. That's about three billion people partying. All over the world, all at the same time.

We've all seen what a million people in one street look like. The Philippines had the only bloodless revolution the world has ever seen when they threw out Ferdinand and Imelda Marcos (she of the three thousand pairs of shoes!) In the TV newscasts we saw a million and a half Filipinos crowded into a Manila park, with priests and nuns lying in front of tanks. It was crowded.

But it was nothing beside the turnout of Filipinos and Catholics from around the world for the Pope's largest mass ever. Nina and I saw four and a half million people in that same park in Manila. (Our travel agency had booked 35 Canadians from Alberta, so we got to go too. I'm not so sure that anyone would have noticed our contribution to a crowd that size!)

I wouldn't be at all surprised to see crowds this size ringing in the New Year and Millennium at many places around the world. But this time we won't be there. We'll be watching from home, via the magic of computerized worldwide TV networks, while it lasts.

If it doesn't last, if the TV fails, that can only mean we're in for a lot of other failures too. Once that happens, we'll be too busy to watch anyway. I strongly suggest you watch from home too.

But if you're out there at the biggest party in the entire history of the world, or worse if you're a cop and you have to work that night, staying in touch will save hassle and could save lives. Maybe yours.

If the world gets bad after Y2k, then for a while it may not be safe to go anywhere without being in touch.

### Calls and Other Recognition Methods

Work out some distinctive calls, so that if your group are ever looking for one another, they'll be able recognize each other. A code name will work, or something else that you can call out. Don't use "Coo-ee," there's 30 million people in Australia. But something like it is OK.

### Backup Plans

Always have a Plan 'B' in case Plan 'A' doesn't work out. A secondary rendezvous point is a good idea. What should people do if they get totally lost? Especially children. What if the fancy radios and cell phones fail just when you need them the most?

### What to Do If Lost

We all need some survival training. It's a good idea even if there's no Y2k disaster. Get a book or two, or better yet take a course or two. Now, not November 1999! Make sure the books and courses suit the climate and region where you live, or places you might go.

### Look over Your Shoulder as You Leave

There is one very effective trick that's taught in hiking and bush survival courses. I learned it in the Boy Scouts years ago, and it works well. In a world gone mad afterY2k it's another of those little things that just might save a life.

As you travel through an unfamiliar place, at every turn or branch in the trail, or every road intersection, *look back behind you as you leave.* Because that's what it'll look like when you're coming back the other way!

This can make a night-and-day difference when it comes to finding your way home. Almost as good as Hansel and Gretel's trail of crumbs.

# What If You Need Help, or Fire, Police or Ambulance?

There may not be any. *There may not be any!* Did I say that twice? Without thinking, I typed it twice over! Let's say it again, then.

### There may not be any help, or firefighters, or paramedics or police!

We all need to be prepared, set up so that we can be self-sufficient. In this book you have received enough information to make that happen. And, I hope, enough information to convince you there's a chance it might all go wrong, so you need to prepare. But only you can make it happen, to ensure the safety of the people you love. *Just Do It!*

You will need quite a bit of equipment, organized into first-aid kits and such.

# Emergency Kits

You'll need to have a set of stuff ready for emergencies. A first-aid kit is an obvious one, but there are other things you'll need as well. You'll need:

| | |
|---|---|
| First Aid Kit | Extinguishers (See page 145) |
| Tool Box | Survival gear suited to your climate. |
| Travel Emergency Kit | Roadside kit (flares, etc.) |

Make sure these things are there when you need them in an emergency. Remember to take them with you when you travel, and make sure they're handy at home. Always pack things so you can get to them quickly and easily. Emergency stuff on top. The problem with emergencies is that we rarely know in advance when, or even if, they're going to happen.

## First Aid Kit

As we said in Chapter 7, you need a serious first-aid kit, and some training, and this we all should have anyway. 9-1-1 and the Paramedics may *not* be there when needed. Buy a serious first-aid kit. Get advice here from a friend in the business.

Add some extra gauze pads, for putting on a wound under a bandage. You'll need some "4x4s" (10cm square), and a few very large ones as well.

Make sure your kit has all the specialized things that your family members may need. Insulin, antihistamines, epinephrine, etc. If you have to leave your home during the Y2k problems – or for any other reason – make sure the kit goes with you.

Take a course in bandaging and basic first aid, and also CPR, especially if you have someone at risk in the family. Buy a small bottle of oxygen, with a breathing nozzle. You must have Pepto-Bismol, or kaopeptate, and/or a package of corn starch and some Imodium or Novo-Loperamide. Be sure to read directions on everything.

. You need some boards for splints. Be guided by what you see on your first aid course. Some pieces of 1x4 lumber or thinner, sanded and rounded, various lengths. It's also a good idea to cut a backboard out some plywood, with holes and ropes. You'll learn how to use it on your first aid course.

Add a whole lot more bandages, of all kinds. Make some extra triangular bandages, and buy some tensor bandages in various widths and lengths. Add rolls of first-aid tape ("sticking-plaster" in English), in various thicknesses, widths and styles.

Include some stretchy tape (Elastoplast or equivalent). Also get some waterproof tape, and as much as possible get "hypoallergenic" tapes, that will not cause allergies.

"Steri-Strips" are not bandages. They're for holding the sides of a wound or an operation together. They're often useful after stitches have been taken out. But they're expensive, so you may be better to spend that money on something else.

Add first-aid sprays, antibiotic creams, oral anesthetic, and lubricant ( e.g. K-Y Jelly). Get plenty of painkillers of various types, ASA (Aspirin), acetaminophen (Tylenol), Ibuprofen, etc. Generics are cheaper than name brands, and they're chemically identical anyway.

Here's an organized list of what should be in a serious first-aid kit:

## Equipment:

| | | |
|---|---|---|
| First-aid Sprays | Antiseptic, Disinfectant | Moleskin for Foot Blisters |
| First-aid Tape | Band-aids, Butterfly Closures | Cotton Swabs (Q-tips) |
| Oral Anesthetic | Tongue Depressor Boards | Insect Sting Allergy Kit |
| Pain-killers | Gauze Pads, All Sizes, | Safety Pins |
| Slings, Splints | Especially Large | Swiss Army Knife |
| Candles | Latex Gloves (Lots of these) | Hot/cold Packs |
| Tweezers | Lubricant ( Such as K-Y Jelly) | Absorbent Cotton |
| Eye Patch | Needles (And Waterproof | Alcohol Swabs |
| Flashlight | Matches) for Slivers (Splinters) | Tensor Bandages |
| Steri-Strips | Triangular Bandages | (Space) Blanket |
| Oxygen | Burn Ointment and Dressings | Antibiotic Creams |
| | | First Aid Booklet |

## Medications:

| | | |
|---|---|---|
| Earache | Antihistamines | • Topical Antibiotics |
| Ear Infection | Anti-Nausea/Motion | • Antiseptic Solution |
| Fever/pain | Sickness | • Anti-fungal Creams |
| Laxative | Diarrhea Medicine, | and Sprays |
| Anti-Malarial | Imodium | Cough Medicine (DM-D-E) |
| Antacid and Gaviscon | Adrenalin, Epinephrine. | Insulin, Antihistamines |
| Antiflatulent | Skin Care: | |

## Tool Box

I've always believed that money spent on tools is never wasted. If things get bad, you and I may have to rely on ourselves to fix a lot of things that we would normally "hire fixed." Around the home, vehicles, electric and gas appliances, etc. You should have a good set of quality tools, and more is always better.

It's a good idea to buy a brand with a lifetime guarantee. One of the better brands is Sears Craftsman. I have been told that specialist brands such as "Snap-On" are a little stronger, but the Sears ones are easier to get, and plenty strong enough.

Travel Emergency Kit: "Go Bag"

You'll need this even if you don't plan to travel. You might have to leave your home, for a variety of reasons. Severe weather, riots, fires, chemical or nuclear spills, or a number of other things could cause evacuations in the weeks after Millennium Day

This kit can be in an airplane carry-on bag, in your backpack, or anywhere convenient. Like the first-aid kit and the toolbox, it must be *ready*, where you can get to it quickly and easily when you need it. And, it must go with you on every trip, of course.

### Contents of Travel Emergency Kit

| | | |
|---|---|---|
| Flashlight | Jackknife (One with Lots of | Real Solid Food Things in |
| Small Candle | Tools like a Swiss Army Knife) | case you're truly starving. |
| Space Blanket | Snacks: Candy, Food Bars, | Access Bars (Page 157) |
| Small Sewing Kit | Fruit, Nuts, Portable Food. | Knife/fork/spoon/bowl |
| | | Waterproof Matches |
| | | Small Plastic Cup |

I used to have a 1-pound (450 gram) hiker's emergency kit, with about 30 items crammed into it. Each item had two or three uses. It had everything from waterproof matches to a teeny tube tent, with a razorblade to slash the tent to make it into a tarpaulin. I've so far been unable to find anything like it, so if you know where to get them, send me an e-mail, please. I'll put it on my website for all to see.

There are more items you may wish to add, listed on page 159 under vehicle equipment.

## Survival Gear Suited to Your Climate.

If our governments and services fail, we may need to exist for a while without the things that we usually rely on to keep us alive. In places where the climate is extreme in any way this may be difficult. Extremes of heat or cold, dryness and lack of water, as in deserts, all create special problems.

Those who live in such places become aware of the special needs, and the special equipment required. In Alberta we know plenty about cold. You must get some good advice from experts in your area, and stock up early on food, goods and equipment.

Don't underestimate what could happen if power, gas, phone and everything else all went down together, along with vehicles and perhaps everything else. Don't let familiarity breed contempt, as the saying goes. It's much safer to overdo the preparations than to underdo them. In such climates, complacency could easily spell death.

## Roadside Kit (Flares, Etc.)

Buy one of those kits that come in a sturdy metal case, if possible one for each vehicle. Some have flares, most these days have safety triangles. These are to put out along the road behind a disabled vehicle. I like to carry a couple of brightly-colored flags as well. I have some old red and yellow semaphore flags that are very visible.

If there are no flares in it, buy some separately. They're more visible in daylight than the triangles. They're also good fire-starters in an emergency. They burn for 20 minutes, so one flare and a couple of wet logs will give a good fire.

Roadside visibility is a critical issue, and can easily be a life-and-death one even in good times. Rally cars are required to carry flares, and get them out on the road and around the corner within seconds of an accident. The next car is usually two minutes behind, give or take about two minutes!

If your vehicle is forced to stop on the road, you must *overdo* the safety and visibility suff. Remember that at 100 km/h (60 mph) a car travels 1 km (1 mi) *per minute!* If you need to turn a car around, for example, 30 seconds is not much time to do it in. 30 seconds represents a half-mile, or almost a kilometer, of empty road!

Most of us grew up judging the speed of vehicles in cities at 50 km/h (30 mph), and learning to cross safely without paying too much attention. But people die crossing freeways. You have to focus, and *overreact*, to be safe with cars coming at you at unfamiliar speeds.

When I was on a training course 20 years ago learning to wave flags and be a corner marshal for race cars, this was one of the biggest issues. At times we would be on the track itself during a race, perhaps picking up a piece of debris, perhaps attending to a damaged car or injured driver. We were trained that if we heard a whistle, we left. Right now. Without looking or thinking. Trust the lookout, and run.

With cars coming at us at 300 km/h (200 mph) this was fairly important.

Cars at highway speeds arrive a lot quicker than you were expecting. Leave them twice as much room as you think you need to.

If you're working around a stopped vehicle, park another vehicle where traffic can see it, and it protects you. Especially at night. But make sure it's at least three or four car lengths away! Every year people die standing between vehicles when the back one is hit. A struck vehicle can go a surprising distance, even with the brakes on. If they do end up parked closer than this, don't ever stand between them.

## The Environment

These days, the environment is a factor in just about everything we do. And rightly so, we've screwed up this planet enough already. We're overdue to start looking after it the way it deserves.

Having said that, so you know where I'm coming from, I must now emphasize that survival must come before environmental concerns. In the lists that you'll see below, by all means buy the environment-friendly options where you can. But always keep in mind that where you meet a conflict, your first priority must be that you and your family should survive all this.

Even at the expense of some environmental damage. Hopefully, the crisis will soon be over, and we can return to our usual ways of looking after our planet. But you can only do that if you survive

Here are the lists. Just about everything here would be handy to have in the house, even if there's no crisis.

# Household Supplies and Equipment

**Candles**. Get wide-based candles and candlesticks that are not going to get knocked over. Find out how long they'll burn for, and try one to be sure. You'll need 3 or 4 hours per room per day, for a month or a year (whichever you think is more likely.) Estimate as if you had no other light source (no flashlights etc., to be on the safe side.

**Batteries** Again, estimate time needed, and over-estimate for safety.

**Fire extinguishers** (See page 145)

**Coal-oil (kerosene) lanterns.** Get "storm lanterns" ( a.k.a. "barn lanterns") because they're safer in bad weather or difficult conditions, and can be hung up. Stock up on fuel, *stored safely*. Over-estimate the amount needed, as for candles and batteries (and everything else!)

**Propane** lanterns, and Propane gas. A very good first choice for emergency lighting. Make your estimates based on 3 to 4 hours per night for a month or twelve, and over-estimate. Store fuel safely, outdoors.

**Camp stove and fuel**. A propane barbecue makes a good backup stove, especially for people who don't go camping. *All fuels must be stored safely, in marked, approved containers.* We don't want a repeat of the fires from 1973. There may not be any 9-1-1 or fire department. There's not much point in doing all this survival stuff, and then having you and your family die in a fire caused by your own disaster preparations!

**Garbage disposal. Plastic bags** in a variety of sizes. Plastic is more hygienic and easier to seal. A good rule of thumb is 4 to 5 per person per week. More is always better.

**Toilet** (in case water is off) Make sure you can get your garbage and toilet waste safely out of your house, to a place where it can wait in case garbage pickup has ceased. A black / green plastic garbage bag slung on the toilet works well. Be sure to have enough so you can double-bag for disposal.

**Bedding** Enough to keep you warm in the coldest weather your location can ever have, and then some because you're bound to underestimate unless you've camped out in it before. Then add some more in case friends, family or strangers come to your door in need. Remember that if all heat sources fail, this is your last shot at staying warm, or perhaps at staying alive. Add some more, just in case.

**Clothing** Hats (for cold and hot), gloves, socks (warm ones), thermal underwear, lots of T-shirts (good for bandages, too), insulated waterproof pants, lots of sweaters and coats. Stock up on sale items, or even second-hand, for backup. Keep plenty in each vehicle.

For cold climates, thermal underwear with a wicking action to keep wetness away from the skin (Gore-Tex or such). Amway Drifab spray will waterproof fabrics and leather.

**Paper goods** Toilet paper, tissues, paper towels. These are not a life-and-death issue, but wise stocking of paper goods could make things much more comfortable if you're stuck in your home for a few weeks after the crisis. To conserve water, you may need to wipe your dishes with paper towels before washing them .

**Can opener** Get a couple of hefty manual can openers – electric won't do! My personal favorite is a brand called SwingAway.

**Disposable plates**, cups, knives and forks, etc. Get the washable/re-useable/disposable kind ("Wash-or-Toss"), just in case you need them for longer than you expected. Styrofoam cups last for a day or two if everyone writes their name on a cup with a ball-point pen.

**Pet supplies,** including food, medications, kitty litter, etc. Plan how you might exercise your dog if the streets are unsafe.

## ehold security

rything off. Especially if you leave. If power, gas or water goes off, check that nouning is left turned on to cause a problem if it comes back on when the house is empty.

Check all locks and access doorways.

Keys for all who might need them. Re-key your locks if you think any undesirable former occupants might still have one. Hungry undesirables may be bad news. Remember to give the landlord a copy.

Fire extinguishers (See page 145)

Smoke alarms. Carbon monoxide(CO) sniffer alarm. Natural gas sniffer alarm. All battery-operated. Get a variety of makes and models, in the hope that at least some of them are Y2k-compliant. Buy some of them early, like *now*, in case of shortages, and buy some more as late as possible, in the hope that these are more likely to be Y2k-compliant.

Motion-detector lights, if you had ideas of installing some. A good idea anyway, even if there's no crisis.

Timers and motion-detectors for indoor lights (especially if you're leaving your house.)

## Weapons

Watch out for angry people whenever there's a widespread problem of this nature, especially if you think they may have a gun. Angry people are more likely to *use* their guns.

While I don't advocate the use of force, if you have guns, look after them properly and store them safely. Hide them well, where a thief won't find them. There are a number of problems with keeping guns in the home:

- More husbands get shot than burglars (by scared wives.) Statistics show you're more likely to shoot a friend or loved one than a burglar.
- In a confrontation, the bad guys can often get the gun away from you, especially if they're more experienced at fighting. Certainly, you can expect that they're less scared, more used to this, have less to lose, and will take more risks in a confrontation.
- If an argument breaks out, you can't use a gun that isn't there. Statistics show that more family members get shot in houses that do have guns.
- Kids can only get at guns in houses where there *are* guns.

That said, there's always a chance that the world may get bad enough that you need guns to survive. Sarajevo is a current example of what it might come to. Store and use wisely.

If you live near any survivalist centers or encampments, keep away from them. Or better yet, move away. Extremists of any color (skin or political, that is) are very dangerous when the controls are missing that keep our society safe. To quote Laurens van der Post, in his book *The Lost World of the Kalihari*, "Mankind is never so dangerous as when convinced he's right."

Survivalists, Aryan Nations, the Klan, and such extremist groups are so convinced they're right, they'll kill you to prove it. Heros are allowed to kill, right? *They* may think so. Stay as far away as possible. Let them do their own thing, someplace away from you.

My advice for dealing with potential violence is to avoid it if at all possible. Stay away from crowded places. If a problem begins to develop, *leave before it gets dangerous.* Travel only in groups, and so on. Remember that if you carry a weapon of any kind, a bad guy could get it out of your hand and use it on *you.*

Check your house for security. Is there anywhere someone could smash a window and reach in to unlock a door? Get tempered glass for that one, and for any windows you fear might be used to get in. Lexan is better, and it's even bulletproof, but it's way too expensive for most of us.

Do you have lights and motion detectors around your house? (Assuming there'll be power, of course.) Do you have bars on your basement windows? Get advice from friends and professionals. Your local police can help with burglar-proofing ideas.

Only get an alarm system if you were wanting one anyway. Make sure you get a Y2k warranty on it.

# Heating and Cooling Your Home

If the lights go out, and/or the gas goes off, we'll have a lot of very cold houses north of the equator. We probably won't at the time feel the least bit sorry for the hot people south of the line, but in fact they'll have their own set of problems.

In addition to taking precautions against freezing pipes and so on, we'll need to have alternative ways to heat our houses. Fireplaces are the most obvious.

## Fireplaces

If you already have one or more, that's a big help. If you have a modern, high-efficiency type, that's even better. If it's an older-style conventional fireplace, check whether it has a fresh air vent. Most of the air used by a conventional fireplace goes up the chimney.

- **Fresh Air Vent.** If you're using the fireplace to supplement other heat sources, such as a central furnace, then you're sending up the chimney large volumes of heated air that you already paid money to heat! A fresh air vent avoids this problem, and can be fitted if you don't have one.

- **Add a Fireplace.** If you've been wanting to add a fireplace to your house, now would be a good time to do that. Be sure either it's a high-efficiency enclosed type, or it has an external air vent. You're probably much safer having a professional install it. But keep an eye on him as he does it. Remember, there may not be any phones or fire department if the new fireplace causes a fire. It's supposed to help solve a problem, not cause a new one.

## Other Heat Sources

For cold climates, it's a good idea to have one or two non-electric, non-electronic, non-digital heat sources. Good old-fashioned uncomplicated propane or kerosene heaters are great. So are catalytic heaters, the kind sold for use in tents, either propane or white spirit (naphtha.) Be sure to use them carefully, and brief children and the elderly about using them safely. Make sure they *practice*, not just watch.

Have plenty of backup fuel, *safely* stored.

## Cold Air Vents

These are an important safety features in houses with central heating. They control the build-up of carbon monoxide. Many people stuff them with a rag or some such, to cut down on the amount of cold air entering the house. Not a good idea!

The furnaces need a lot of air for burning, and if you block off the vent, then like the fireplaces, they burn expensive preheated air. The best idea is to build an insulated "cold room" around the vent and the furnace. Then you can store vegetables and such at a cool temperature. At the same time you'll be saving on heating, and protecting your family against carbon monoxide poisoning.

## Pilot Lights

For every gas appliance in your house, you must check out how it behaves when the power or the gas goes off, or both. Does it fail safe? What happens if the power and the gas come back on, or either one without the other? Is it still safe? When things fail, what must you do to keep them safe? Do you need to relight pilot lights? Make sure you know how.

## Add Insulation

In both hot and cold climates some extra insulation is a good idea. If you rely on air conditioning in a hot place, can you cope without it? Insulation will definitely help. Make sure you also have some way to get some air flow (and I don't mean electric fans!)

Storm doors are good for cold climates, and screen doors for hot places. In Canada we use a combination door that does both. A second layer of glass or plastic over your windows will greatly reduce heat loss. It could be storm windows attached on the outside, or it could be a layer of thin plastic on the inside. A layer of Lexan fixed on the outside has the bonus of being bulletproof, in case that's a concern for you.

If you've been thinking about adding some insulated siding to your house, or some insulation in the roof, the early summer of 1999 would be a good time to do that.

## Additional Cooling for Hot Climates

Whatever you do, it needs to be non-electric, and non-digital. You need to find some way to get a breeze through your home without electric fans.

And with or without fans, you can cool the air entering your home by passing it over or through water. A fountain or spray of some kind is perfect. As some of the water evaporates into the moving air, it cools the air quite a bit.

Your water reserve will need to account for this. As well as needing more water per day per person in hot climates, you'll need to estimate how much you'll need for this kind of thing. And on the streets of New York, don't count on having fire hydrants for the kids to cool off in, if the water supply becomes a problem.

# Food and Drink

## Cooking

If power and/or gas go off, cooking will be a problem. You could use an open fireplace, but make sure you have suitable, safe, stable grills to put the food on, and tools for putting food on and off the fire. *Practice before The Day!*

A barbecue or camp stove will also do well. Make sure you have a good supply of fuel; wood, propane, naptha or whatever. Store it *safely*, where it won't get stolen. Take special care to put the stove or barbecue in a place where it can't catch something on fire. There may be no 9-1-1 or fire department, remember.

Have extinguishers and/or water buckets handy at all times. Check that smoke alarms are working properly. If you must disable a smoke alarm while you cook, make *damn* sure the battery goes back in after you finish. Much better to try and place the alarm so that you can cook without setting it off, but still get full protection from it.

Make sure you cook everything well, because even minor food poisoning could become a major problem if there's no hospitals, or no way to get to them.

## Freezer

Make sure it only has stuff you could use up in about three days, because that's about as long as it'll keep things frozen without power. As long as the food still has ice crystals in the center it's safe to cook and eat. Store some of your drinking water in not-quite-full plastic containers in the freezer. This will keep it cold for longer without power.

Have an icebox cooler available, and some ice or frigi-packs ready in the freezer, to take over for the fridge if the power fails. That will at least give you a day or two to get the contents of your fridge cooked, so you can keep them long enough to eat them.

## Containers and Storage

You would do best to buy some stackable plastic tubs, and best if they all match, so they'll stack better. Then, to make them rodent-, child- and insect-proof after you fill them, tape around the lid with duct tape or electrician's tape. You need to do this especially with things like flour and grains(for weevils), and sugar, honey and sweet things (for ants.)

Remember, depending on how seriously you're planning all this, you need this food to stay good for one or more years. Leave the food in the original packing, unopened, and place it in the plastic tubs. Then tape the lids carefully so they're completely sealed.

Mark everything on the side and top, so you can see what's in it when they're stacked to the ceiling. Keep a list, so you know what's there, and what you still need. Plan carefully.

### Childproof Storage

Since fire may become a critical matter with both power and water out, be especially careful about storage of matches and flammables.

And watch for cheaters. Sure, I'm quite certain, as you are, that you can trust everyone in your group. But just in case someone did steal food or water, they could potentially be endangering the lives of the rest of the group. All group members and group leaders must be aware of the exact situation about essential supplies, especially food and water.

# What Foods to Stock Up On

The Survival Center (see Appendix) has "Family Food Units" of high-quality air-dried and freeze-dried foods. These are real meat and vegetables, and when prepared they're just like regular food. Very expensive at approx. US$3000 (feeds 2 people for 1 year) or US$1500 (2 people for 6 months.) Keeps forever, expensive but excellent. We plan to get one as our backup supply in case the crisis runs more than a year or two. But buy now before the rush.

**Rice.** I recommend rice because it keeps better than potatoes, and is so much easier to cook and use than other grains. A 20kg (40lb) bag will do four people for a month of heavy use, or three months of light use. If you expect to have the power to run it, an automatic rice cooker is great. Get one from an Asian food store if your hardware store doesn't have them.

**Other Grains** Our western palates are more accustomed to wheat and such like, but the problem is that these grains must be ground before they can be used. Make sure you have a pestle and mortar, or some other way to grind your grain into flour.

And *try it out long before Y2k!* Early 1999 is the time to be discovering that these things are not as easy as they may seem. Not early 2000! Leave yourself lots of time to switch to another method, or to learn how to cook rice instead.

**Potatoes** Don't throw away the sprouts.

**Flour** Mostly *whole wheat*, for fiber and nutrients. Seal in a plastic tub, taped around the lid to keep insects out. If insects do get in, use the Navy method and cook them too.

**Pancake mix, biscuit mix.** Very handy, especially if your kids get tired of what you've been giving them. Again, get the whole-grain style. You could also get some cake mix for treats.

**Syrups, sauces, ketchup, sugar, salt, etc.** Stock up on the condiments you usually use, and spices too. You may need a little help to make the food palatable if the crisis drags on.

**Noodle soups.** Very handy. Good on carbohydrates. Buy plenty.

**Pasta:** Load up on this by the case lot! Easy to cook, lots of important carbohydrates. Get mostly the *whole-grain* type for nutrients and fiber.

**Dried Peas, Lentils, Beans, etc.** Good sources of protein and vitamins. Get plenty, in 10 or 20 Kg (20 or 40 lb) bags. Seal in plastic tubs.

**Canned goods.** Fruit, vegetables, meat, soups, *everything*. Buy plenty. And openers.

**Access Bar** This is a highly nutritious energy bar, very different from the others. Developed by Dr Lawrence Wang, biochemist at the University of Alberta, it can give enhanced physical endurance, and it can *double your survival time in extreme cold.* It was built from an analysis of the foods bears eat to hibernate, and it works by making the fat stores more accessible to your body. Order from a Melaleuca distributor, or www.melaleuca.com, or call 1-800-742-2444 (US & Canada).

**Power Bar** An athlete's nutrition bar, developed by a marathoner/running coach, a PhD chemist, and a food and nutrition major at UC Berkeley. Order from www.powerbar.com or any athlete's store, and many food stores.

**Amway Food Bars** One of the earliest and most successful in the field. You can contact the web site, but you're better off to check your Yellow Pages under "Cleaning Produc5ts," or just ask around for an Amway distributor. Everyone knows someone who "does Amway." www.amway.com

**Meat** Get plenty of canned meat. Don't worry about the fat content. It's no worse than a hamburger, and if survival becomes an issue, you may need that fat and all its calories. Freeze-dried meat is wonderful, tastes good and lasts forever. Expensive! Cook a large roast of beef or pork, or a ham or a turkey or two for a New Year dinner so you can make it last for a couple of weeks.

Limited amounts of frozen meat are OK, but be prepared to cook and eat the whole lot if the power and/or the freezer fail. Live meat is a great idea, as long as it can feed itself in your back yard. It could live there months if needed, to give fresh meat when you start running out.

A sheep or a goat to cut the grass is a great idea, and a great reserve of meat. But watch it doesn't get stolen from your back yard! An average family could live for a year or two on the meat from a steer, but storage may be a problem.

If there's no disaster, you can take it somewhere to be turned into meat. In a real emergency, you may have to do a number of things you never thought you could. Killing, skinning and butchering might be skills you'll be forced to acquire to keep your family fed.

## Water

This is a most precious and important substance. We need water to survive, more than we need food. Take some extra precautions here, and store way more than you think you'll need. Watch for the word "Potable" on bought water, or on taps in unfamiliar places. For those who may not have encountered this word before, it simply means "drinkable."

Buy bottled water – *big* bottles. Allow 4 liters (1 gal) per person per day for cooking and drinking. In severe times, down to 1 liter a day for drinking. Below this, you're running near the body's limits, but if all you have is a glass a day, share it and control it carefully.

Most water utilities do not have backup generators to run their water pumps. The ones that do will hopefully start in Y2k. No guarantees.

Fill a bunch of *clean* containers with (drinkable) tap water well in advance, say November 1999. Or earlier won't hurt. Plastic jerrycans, camping containers, 20-liter (5-gallon) pails with tightly-sealed lids, 45-gallon plastic rainbarrels or (new and clean) garbage cans, and so on will all do the job. Fill all the tanks in campers and trailers. This is just an extra hedge in case water supplies are interrupted *before* Millennium Day. To avoid plastic taste, you may wish to empty and refill them around Xmas day, a week before Millennium Day. Do them *one at a time*, just in case the water goes off as you work!

Early on December 31 fill a bathtub. Don't leave the last-minute things like this *too* late. The problems will start happening as midnight rolls across the continent and around the world, so don't wait literally until the last minute.

Estimate how long you think the power and water might go off for. And what the *maximum* outage might be. Normal usage, living comfortably without struggling, you would need 8 liters (2 gal) of water per person per day. This would be about 2 liters ( gal) to drink, the same for cooking, and 4 liters (1 gal) for washing.

For drinking, include water, juice, milk and soft drink supplies in your calculations. Store clean tap water for all this. Washing water should also be potable (drinkable) in case it becomes a backup supply for drinking. Don't forget there's another 80 to 160 liters (20 to 40 gal) of potable water in your hot water heater, and 12-20 liters (3-5 gal) in your toilet tank. Don't waste that.

If you need to be careful about conserving water, you can cut these numbers in half. One liter or quart each for drinking and cooking, and two for washing, would total to 4 liters or 1 gal per person per day. In an extreme crisis, you could cut that in half again without doing anyone any long-term damage. In a real emergency you would quit washing for a time.

Flush toilets use a lot of water. Avoid using them if possible in a water shortage. The toilet tank holds between 12 and 20 liters (3 – 5 gal) of water, useful if you're running out.

Be sure you have some way to go hunting for water in case you run out. (Backups, remember?) In rural areas, locate a clean lake, stream or spring. Before the crisis, not during. Have one or two large tarpaulins or sheets of plastic to spread out to catch rainwater, and a couple of 20-liter (5 gal) pails or bigger to collect it in. In Northern climes, remember the first rule of winter survival: "Don't eat yellow snow!"

In rural areas, if you can find a stream to dam, or a suitable pond, it can come in handy for firefighting. You'll need a pump. Your fire department no doubt has one, but we're not counting on them.

You should get some water treatment tablets, or filters. Get something that's advertised for travelers in the tropics, or for backpackers. But don't trust the filters. If at any time you must use suspect water, you need to *boil* it **20 minutes** to be sure of killing everything.!
**Juices**. Get the non-refrigerated type. If possible get the ones with lots of pulp. There is very little nutrition in juice, just a bit in the pulp.
**Alcoholic drinks.** Beer and liquor are not a good idea, except in limited quantities for an occasional treat. But only if you're very confident of being able to manage yourself and your group in relation to alcohol. If anyone in your group has any slight problem or history with alcohol, then don't bring any at all.

If it happens that things get really bad, we may be asking ourselves and our families to cope with something like they've never seen before. It happened this way to ordinary families in Europe during the Second World War. Some families starved, some coped, and some people couldn't cope.

If alcohol is available in your group, someone who loses control for a short period and gets drunk might be putting himself and others at risk. Better to avoid the possibility altogether unless you are very confident of your entire group.

I love to drink single-malt Scotch: Lagavulin is my all-time favorite. But I would willingly forego this pleasure through a Y2k crisis if I become aware that someone in my group has or used to have a problem.
**Other drinks.** Lay in a good supply of all your family's favorite (non-alcoholic) drinks. Add a bunch of powdered or concentrate drinks as backup. Nothing refrigerated, of course.

# Vehicles

The simplest and best solution if your vehicle fails on Millennium Day is to go right out and buy another one. Drive the new one around the block first, though. A few of us may actually be fortunate enough to do that, but not me! Most of us can barely afford to keep the one we have running, never mind throwing it away and getting a new one. As the Sinatra song says, "Nice work, if you can get it."

I plan to keep my 1981 Chevy van and 1986 Camry. If you have, or buy, something from the very early 1980s, or a 1999 or 2000 model, you should be OK. No guarantees, except for Volvo and Audi, so far. And then only their 97-99 models.

It has been suggested that apartment dwellers in large urban areas might want to leave the cities. Jennifer, in one of my classes, suggested a motorcycle and trailer, to go cruising America until the troubles die down.

I think this might be a good idea in a truck and camper, or a motorhome, but *not* on a motorcycle. (See my upcoming novel, "*Acres of Fire*.") And don't go too far before the crisis. Wait until we see how bad things may or may not get, before you venture far from home. Highways and campgrounds may become dangerous places.

You'll need some solid protection around you at night and while traveling, not a motorcycle. If things get really bad, traveling anywhere could be dangerous. So make sure you're in a nice, safe spot for Millennium Day, in case you end up parking there for some weeks or months.

Buy a pre-1982 or post-1998 model if you want to be sure as possible that it'll run.

## Vehicle Equipment

In the Prairie provinces, and in places like Alaska, Finland and Siberia, we learn about cold winters and driving. In hot countries they learn a different set of skills and precautions.

Below you'll see a list of the things I think you should have in your vehicle, divided up into a section for everybody, and separate sections for extreme hot and cold climates. Each of these sections is then broken down into things you must have, should have, and it would be nice to have.

While it's always important to have your vehicle well equipped with emergency items, in extreme climates it can easily become a matter of life and death. And of course

## For Everybody:

| Must Have | Should Have |
|---|---|
| Spare Wheel – *preferably two.* Wheel wrench. Spare wheel nuts Jack. 2x6 board or larger to put jack on. Battery jumper cables Towrope – Breaking strain should be 5 times the weight of vehicle. Toolbox,   First Aid kit Extra gas, *safely* stored in an *approved* safe container. Flares, safety triangles or both. Buy a roadside  emergency kit. Food – snacks, food bars, real food (can of beans), Hand-held spotlight. Fire extinguisher- Nice to Have Flashlights and spare batteries Extra keys. *Two* for you to carry, and some for  your passengers. Waterproof matches Red / yellow warning / signaling flags Fan belts. A spare for every belt on the front of the motor. Toilet paper. Store the roll in a tin can. Paper towels,  Tire gauge | Knives. A small hunting knife, plus a multi-use  folding knife (Swiss Army or equivalent) Shovel, axe(s) Coveralls. Keep clothes clean, and double as warm overclothing Boots. For digging, working, getting help. Extra fluids: Oil, Automatic transmission, Power steering, Brake, Antifreeze, Windshield washer. Silicone spray, for lubrication, and for drying wet ignition and spark plugs. Space blankets, for hot (shiny side out) and cold ( shiny side in) Extra rope. Break strain 300Kg (600lb) **Nice to Have** Cell phone, CB radio, scanner, TV. Hand cleaner. Amway "Work Mate" Planks or metal channels, to put under wheels when stuck Bug spray, sun block Crow bar and sledge hammer Air pump . Tire chains. Tarpaulin Airbag lifter jack. Solar trickle charger Fire starter cubes Access Bars (See page 157) |

it happens when you least expect it. If things get bad after Y2k, traveling may become very dangerous, especially by car. If you must drive, even short distances, there may be no one to call on for help if something goes wrong.

In other words, all those minor inconveniences that are no big deal in our civilized world could become life-threatening after Y2k. Running out of gas, minor breakdowns, getting stuck, overheating, all could become very serious if there's no one to call, nowhere to get supplies or parts, and bad guys roaming the highways.

As usual, you should consider the lists here to be the minimum. You can always add to them. All this is a good idea, even if Y2k is no big deal.

For hot climates, extra cooling for the engine is always a good idea. An engine oil radiator in front of the regular radiator can make an engine last much longer in hot conditions. Vehicles working hard at below 30 km/h (20 mph) in hot weather can often overheat from a lack of air flow, especially off-road in rough terrain. Adding a thermostat-controlled electric fan can prevent this.

Another issue closely connected with vehicles is the supply *and safe storage* of flammable fuels.

## Gas, Gasoline and Other Fuels

### Chain of Supply

My friend Kathy has booked a trip to Las Vegas for December 26, 1999, returning home to Edmonton January 2, 2000. I have assured her that if there's no disaster I'll be at the airport with flowers and humble pie to welcome her home. On the other hand, I told

### Cold Climates:

| Must Have | Should Have |
|---|---|
| Access Bars (See page 157) Extra radiator antifreeze Extra windshield washer antifreeze Warm clothing: Gloves, hats, socks, sweaters, sweatpants, jackets, ski suits, skidoo suits. Methyl Hydrate, a.k.a. Methyl alcohol, Methylated spirits. For water in gas. Candle or other heat source. Big, wide, stable, safe, long-burning candle. | Ether starting spray Lock de-icer spray Sleeping bags, blankets, rugs. Tire chains |
| | **Nice to Have** |
| | Sand and/or driveway salt, to put under wheels on ice. Spare battery, permanently mounted or securely and safely stowed Big, warm friend (a large dog is great.) |

### Hot Climates:

| Must Have | Should Have |
|---|---|
| Water, for the people as well as the vehicle. Salt, for the people in case of heat stroke. Bug spray, sun block | Tire chains. For mud. Useless in sand. Extra engine cooling. |
| | **Nice to Have** |
| | Umbrellas or tarpaulins for shade |

Kathy that if the planes are not flying, to call me, if the phones are working. I'll load up my trailer and my dear old 1981 Chevy van with barrels of gas, and come and get her. I promised that if I hear nothing by January 31, I'll go get her anyway, but I'm not so sure I'll have enough gas . . .

Going places in a vehicle, *you gotta have gas*. So the wells and pipelines and tankers have to get the crude to the refinery, and the refinery must be operating. The pipelines, trains and tanker trucks must get the refined gasoline to the gas station.

Then the power has to be on, the gas station open, and the pumps actually working, to get it into your car. Finally, you need a credit card that works, or enough cash, to be able to pay for all this. And a credit card needs a chain of banks and a (computerized) communications network. You see how a chain is no stronger than its weakest link. And remember that if 5% of the *links* break, we could have 20% to 40% of the *chains* in our society fail.

### Gasoline: Lineups and Safe Storage

Those of you old enough to remember the 1973 gasoline (petrol) crunch will remember that, aside from the fights and shootings in the lines, the shortage was deadly in other ways. Once they got that precious fluid, they took it home and hung on to it. Often in unsafe containers.

There were vehicle fires, house fires, apartment fires and garage fires. Apartment fires were especially a problem, because apartments usually don't have garages or some such to store flammable things like gasoline. So people would have gas in their bedrooms and living rooms. And they'd smoke.

Apartment fires always affect a great number of people, even when only one unit in the building burns. But with a few cans of gasoline to get it going, a fire can easily spread to several suites before it's stopped. In early 1999, buy the *right* kind of storage container for the fuel you will need to stockpile. It should say quite clearly right on the container what it can and can't be used for. Do it *right*. No amount of money saved is worth dying for. Or losing a kid for.

### Home Heating Oil

This is very much a chain-of-supply issue. One link out, and you freeze. And don't forget your oil-burning furnace has a chip in it, and needs electricity to run. So it's at risk in three ways: fuel supply, its own chip, and power supply!

In early 1999, get some *safe* storage tanks for additional heating oil, at least enough to get to the end of that winter. Keep the spare oil out of the house, and the gasoline too. But not loose in the back yard. There could well be gangs of kids roaming the streets and alleys, and anything left out may walk off. A lockable shed or other outbuilding will do nicely.

But once your house is warm and OK for the winter, then what are you going to do?

# Radio and TV

You'll need these for more than just entertainment. You may need them for some critical safety information if the world goes bad. Here are some ideas:
- Battery TV
- Lots of batteries
- Some rechargeable batteries
- An old short-wave multi band battery radio.
- Guaranteed Y2k compliant Battery-operated scanner for short-wave and other channels. Get one with as many channels as possible. Since scanners are always digital, insist on a Y2k guarantee.
- Chargers that run off a vehicle, as well as household chargers. (An inverter helps.)
- Stay low-tech, no digital displays. Sliding-rule tuning.

# Chapter 9:　　　　Conclusion

Maybe Y2k won't be all that bad. Here's my thinking on some possible scenarios. I believe that my Best-Case Forecast (Scenario 1) is the very *least* we should expect. If that's all it's going to be, then we'll be very lucky indeed. But I don't think so.

On the other hand, I don't think my worst-case scenario will happen either. We'd have to be very, very, *very* unlucky for it to happen like that. What you'll find here under Case 5 won't happen. But it's not impossible. I've included it to show some of the worst things that could possibly happen, so we can all think about them and be ready.

Having these things all happen together is about as likely as you and me sharing the lottery jackpot. It always happens to someone else! But it's *not impossible*, just most unlikely. But *some* of these things might happen, if we're very unlucky.

## The Five Cases

What you see here are six versions of what might happen, but only five of them count. Further on, we'll examine each one in detail.

0. Nothing Much Goes Wrong　　*Totally Impossible!*
1. Best Case:　　It couldn't possibly be less than this.
2. "If We're Lucky" Case:　　Everybody should prepare *at least* for this one.
3. Expected Case:　　This is what I personally expect will happen.
4. Worst Expected Case:　　I think it just might conceivably get this bad.
5. Worst Disaster Case:　　This is as bad as it could possibly get.
　　***This is not impossible.***

Case Zero: "Nothing Much Goes Wrong" shouldn't even be in the list. ***Yet most of the population of the world will make that assumption!*** Most people will do *nothing* about protecting themselves and their families from Y2k. Whether because they're sleeping and don't know it's coming, or don't believe it, or don't get around to it. For whatever reason, they will ***not*** prepare.

People in some parts of the Third World may never hear about Y2k. Or if they do, they have no money or flexibility to make plans and preparations. These are people who spend their entire lives just staying alive. There's truly nothing they can do about it. These are the same people who suffer badly in typhoons and hurricanes, and have little choice but to pick themselves up and try to rebuild their villages.

For those of us in the developed world, especially those who have read this book, there's no excuse for being unprepared. You can, and you must, make *some* preparations, for the sake of your family and loved ones. Those of my readers who are in the habit of buying car, fire and life insurance must surely see the need for this new form of insurance.

Those who are *not* in the habit of buying insurance are probably not reading this book either.

My advice, for everybody, is for you to *make up your own mind* which of these scenarios you think is going to happen. Then I believe you should prepare for that one, *and for the next worst one* in the list.

Suppose after reading this book you decide that you think Case 2: "If We're Lucky" is what's going to happen. Well, that's the right thing to do. You've made a choice, an estimation, ***which 95% of the people will not do!*** And now you must prepare, and 99% will *not* get around to that.

So now you're prepared and ready. But what if you're wrong? Not totally wrong, just out by one number. If Case 1: Best Case is what happens, you're in great shape! So you'll end up with a month or two of food to use up, but you were planning to eat for that period, anyway. And you now have candles, first-aid kit and fire extinguishers in case you need them.

Most of your preparations should be things that would have been a good idea anyway.

But what if you're out by one number in the other direction, and what really happens is Case 3: David's Expected Case? If you prepared for Case 2, then after two or three months you'll be out of food. Or you may be living on very restricted rations to try and make the supplies last. Either way, this is not going to be comfortable.

And if you're responsible for young children, aged parents, or someone with special needs, things could get serious. *Someone might even die.* If you're one of the decision-makers in the group, then I know I needn't remind you of your duty to these people who are at risk.

So if you believe that Case 2 will occur, you need to be prepared for Case 3, and then you're reasonably well covered. But there are no guarantees either way in this business.

### Hope for the best and prepare for the worst.

And what if you expect Case 2, and prepare for Case 3, but Case 4 happens? Prepare by adding a little more to everything, in case things get a bit worse than you expected. Buy a few more bags of rice, peas and lentils, just in case. You can't second-guess everything, so you must make an estimate get to work preparing.

Now I realize that in many family groups, perhaps even most families, the teenagers and young adults often are not consulted on decisions like these. If you're a parent or elder in a family or extended family group, you must for everyone's sake consider all of this very carefully. Then you need to involve every group member, including the younger folk, in the decisions, the planning, and the carrying out of those plans.

Each person should be involved to the limit of what they can handle. Children and teens need to contribute, and should be allowed to. If nothing else, this will ensure that they understand the seriousness of it all, and it'll help to prepare them in case they have to assume responsibility if you're hurt or absent.

Every airplane has two pilots. Every ship has a First Officer who could bring it home without the Captain. You must make sure everyone in the group is able to deal with whatever may happen. They must all know who is in charge if you have to leave, and know how to fill in for you or someone else if necessary.

On the other hand, if you happen to be one of those often-ignored teens or young adults, your duty is to make sure the parents, leaders and decision-makers in your group are aware of the problem. You must bring it to their attention, and this book too. Then pitch in and help.

If after all that they just don't see it, and they think you're nuts, you'll need to prepare as best you can, with whatever resources you may have. You need to prepare to save yourself, and I would hope you would extend that protection to the rest of your group if things get bad. This is one sure way to become a hero!

Remember, things you do should be things that would have been a good idea anyway.

Now let's take a look at the Five Cases That Count, and what you should do for each.

### 1. Best Case: It couldn't possibly be less than this.

I'm convinced that at a minimum there'll be thousands upon thousands of Year2000 problems that will not be very serious. Every one of us will be affected by at least a few of these problems. Most of the things that go wrong will be of the nuisance variety, or if they're serious they won't last more than a few days.

If your watch doesn't work, you may need to buy a new one. If your VCR or cell phone or microwave doesn't work, you may need to do things the old-fashioned way until you can repair or replace it. Hospitals and police may be overloaded, but they'll be there, and continue looking after us. Life will go on, after a short pause, maybe a few days.

But it'll take weeks and months to clean up the damage.

If the Y2k problems are this short, they'll be like a tornado, hurricane or blizzard. These storms last an hour or two or a day or two, and leave damage and debris that takes weeks and months to fix. Earthquakes are the same.

Programmers and others will be working long hours to get the software cleaned up and running again. Engineers will be fixing factories and power plants. After a year or so it'll all be a memory for most of us.

We'll need to be prepared for a few days of no power, phone, shops, work, school, airplanes, and no way to get to work or anyplace else. Planning for this would be like planning for a weekend camping trip without going anywhere.

## 2. "If We're Lucky" Case: I think everybody should prepare *at least* for this one.

On top of all that might go wrong in Case 1, I think there'll be many problems that will have somewhat more of an impact. You may have trouble getting to work for a few days – or perhaps longer. The lights may go out, the phones, newspapers and Internet may not work, and the TV may go off the air, for a few days – or more likely a few weeks.

Stores may run out of food and other supplies. Hospitals may not be able to cope, at least for a while. There could be riots, which would also mean fires and looting. If there's no water pressure the fires could get serious. If there's not enough cops, the riots could too. This might last a month or two or three.

But it'll take months or a year or two to fix it all and get everything working smoothly again. In addition to the software that will have to be fixed throughout 2000 and 2001, there'll be a lot of other damage as well. The recession will be about like the one in the 1970s, and probably will last a year or so, but might last most of a decade.

There'll be physical damage from riots and fires, economic damage, and people who lost their income or savings trying to put their lives back together. Many businesses will close, and jobs will be lost. All this could mean a lot of emotional damage to recover from.

## 3. Expected Case: This is what I personally expect will happen.

My personal outlook is that there'll be *serious* problems for a year or so. Businesses and government departments will fail. In some countries, I expect governments will fall, and their agencies come to a standstill. This will happen mostly in the Third World, where governments tend to be less well organized.

But not entirely. Some of the richer countries could be in trouble, too.

I fully expect the lights to go out right across North America. I'm sticking my neck out here, and I hope I'm wrong, totally wrong. But I must do it in the hope and belief that I'll achieve my goal: that some of you out there will be better off because you read this book, whatever happens or doesn't happen.

If America becomes the new Dark Continent, there won't be a lot of light elsewhere either. How long will we be in the dark? I expect pockets of local light will flare up within a very short time, as they fix things and bring a powerplant or two back into service here and there. But if the experience from the New York and Hawaii tests are anything to go by, powerplants will be up and down all over the place for quite a while.

The view from space-station Mir in orbit could be interesting, if Mir is still working that is. First the lights will go out, beginning with Tonga and New Zealand, and spreading around the world. Then little patches of the world will be lighting up and turning off again at random for quite a while.

And if the 13 days from the New York test turns out to be the maximum down time for powerplants, so the average might be more like six days, that's still a long time to be without heat and light. But who knows what the average might turn out to be?

Unfortunately, we're going to discover what that average is when the WFITFAFIT method kicks in. (That's "Wait-For-It-To-Fail-And-Fix-It-Then," a.k.a. "Fix-on-Failure"). Just like the New York test. So many factories, petrochemical plants, railroads and other parts of our industrial machine are planning to do it this way. This scares me, and I think it'll hit us hard, very hard.

The power grid in North America, like those in many countries, will need only a few plants to go down, to put the whole grid down. But if WFITFAFIT puts *many* of them down rather than just a few, then "Houston: we have a problem!" Like Apollo 13, we won't have enough power to run things, and we could lose all power and maybe die. Literally die, or perhaps just the economy.

Because of this WFITFAFIT approach to fixing things, it could be very difficult to get enough generating plants and transformer substations all up together, to make the grid operate. I'm expecting blackouts and brownouts, power off and on unpredictably **all over the world**.

*The responsible thing for chip manufacturers to do is stock up in advance,* **whether or not** *they've told their customers about the impending failures.* If chip manufacturers are overloaded, running out of stock, and some go out of business, WFITFAFIT itself may grind to a halt.

We'll get surges and spikes that could kill your expensive computers, stereos, home theater TVs, fax machines, and all those fancy electronic items we've come to depend on. Everything with a chip in it is vulnerable to power spikes.

Since 99% of the people are not going to be prepared, yours might be the only house in the neighborhood with a microwave that still works. You and I, of course, will have all our electronic gadgets plugged into nice new power bars, all over the house. A good idea even if there's no disaster.

Besides, the factories and so on can't even get going on the WFITFAFIT procedure until the power comes back on! So the power plants could be out for an average of six days each (if the New York experience turns out to be the max), or some number of days, we really can't tell how many.

But then, however long it takes powerplants to come back on stream, the factories might take about the same average too. Where does that leave us? The lights come back on, after however many weeks, and we still can't go back to work. And if they can't get replacement chips, will we ever go back to work?

Also, there could be physical damage to the power system, and the repairs would add more down time in some places. If this is extensive, the crews could be overloaded, and it might take a long time to fix it all. Small towns and rural areas can expect to be at the bottom of the priority list, so they could be out for months even after the cities are lit up again.

And then some of the factories will suffer the same kind of fate as the New Zealand aluminum smelter. And a few weeks later, as some of the power plants and factories are just getting going, companies will start going under. The recession will begin, if it hasn't already.

As welfare checks don't arrive, and food and supplies run out, the riots will begin.

Riots, fires and disturbances will be extensive. I believe we'll have riots like the ones in Los Angeles, but in a number of cities across the continent, and around the world. Police and military will need to act quickly, before things spread. With no street lights, nights will be extremely dangerous. With no water pressure, fires will be deadly.

I don't think Saddam will attack, but you just never know. He could. And some of the others are even less predictable. As I write this paragraph in October 1998, Saddam is getting more and more militant in refusing to allow UN inspectors to see his weapons factories. This scares me. Could he have plans for Y2k?

I fully expect a number of terrorist acts, including one or two on January 1ˢᵗ, 2000. And with the riots, I really don't think we can afford to be at all lenient. If they start fires, we could really be in trouble. I'm staying away from crowded places that night. I'll watch everything on TV (while it lasts!)

I'll be getting a satellite dish, for backup, in addition to my cable feed. I want to see what's going on, one way or another. I'll also be taping CNN and CBC News nonstop all that night, with battery power backup.

I think most vehicles will run, many of them with the digital dash not working, or something trivial like that. The keyless entry may fail, or the burglar alarm. But I do expect a sizable number will become *unuseable*, perhaps one to 5%, perhaps more. And I'm not holding out hope that warranties will cover this. Getting *anything* fixed may take a long time.

My personal belief is that all this will take about a year to get under control. I believe you should have at least enough food to live for a year or more. Nina and I have enough to eat reasonably well for a couple of years. At the time of writing we're still gathering enough so that we could live on reduced rations for five years or more if we had to.

Then I expect we'll take most of a decade, say seven to 10 years or so, to recover from the recession. I'm hoping it'll take us less time than after the 1929 crash, because I believe we as a society understand our own economics better in this day and age. At least, I hope so.

These are the things I think will happen. I hope I'm wrong, all wrong. I hope you all laugh your heads off – *after* Y2k. I don't think so, but I sure hope so. If you're laughing right now, that saddens me. I have a feeling you might be headed for some trouble.

Meantime, my plans are built around this case, and also Case 4: Worst Expected Case.

## 4. Worst Expected Case: I think it just might conceivably get this bad.

My personal worst case scenario is for major trouble lasting well over a year, followed by a severe depression, much like the 1930s, for *a decade or two*. It might take us 20 years to recover fully. And then the UNIX rollover is only 18 years away! I trust that will get looked after a little better.

If this comes to pass, we'll have all the problems we discussed in Cases 1 to 3, and a whole lot more.

I would not be surprised to see governments fall in many countries, with depression, famine and starvation following. These could be serious in many countries. In the developed nations, however, it'll probably be only a minority who are starving. *Probably.*

In many countries, including some of the rich ones, I would see numerous government programs simply ending, because there's no one working to pay taxes, and no way to collect them if they were.

### Electricity and Utilities

I can foresee, as a worst case, electricity being off maybe for months, and then unreliable for perhaps a year or two. Imagine what that would do to our industries, worldwide. And if WFITFAFIT then affected the few factories who hadn't closed their doors, they could take more months to get going. The ones that make it at all, that is.

No goods to trade, no way to earn money. No taxes, governments laying off. In this, the worst case that I think could actually happen, I can see the downward economic spiral gathering a lot of momentum. It could bottom out at a devastating level.

That's why, if it gets this bad, I can see us taking up to 20 years to recover. And there's always just a chance we could be plunged into another Dark Ages, as Davidson and Rees-Mogg predict in *"The Great Reckoning."*

## Law and Order

The riots would begin. Our ability to control them will be even less than I pictured before. With no streetlights, we would live in a jungle every night. Dog eat dog. Even staying off the streets won't always be good enough.

In South Africa, so I read, during the time of trouble before the emancipation of the black majority, there was very little law and order in many of the "black townships." Groups of young men would routinely capture a young woman off a street corner, secure in the knowledge that there were nowhere near enough police to bother them.

Since they were armed young thugs, they had no fear of repercussions from the people around them either. Typically, they would drive the girl out into the bush, beat and gang-rape her, and usually deposit her, devastated, back in town. Frequently infected with HIV.

Sometimes they didn't need to bother with the last part. Just leave the body in the bush.

If our society begins to break down, God only knows what the gang elements may do for "fun." Even now, we know that groups like Hell's Angels and The Mob can rape, pillage and kill almost at will. Take away large chunks of the power and ability of our police forces, and that could be us they're doing it to.

This is why I'm advocating that our authorities need to be armed *in advance* with *all the weapons* they might need. I mean not just the firearms, but the legal weapons also. Governments must be *ready* to declare martial law, and hope like hell they don't need to. If we need it, we'll need it around 12:05 a.m. on January 1, 2000.

Generals must be *ready* to order massive counterattacks, urban or international, and hope they don't need to. If it gets this bad, I'm just afraid they might need to. Riots and disturbances will crop up everywhere, day after day, week after week. And I'm not sure how much we can demand from our soldiers and police. They too have families to worry about

Military bases and police forces must have contingency plans in place. They may need to gather in and protect the families of police, soldiers and essential workers while those guys are putting their lives on the line to protect the rest of us. This is one of the steps included in Operation Abacus. They need to have an escalating series of plans for dealing with minor, major or critical disturbances.

## Fires

With power out, and water out for so long, I would not be surprised to see much of Manhattan alight. Once a fire gets going in a high-rise building, it'll easily spread to the next one if there's *no water whatever.* No sprinklers to slow down a fire. No hoses playing on neighboring buildings.

A high-rise building doesn't just burn neatly down to the ground like a candle. So far in our history, we've been fortunate enough, and our engineers and firefighters good enough, that we've only once had a skyscraper burn all the way to the ground (that I know of. Somewhere in Brazil, I was told.)

Even when an airplane flew into the Empire State Building in the 1930s, the damage was confined to a few floors. It was completely repaired.

But buildings fall over when they burn. A skyscraper is much taller than it is wide. If we have no water, and a skyscraper burns to the ground, at some stage the burning building will fall on top of a couple of nearby buildings. It'll be like trying to burn one stalk of grass in a dry field.

Not every fire will spread like this, but some will. I expect that, if things get this bad, there may be *"Acres of Fire"* in the heart of several major cities around the world, sometime in the first few weeks and months of the new millennium. And some will be in the rich nations, because some will be started by terrorists and ghetto rioters.

## Terrorists

In the worst case, there would be a large number of terrorist acts around the world on January 1ˢᵗ and in the days following. Many of these groups will have planned it that way. And Hell's Angels and their ilk will be out there too.

We can be *totally certain* that people like this will take advantage of what's going on, to destroy a few buildings and people here and there. Then, as it becomes apparent that we're having trouble controlling things, more will jump on the bandwagon.

There is cause for concern in the recent gift of US$25 million *of the Saudi people's money* from the Saudi royal family to the Hamas terrorist group (Sunday Times April 12, 1998). This group has killed scores of Israelis in a series of suicide bombings since 1996.

I imagine it would take them only a year or so to spend that kind of money stocking up on bombs and guns – just about in time for Y2k! And it has all taken place in another country, where you and I and the United Nations can do nothing about it.

I strongly recommend that the Jewish community worldwide arrange for their businesses and synagogues to be patrolled at all times throughout the crisis period. Police forces should also be helping, but may be spread too thin. Like everyone else at that time, the Jewish people will be forced to rely on their own resources.

We can *hope* for help from the authorities, but we shouldn't expect any. Stock up on water, extinguishers, smoke alarms. Don't rely on the Fire Department or the water pressure.

Just like the rash of copycat airplane hijackings we had in the 1970s, they'll all want to try it. And when they realize we can't put out fires, they'll have a wonderful new weapon. The venerable Molotov cocktail will come into its own as the world's cheapest and most effective terrorist tool.

And, unlike fancy police laser scopes and army rocket weapons, it doesn't use any microchips! The Molotov cocktail is guaranteed to work in Y2k because it's nothing more than a bottle of gasoline (petrol) with a rag stuck in the neck.

Light, throw, burst. These things were used very effectively by Hungarian freedom fighters against Soviet tanks in their 1956 revolution. Once they got the tank commander to open his trapdoor, that is.

The World Trade Center in New York is well equipped with sprinkler systems. It's a modern building, designed to be as fireproof as they come. The building stood up quite well to the bomb blast, and has long since been fully repaired.

But what if there was no water? What if these guys loaded up two or three more vans with barrels of gasoline, and parked them a little way from the bomb truck? We would then be the recipients of the world's largest ever Molotov cocktail! And no way to put it out.

If it gets like this, I don't think I want to work in a high-rise in a major center after Y2k.

## Vehicles

I believe that it *could* get bad enough that maybe half of the vehicles on our roads will not run. But even 10 or 20 percent would be disastrous. This would place an unbelievable strain on everything else. Emergency services, government, industry and our daily lives depend on automobiles second only to computers.

The costs would be horrendous. The cost would be bad enough to fix the ones that can be fixed. Then there's the replacement cost for the ones that can't be fixed. But if the power and the factories are down for a year or two, how would we replace them anyway?

And how would we fix the fixable ones, if the dealerships close, and no one's making the replacement chips? If it gets this bad, it'll be a year or two before our industries are producing again. We might see millions of valuable, perfectly fixable cars and trucks abandoned by the roadside.

Rusting, deteriorating, vandalized. Looking a lot like the highway from Kuwait into Iraq after Desert Storm. (See "*Fires of Kuwait*," IMAX.)

We know they won't last long there. They'll be vandalized and stripped in short order, and there would be very little the police could do. Far too many, and the cops will be tied up just trying to keep war from breaking out.

Imagine the effect all this will have on the economy. Add all these things together, and I think you'll agree that in this case it could take a couple of decades for the world economy to recover.

When our society does eventually recover, some parts of it could be very different from what we're used to. If we have to rebuild society, I think it likely we'll focus on the essentials, and drop a lot of the extras. Professional sports and entertainment are areas that might be greatly reduced. Highly-paid athletes, actors and "musicians" might become a thing of the past.

Jobs and careers may disappear. Income tax may be at a flat percentage rate.

Some of the changes in our society might be things that are unthinkable in today's political climate. Government payouts like welfare, unemployment, medical and old age were unheard of last century. It's conceivable that we might end up back in a similar mode to that period, at least in some aspects of society.

If our society has changed by the time we recover, this will be very difficult for most older people to handle. Not that it'll be easy for the youngsters, either. But for people my age, we have lived with one set of post-depression, post-war rules all our lives. A totally new set of rules about how life works may be beyond the understanding of most older people.

The biggest modern-day example of such a change of societal rules is post-communist Russia. Their experience shows graphically how difficult it can be to adjust to a new order. They have had social unrest, rampant crime, and severe depression. There have been riots, and people have died in them. Y2k might conceivably get that bad for us. And no-one to call on for help.

This is stuff that can't even be thought about in "normal" times. But when we as individuals, as well as our society, are faced with actual survival issues, all the rules may change. I sure don't presume to say what's right and what's wrong here.

I'm just the messenger, prodding you to think about these things and be ready in case you do have to face them. And we must all do some thinking, even about the unthinkable.

## 5. Worst Disaster Case: I believe this is as bad as it could possibly get.

I really don't think this is going to happen. And I surely hope it doesn't. You see it here because I feel I would be doing you a disservice if I simply ignored the possibility. You'll need to read what's here, and come to your own conclusions. Remember, you owe it to your loved ones to *"Hope for the best and prepare for the worst."*

### *This is not impossible.*

#### It won't happen this way (but it's not impossible.)

The last time something like this scenario happened, it was called the "Dark Ages," and Europe was plunged into chaos and anarchy for 500 years. In *"The Great Reckoning,"* Davidson and Rees-Mogg point out that historians now agree that the Dark Ages were caused by the *invention of the stirrup* about a hundred years earlier. How could that be, you say?

Until then, men could not fight on horseback. They rode horses *to* the war, and had to get off to fight. With the stirrup, they had enough stability and control to fight from the saddle. This changed the shape of warfare, *as surely as the microchip is today.*

Over the next few decades, there arose the concept of the *knight*, an expensive, highly-trained warrior who fought on horseback, with stirrups. When these paid killers were not fighting a war for some lord or king, they sat at home, bored. Hence the tournaments we read about in medieval literature like *Ivanhoe* and King Arthur.

What these men noticed next was the stream of goods and wealth in the form of taxes, going from the countryside into the major cities like London, Rome and Paris. Naturally, they helped themselves, and the wagons were defenseless against them.

Soon the central governments of the European nations were starved of supplies. Governments became weak and disorganized, and depression, chaos and anarchy ensued. It took five hundred years to recover.

Sound familiar? These days the "knights" are gang members and drug dealers. A hundred years ago the "knights" were robbing stage coaches in the Wild West.

## The Worst That Could (But Won't) Happen

The list below is all the things I can imagine that *could* go wrong. I fully expect that a few of them *might* happen. I really can't imagine all of them happening. But we, and our governments, must be ready, to nip them in the bud if they do occur.

What if *everything* I've talked about in this book comes to pass, and what if each one happens in its worst or near-worst form? Here's the list:

- Commerce and industry halted by MIS computer problems.
- Government payouts cease altogether – welfare, unemployment, medical, old age, etc.
- Police, military and emergency services are totally overloaded, none of their equipment works, and their staff want to stay home to protect their families.
- Hospitals and medical services are totally overloaded, none of their equipment works, and their staff want to stay home to protect their families.
- Telephone systems are totally overloaded, none of their equipment works, and their staff want to stay home to protect their families.
- The lights go out right around the world, and stay out.
- WFITFAFIT grinds to a halt through a lack of replacement chips. Lights stay out, factories stay silent, and trains don't run.
- With no power, there's no central heating in cold climates. Pipes and people freeze.
- With no power there's no water pressure.
- Firefighting services are totally overloaded, none of their equipment works, and their staff want to stay home to protect their families. And there's no water pressure anyway.
- Airplanes get lost and some miss the airport. Some reach the airport and crash trying to land in the dark. A few collide in mid-air. Radar is out.
- Ships run aground, railroad signals don't work and trains collide.
- Driverless trains run off the end of the tracks.
- Emergency services are totally overloaded, none of their equipment works, and their staff want to stay home to protect their families.
- One nuclear plant suffers a total meltdown, and releases clouds of radioactive material.
- A dozen others around the world have partial meltdowns, and release "small" amounts of radiation. People die. It's like Chernobyl and Bhopal rolled into one.
- One actually blows up. Properly mistreated, they all have the *potential* to become A-bombs. Rescue teams from other countries are all busy at home. Fallout drifts over neighboring countries.
- Nuclear emergency services are totally overloaded, none of their equipment works, and their staff want to stay home to protect their families.
- Terrorists hijack planes and ships (the few that are working), terrorize and kill people, but find there's no gain in it for them.

- We don't have an airplane that will make it with them to Cuba. And Cuba doesn't want them right now. They're busy, and the lights are out.
- Terrorists hijack buildings and airports, terrorize and kill people, but find there's no gain in it for them.
- Terrorists burn buildings.
- Riots break out in the inner cities all over the world. Rioters burn buildings.
- Riots break out in prisons. Rioters burn buildings.
- Prisoners break out of prisons, or are (perhaps unwisely) released by wardens who refuse to starve them, or refuse to allow them to die in their own fires.
- Released and escaped prisoners add to the crime, looting, rape, AIDS, violence, fires.
- *"Acres of Fire"* form in the center of every major city in the world.
- Saddam, Moammar, Mladic and half-a-dozen others attack various unprotected states.
- Saddam drops every Scud he has on Israel. Patriot missiles malfunction. Scuds score.
- Israel retaliates with whatever is still working. All of it. Everything.
- Palestinians attack Israel.
- Jerusalem and Baghdad are on fire. There's no water, no help from other nations.
- Karadzic and Mladic come out of hiding and restart the Serbian "ethnic cleansing."
- Ethnic Albanians in Kosovo province rebel against Serbian rule.
- Ethnic minorities revolt all over the world.
- The U.N. peacekeeping forces are totally overloaded, none of their equipment works, and their soldiers want to stay home to protect their families.
- Our own military forces have been badly depleted by cutbacks. They're totally overloaded, none of their equipment works, and our soldiers want to stay home to protect their families.
- Saddam detonates a Soviet nuclear device on Tel Aviv.
- Saddam releases anthrax over western Europe.
- Ebola breaks out in Africa. Refugees carry it with them as they flee.
- Humanitarian and medical relief services are totally overloaded, none of their equipment works, and their staff want to stay home to protect their families.
- Interruptions in the supply chain cause shortages of food, drugs and medical supplies.
- Shortages of condoms causes increased spread of AIDS.
- Rapes by rioters, gang members, prisoners, terrorists, rebels and invading aggressor armies cause uncontrolled spread of AIDS. Rioters, gang members, prisoners, terrorists, rebels and invading aggressor armies don't bother to use condoms even in "good" times.
- Hospitals and medical services are totally overloaded, none of their equipment works, and their staff want to stay home to protect their families from rioters, gang members, prisoners, terrorists, rebels, invading aggressor armies and AIDS. And they've run out of condoms.
- The planets all line up on May 5. Disasters begin in March, peak through April and May, and continue diminishing through June, July and August.
- Hundreds of thousands die in earthquakes. Millions die in coastal floods.
- Hospitals and medical and emergency services are totally overloaded, none of their equipment works, and their staff want to stay home to protect their families. Disaster services collapse.
- The world economy totally collapses. Wall Street burns.
- There are *"Acres of Fire"* in Manhattan.

If all of this did actually happen, we might possibly begin a new Dark Ages. This time the whole world, not just Europe. The new world order would look worse than Brooklyn, worse than post-communist Russia, worse than the post-war Chinese warlords, worse than Sarajevo. The Mob, the Hell's Angels, the drug lords and the warlords would take over.

If that happened, the world would look like Mad Max, the Road Warriors and Waterworld rolled into one.

Right now in 1998 the world is tightly controlled, and has been for almost two centuries. All countries have police forces and armies. Despite their various levels of reliability in some countries, these forces all contribute something to a state of relative peace and stability, law and order. Take away a sizable chunk of that control, and the bad guys will have field day. It's automatic.

They're *not* going to sit around waiting for us to rebuild a world which they're hellbent to destroy anyway. Hell's Angels, The Mob and Mafia, petty vandals, thieves and murderers will go out and "just do it" if the cops are busy elsewhere, if there are any cops around.

We've all seen the looting that ensues once a riot has got out of hand, even in "good" times. Most of the looters are "good" guys, ordinary people who would not normally be considered criminals. But when the controls are gone, they will simply help themselves.

We've seen it. And the bad guys will do worse, far worse. And all the thieving of perhaps billions of dollars worldwide will weaken businesses and strengthen the depression.

Stay out of crowded places. Prepare your home and business to be as burglar-proof as you reasonably can.

## Epidemics

What if Ebola or plague broke out in Africa? Last time it took a concerted and expensive effort from the developed countries to stop the outbreak. Many doctors and nurses from what was then Zaire, and other countries as well, volunteered and placed their own lives in danger. Some in fact did catch it, and some died.

During the outbreak, it was found that one-fourth of the infected patients survived. It seems that one-fourth of the population have a natural resistance to Ebola, enough to survive. It's no doubt genetic, though there's no real proof of that yet.

But this suggests that if Ebola or something like it *did* break out in a Y2k disaster, we might be left with only the resistant one-fourth of us to populate the planet.

That's basically what happened in the "Black Death" plague epidemics in medieval Europe. The resistant two-thirds of the population of Europe survived. Plague, TB, influenza, polio, cholera, typhoid, typhus, dengue, all have potential for epidemics if things get bad.

Get *all* your shots.

## A Different World

Even if society doesn't collapse totally, some writers are predicting that the world may look very different. A flat-rate tax structure would sure affect the life and livelihood of an accountant or a tax lawyer! There would be no complexity left in it for them to try and explain to you and me. They'd be out of a job.

There could be a lot of changes like this. Maybe not that one, but others like it, or some that we really can't imagine.

But not the total destruction of society.

That's the kind of scenario we've seen depicted in movies like "*The Morning After,*" a made-for-TV movie about the aftermath of a U.S.-Soviet nuclear exchange. Numerous other apocalyptic movies have suggested what might happen when our civilization collapses totally, but I think "*The Morning After*" was one of the most realistic (See Chapter 5).

One scene has always stuck in my mind. Some months after the holocaust, the family are eking out an existence on the farm. The farmer finds refugees from the city squatting on a corner of his land, and orders them off. So they shoot him. Just like that. End of story. End of life.

In a scenario like this, life could become very cheap. Most unlikely, but not impossible. Watch out. Stay away from crowds, stay indoors if things get bad.

If we had a total collapse of our society like this, which we won't, but if we did, the world might look very different. Those who survived would likely be subsistence farming, far from the shells of the cities.

It could be just like the pioneer days in America, with a dose of the Wild West thrown in. Cowboys and gunslingers with M-16s. Fighters looking for a fight. Just like medieval Knights.

In the Wild West, an angry man with a gun could only kill so many people. If things got as bad as this, an angry gang member with an Ouzi or an M-16 stolen from a dead soldier could kill hundreds or even thousands, and still not get caught.

Nina and I recently watched the movie "*Welcome to Sarajevo*." We were shocked at the sight of the devastation in the once-beautiful cities of the former Yugoslavia, a legacy from President Karadzic and General Mladic. "Broken English," a New Zealand film about a family of Croatian refugees, also shows some footage of Sarajevo streets.

Once the host city for the Winter Olympics, abandoned burned-out buildings now stretch for blocks and blocks. Ravaged shells of high-rises tower over the ruins. I believe these films depict quite accurately how people are living, barricaded in doomed buildings,

# In the 90s.

These massacres and these monsters still exist in our society after five thousand years of "civilized" rule. Hitler and Idi Amin were products of this century. If the chains of civilization are removed, monsters such as these will be loosed on defenseless people, *all over the world.*

Could it happen? I think it could, in some places. Controlling our own cities may mean mobilizing as for a full-scale war. Who knows, perhaps even conscription might be necessary. But definitely we must stay away from crowds, fights and riots.

I don't think it would take 500 years to recover, like the Dark Ages did. But it could take quite a few decades. *If* it gets that bad, count on educating your children and grandchildren by candlelight, around the fireplace after working in the fields, on how to rebuild society.

I don't think this will happen. I have too much faith in human nature to expect it. But I feel I must recognize that this is not impossible. If you happen to have a "little house on the prairie," make sure it's ready, just in case.

## The Final Word

You don't have to stick your neck out the way I am. But of course, you can if you too feel the need. Certainly you need to alert those you care about. At the very least buy them a copy of this book. Insist that they read it, and tell them that if they're *still* not convinced, you'll promise to leave them alone.

Commercialism notwithstanding, I really believe that one of the most important things you can do for the people you love and care about, is to give them a copy of this book.

And if even then they still don't get it, you *will* have to leave them alone, if just to keep the peace. What this means is that you'll need to put aside a few more bags of potatoes and rice, and some extra cans of creamed corn, asparagus and corned beef. You'll need to be prepared for the time when they come knocking on your door like the "friends" of the Little Red Hen.

But you and I will need to be a little more forgiving than she was, because these are people we love. Even if they don't listen too well. If there's no disaster, it just means you're stocked up with the necessities for two years instead of one, or four years instead of two, or whatever it was that you decided upon. No big deal.

And the few bucks it cost you can be counted as extra insurance premiums that you gladly paid because you love those guys.

Don't start a fight over all this. If you drive them away, that just makes it more difficult and less likely for them to come to you for help when the crisis does hit. This could be your chance to come through as the shining, forgiving hero. Or just as someone who cares.

And if it doesn't happen, send me an e-mail. The 'Net should be up.

If it does happen, send me some e-mails anyway. Once the 'Net comes back up in a month or two or a year or two. Tell me all your stories, disasters and adventures, your tales of heroism, hardship and survival. Tell me about heroes you think should be recognized, and about those whose shortsighted attitude caused pain for themselves or people around them.

Include your name, address and e-mail, and a note giving permission to publish your story. I'll collect them and publish the best in a book celebrating the people who survived. You will, of course, get the credit for your stories that are included, with your name beside them in the book.

And if there's no disaster, we'll just chat by e-mail while we munch for a year or two on the survival supplies.

Good luck.

Sincerely,

David.

# Appendix: To Find Out More

## Books:

John Davidson and Lord William Rees-Mogg
  *"The Great Reckoning" "Blood in the Streets,"*      Simon and Schuster
Ed and Jennifer Yourdon *"Time Bomb 2000"*            Yourdon Press / Prentice Hall
Capers Jones *"The Year 2000 Software Problem"*       Addison Wesley
W. Michael Fletcher, *"Computer Crisis 2000,"*        Self-Counsel Press
Bryce Ragland *"The Year 2000 Problem Solver"*        McGraw Hill
Garth Brooks: *"The Mythical Man-Month"*              Addison-Wesley
Jon Krakauer *"Into Thin Air"*                        Soft-cover: Anchor Books
                                                      Hard-cover: Villard Books

## Websites:

Orders (single or multiple copies)      www.trafford.com
                                        1-888-232-4444  Fax:250-383-6804
  (Multiple copies)                     flyingkiwipress@home.com
                                        250-477-3617
Author, David Wm Brown                  flykiwi@home.com
Travel Services:                        maligaya@oanet.com
                                        403-448 - 7310 Fax 403-429-3250
OOABook                                 http://catalog.wiley.com/ss/.1256953645/
                                        index.cgi?script=remsrch&query=An+
                                        Introduction+to+Object-Oriented+Analysis+
                                        www.wiley.com
Peter de Jager                          www.year2000.com
Ed Yardeni                              www.yardeni.com
Ed Yourdon                              www.yourdon.com
Gartner Group                           www.gartner.com
Capers Jones                            www.spr.com
Gary North                              www.garynorth.com
Ross Stewart                            www.year2000.co.nz
                                        www.infotech.co.nz
Michael Fletcher (See book above)       www.highspin.com
2k-Times                                www.2k-times.com
Westergaard                             www.y2ktimebomb.com
Plesman Communications Inc.             www.plesman.com
Canadian Technology Seminars
Y2k Investor (Tony Keyes)               www.y2kinvestor.com
Loma Prieta Earthquake USGS             www.eqe.com/publications/lomaprie
North American Electric Reliability
  Council (NERC)                        www.nerc.com
Nuclear Power                           www.eia.gov
                                        www.eia.gov/fuelnuclear.html

TEERS  A volunteer organization with extensive experience of rescues around the
world. They have dealt with earthquakes and all kinds of disasters, and their aftermath,
and have much to say that's also relevant to Y2k and could be useful. Or could save
your life.                    www.teers.org
                              www.amerrescue.org

Union Pacific Railroad

www.unionpacific.com
www.uptweb.com
www.up.com
www.unionpacific.com/overview/technolo.htm

U.S. Treasury Dept

www.ustreas.gov
www.ustreas.gov/treasury/bureaus/irs/prime/
primerfc.htm

(U.S.) President's Commission on
Critical Infrastructure Protection
(PCCIP)

www.pccip.gov
www.pccip.gov/eo13010.html
www.pccip.gov/report_index.html

Computer Information Center

www.compinfo.co.uk/y2k.htm

Electric Utilities

www.accsyst.com/writers/ele2000a.htm

Information Technology Association
of America

www.itaa.org

Rodney King riots LA 1992

www.citivu.com/ktla/sc-ch1.html

Wahine Storm

www.wellington.net.nz/about/past/
traged01.htm

Piper Alpha Disaster

www.bbc.co.uk/education/disaster/
piper.shtml

Bhopal

http://members.aol.com/ggmathew/
bhopal.htm http://www.bhopal.com/
http://www.infoasis.com/
people...UnionCarbideIndia_environ.html
http://www.earthbase.org/home/timeline/
1984/bhopal/

Survival Center

http://www.survivalcenter.com

Access Bars:

www.melaleuca.com

Power Bars:

www.powerbar.com

Amway (Food bars and numerous
products useful for Y2k)

www.amway.com

(Also see your Yellow Pages under
"Cleaning Products")

Heritage Farms 2000  (Many links to
other Y2k sites)

www.heritagefarms2000.com
1-800-383-2489

ISBN 1-55212-224-7